D1257903

The Edge of
Beyond

Ralph Vaughan Williams in the First World War

Stephen Connock

Albion Music
Ltd

Albion Music Ltd.
© Stephen Connock 2021
ISBN 978-0-9956284-5-8

Published by Albion Music Ltd. 2021
www.albionmusic.com

Designed by S. L. Chai (chaisl@intune.co.uk)
Printed in Great Britain by Mutual Media (UK) Ltd.

Vaughan Williams in 1915, with cap askew!

To my father

Cpl Leslie Thomas Connock (1921-91)
Royal Air Force, Burma

'Groping our way along the trenches in a Stygian darkness, guided by the voice in front, the duckboards beneath our feet and the touch of invisible walls of sodden clay on either side, I realised for the first time the hopelessness of that distant place known as the Edge of Beyond…'

Pte. C. Young, 2/4th London Field Ambulance, Royal Army Medical Corps. Autumn 1916, Neuville St Vaast, Northern France

The Edge of Beyond
Ralph Vaughan Williams in the First World War

Preface

Having formed the Ralph Vaughan Williams Society in 1994, with Dr Robin Barber and the late John Bishop, I was determined to visit the area in Northern France to which Vaughan Williams had been deployed as a private with the 2/4th London Field Ambulance, 60th Division on Midsummer's Day 1916. I shared this aspiration with Ursula Vaughan Williams over dinner in April 1999 and, in typical Ursula fashion, with a glint in her eyes, she disappeared down to the cellar in her elegant home in Camden, north London leaving me alone with the Epstein bust of Vaughan Williams glaring down at me. Some ten minutes later she returned with a number of trench maps that had belonged to her husband from 1916 when he was based in Ecoivres, just north-west of Arras in France with the Royal Army Medical Corps. With these maps in hand, plans were finalised to make the trip with Robin Barber and two American members of the RVW Society – Alan Aldous and Kelly Wise. We left by car on Thursday 20 May 1999, bound for Arras, and returned on Sunday 23 May via Boulogne. The results of this memorable first trip were described in a series of articles for the *Journal of the RVW Society* in October 1999.

At least a dozen visits to this part of France followed over the next 20 years. Many buildings from Vaughan Williams's time in France are still there, including the Main Dressing Station at Ecoivres. The chateau opposite this building that the officers of the 2/4th London Field Ambulance used as billets in 1916 has since been demolished. Of course, the twin towers of Mont St Eloi remain today much as they were in 1916, still a guide for anyone unsure of their location. The *estaminet*, a rather downbeat café in Mont St Eloi which was frequented by the officers of the Royal Army Medical Corps – and sometimes by the ranks including Vaughan Williams – was open for refreshments in 1999 but is now, alas, a private home. The road from Mont St Eloi to Neuville St Vaast is today surrounded by peaceful meadows so that it is possible to walk the approximate area that Vaughan Williams would have taken with the motor ambulance, night after night, in the summer and autumn of 1916. Neuville St Vaast was largely destroyed in the *First Battle of Artois* in 1915. Although now rebuilt, it remains a sombre location.

This description also applies to Croisilles and Mercatel, to the south of Arras, the area where Vaughan Williams served as a Second Lieutenant in the 141 Heavy Battery, Royal Garrison Artillery in 1918. Here Vaughan Williams took part in intensive artillery bombardments during operation *Mars*, part of the German *Spring Offensive* which began on 21 March 1918. In the weeks after this attack began, Vaughan Williams was in greater danger than at any other time during the war. In early August 1918 he was involved in the largely successful *Battle of Amiens*. After this battle, from late August 1918 and into October 1918 he travelled with his Battery in a great trek through northern France and into Belgium. During this period he contributed to both the *Fifth Battle of Ypres* and the *Battle of Courtrai* before reaching the outskirts of Antwerp a few weeks before the end of the war. There was little time for Vaughan Williams to relax after the Armistice as his Unit, now known as the 86th (Mobile) Brigade, was chosen to take part in the Army of Occupation, involving yet another arduous march of over 130 miles through Namur and Charleroi to the Rhineland.

In 2005 I also visited Salonica and Katerini, following the path taken by Vaughan Williams and the 60th Division as they crossed the Mediterranean in a difficult 11-day sea journey from Marseilles in November 1916. The landing areas near Salonica were much as they were in 1916 although the towns have changed beyond all recognition. The dust and grit, however, have not diminished, nor will they ever.

From that time I wanted to write a book on Vaughan Williams's wartime experiences. However, this had to wait until my volume of recollections of the composer was published in 2018 under the title *Toward the Sun Rising – Ralph Vaughan Williams Remembered*. Then it was possible to concentrate on the First World War with a view to publishing a hardback volume in good time for the 150th anniversary of Vaughan Williams's birth in 2022.

This book aims to provide greater understanding of Vaughan Williams's wartime experiences which are covered only in very general terms in most biographies of the composer. There is, I feel sure, much new material in this book which will add to our appreciation of what Vaughan Williams went through in the crucial years from 1915 to 1919. This book also seeks to explain the impact of the war on the music of Ralph Vaughan Williams, especially a number of key works written in the 1920s when memories of the war remained raw. This section focuses on what I term his Great War Trilogy: the *Pastoral Symphony*, *Sancta Civitas* and *Riders to the Sea* with *Along the Field*, the *Mass in G minor*, *O Vos Omnes* and some other pieces added for good measure. This pivotally important chapter is called 'With rue my heart is laden' from the poem by A. E. Housman set by Vaughan Williams in *Along the Field*.

More generally, the book follows the composer in chronological fashion, from his enlistment in the Royal Army Medical Corps on New Year's Eve 1914 to his final demobilisation on 15 July 1919. I have added an opening chapter on Vaughan Williams's life from his birth in 1872 to August 1914 and then a further chapter on his life and music after the war ended to the composer's death in 1958. These provide what I hope is useful context, especially for those relatively unfamiliar with the details of Vaughan Williams's achievements.

This is a book on a composer during the Great War, not a military history. However, where appropriate, I have added relevant technical details such as the firing capacity of the 60-pounder guns that Vaughan Williams was responsible for transporting in 1918 when he joined the 141 Heavy Battery, 86th Brigade, with the Royal Garrison Artillery. There is also information about the horses which did the heavy pulling and often died from fatigue, gas poisoning, shelling or the bitter cold. For Vaughan Williams's period in the medical service, I include detailed plans covering the evacuation procedure for the seriously wounded on the Western Front in 1916 and information on the manpower and organisation of various dressing stations near the Front.

Elsewhere I have added material of a more strategic nature on the course of the war at particular times when this is relevant to the activities of Vaughan Williams and his colleagues. This places their actions in a broad historical context. I have kept all this to a minimum to avoid dwelling on too many military details. There are many fine texts on military aspects of the First World War which are referred to in the references at the close of each chapter and in the *Select Bibliography* at the end of this book.

Vaughan Williams was not kind to future biographers, especially any who might care to focus on his experiences in the Great War. There is very little correspondence from the period – unlike, say, the numerous letters from Ivor Gurney to Marion Scott in 1915-17, or those from Wilfred Owen to his mother in 1918, or the hundred-plus letters from Winston Churchill to his wife, Clementine, written during his brief period in the wartime Army. There are no war diaries such as those kept by George Butterworth or, in pained, unhappy prose, that of the poet Arthur Graeme West (both published posthumously), or by Siegfried Sassoon or the broadcaster Norman Ellison. There is no novel like the one written by Robert Graves that would ultimately be the source material for his wartime autobiography *Goodbye to All That* (1929, revised 1957). Similarly, there are no war memoirs such as those written by Edmund Blunden (1928), Huntly Gordon (1967), Max Plowman (1928), J. B. Priestley (1962) or Dennis Wheatley (1978). We are fortunate to have some recollections from those who served with Vaughan Williams from 1915 to 1918 and a few letters to his friend Gustav Holst – and that is about all. The absence of any letters from Vaughan Williams to his mother or his wife between 1915 and 1918 is noteworthy in itself. If there were letters to and from Adeline, which seems very likely, these were almost certainly destroyed after her death in 1951 when Vaughan Williams had a major clear-out at his home in Dorking, burning all the material he did not want.

This book therefore fills in the details, where possible, from Army records, including the *War Diaries* of the 2/4th London Field Ambulance and the 86th Brigade, Royal Garrison Artillery, although these never mention Vaughan Williams by name. At least they do inform us about his Unit's whereabouts and, more generally, what was happening day by day. Given the organisation and discipline of the Army, we can state with certainty that if the 2/4th London Field Ambulance or the 141 Heavy Battery were in a certain location, then so was Ralph Vaughan Williams. Secondary material is also included when this provides helpful background information. We are, for example, particularly fortunate to have the recollections of the personnel of the 2/4th London Field Ambulance published as a book in 1935 called *Tales of a Field Ambulance*. Although Vaughan Williams did not contribute to this book his friend, Harry Steggles, did. There is no similar work on the 141 Heavy Battery, 86th Brigade, with whom Vaughan Williams served from March to December 1918 in France, Belgium and Germany.

I hope this analysis of Vaughan Williams's wartime experiences will inspire you to visit Arras and the area to the north around Neuville St Vaast, including Ecoivres, Mont St Eloi and the southern and western slopes of Vimy Ridge. Hopefully, time will also allow a visit to Croisilles, Neuville-Vitesse, Mercatel and into Belgium to see Ypres where Vaughan Williams was involved in the *Fifth Battle of Ypres* from 28-30 September 1918. We can also follow Vaughan Williams in the march through Namur and Charleroi from 17 November to mid-December 1918 when he was part of the Second Army, within the Allied Army of Occupation, heading for the Rhine. In these locations we can visualise what he and countless others had to endure, often in appalling conditions, between 1916 and the weeks following the signing of the Armistice on 11 November 1918.

Many of the composer's friends, such as George Butterworth, Bevis Ellis, W. Denis Browne and Ernest Farrar, did not return and others, such as Ivor Gurney, Patrick Hadley and E. J. Moeran, were seriously wounded. Vaughan Williams also lost two brothers-in-law, Charles and Edmund Fisher, between 1916 and 1918. Fortunately, Vaughan Williams survived the war without serious physical injury, except for damage to his hearing caused by close proximity to heavy artillery during 1918. It is clear, however, that there were profound emotional consequences and these are best illustrated and explored by listening to a number of important musical compositions of the 1920s. These include the poignant *Pastoral Symphony* and the haunting *Along the Field*. If possible, listen to the *Pastoral Symphony* on a portable device while sitting near the towers of Mont St Eloi, looking west at the 'Corot-like country' which inspired it and which became so familiar to the composer.

We should all be deeply thankful not only that this great composer emerged almost unscathed from the First World War but also that Vaughan Williams's frontline experiences served as an inspiration for some of the most memorable works of his long and illustrious composing career.

Stephen Connock MBE
1 March 2021

Acknowledgements

My initial thanks are to Ursula Vaughan Williams who was always encouraging me to write this book and provided most of the photos of Ralph Vaughan Williams that are reproduced in the pages that follow. The late Simona Pakenham was also most helpful and gave me other photographs. John Francis provided invaluable editorial assistance including scanning all photographs and illustrations and adding many helpful comments based on his own research into aspects of Vaughan Williams's life and music. I have also received considerable help from Albion's Technical Editor, Gary Dawkes, whose assistance removed many errors in my writing. In addition, George Blair, Hugh Cobbe, George Spencer, Frank James Staneck and John Whittaker all contributed many important suggestions to early drafts of this book. P. J. Clulow kindly helped with musical illustrations and Tad Kasa provided the colour-tinted photo of Vaughan Williams on the front cover. S. L. Chai was invaluable as a designer and Hugh Cobbe, on behalf of the Vaughan Williams Charitable Trust, also kindly gave permission to reproduce many of the photographs included in this book. I am grateful to them all.

Thankfully, certain editions of the *War Diaries* of the 2/4th London Field Ambulance and 141 Heavy Battery of the 86th Brigade, Royal Garrison Artillery, are available online through the Public Record Office website, although gaps remain. The staff in the Public Record Office in Kew were always helpful as were librarians at the Imperial War Museum and the British Library in London.

Any gaps, errors or oversights that remain are, of course, my responsibility.

List of Illustrations

List of Photographs

Front Cover – Ralph Vaughan Williams in late 1917, with his Sam Browne belt.
After title page – Vaughan Williams in 1915, with cap askew!

1   1872-1914: From Down Ampney to The Lark Ascending

Ralph Vaughan Williams remembered little of his father, Arthur, who died on 9 February 1875 when he was barely into his forties. Arthur was the second son of the judge Sir Edward Vaughan Williams and Jane Margaret Vaughan Williams (née Bagot) and became the vicar and school manager in the small Gloucestershire village of Down Ampney. He died from what was reported as tuberculosis although his illness may have been bronchial pneumonia; precise diagnosis of such chest infections was difficult in Victorian times. In any event, his health had deteriorated quickly; his last reported baptism took place on 13 December 1874. With Arthur gone, there was nothing to keep his widow, Margaret Vaughan Williams, and her three young children – Hervey, Meggie and Ralph – in Down Ampney so the family moved back to Margaret's family home at Leith Hill Place, high on the North Downs in Surrey.

Of mixed English and Welsh descent, Ralph was born in Down Ampney on Saturday 12 October 1872 and baptised on 1 December 1872. The return to Leith Hill Place was welcome to the children who could enjoy the gardens and fields of the house high on

Photo 1: Arthur Vaughan Williams.

the North Downs, with its magnificent southerly views over The Weald. Now owned by the National Trust, Leith Hill Place had originally been bought by Vaughan Williams's maternal grandfather, Josiah ('Joe') Wedgwood III (1795-1880) in 1847. He had married Caroline Darwin (1809-1882), the sister of the botanist Charles Darwin, and they had three children – Sophy (1842-1911), Lucy (1846-1919) and Margaret (1843-1937) who was to become Ralph's mother.

Joe and Caroline Wedgwood were quiet and undemonstrative much like Ralph's father. Margaret, however, was remembered for

Photo 2: Margaret Wedgwood (née Darwin), Ralph's mother, on 18 July 1856, aged 13.

being intelligent but strict. She was described as quite dominant and firm with her children who had no father around to deflect criticism. Living up to the expectations of an intelligent, dominant yet benevolent mother can be challenging for any child. It may explain in part a certain insecurity in Vaughan Williams's later character and possibly his sister Meggie's descent into eccentricity and ultimately to madness.

Generally, it was a sheltered life with servants to do the household work. This meant there was more time for intellectual pursuits including painting, literature and music. Vaughan Williams's mother, who called him 'Ralphy', read

Bunyan's *The Pilgrim's Progress* to him as a young child. 'Reading aloud' was an important feature of his domestic life, a tradition Vaughan Williams continued throughout his adult life. The *Authorised Version* of the Bible and Shakespeare were both vital elements of Vaughan Williams's early childhood reading, as were the poetical works of Percy Bysshe Shelley, Alfred, Lord Tennyson, Matthew Arnold and George Herbert. Such books were given as gifts for birthdays and Christmas, generally by his mother, who inscribed them in formal, typically Victorian, terms: 'Ralph Vaughan Williams from M.J.V.W.'

Photo 3: Ralph in 1876.

As to music, Vaughan Williams received his first lessons from family members when he was five, and wrote a short piano piece, *The Robin's Nest*, when he was just six. Indeed, he was only eight when he signed up for a correspondence course in music organised by Edinburgh University and passed both the preliminary and advanced examinations. He was taught the piano, which he said 'I never could play', and the violin, describing the latter as 'my musical salvation'.[1] He also played duets with his brother and sister and enjoyed singing in a clear treble voice.

Vaughan Williams took his violin with him to preparatory school at Rottingdean, in East Sussex, joining in September 1883. Here he was able to focus on his musical studies under William Michael Quirke (1848-1918), an Irishman described by Vaughan Williams as 'a

Photo 4: Hervey and Meggie on 28 January 1873.

Photo 5: Ralph at Rottingdean, March 1885.

fine teacher' from whom he learned much. He played Raff's *Cavatina* at a school concert and, on 15 December 1886, aged 14, he took part in another concert at Rottingdean School when he played in violin trios and in a violin solo by Gounod. He was introduced to Bach while at Rottingdean along with Mozart, Schubert, Haydn and early Beethoven. Vaughan Williams later described the Novello *Bach Album* as: 'A revelation, something quite different from anything I knew, and Bach still remains for me in a niche by himself'.[2]

Following five years after his brother Hervey, Vaughan Williams entered the public school at Charterhouse, near Godalming in Surrey, on 7 January 1887. Initially placed in the Headmaster's House, he transferred to the new Boarding House in 1889 and remained Head of House until he left the school in the summer of 1890. Other than a note on music at Charterhouse written for *The Carthusian* in 1952, Vaughan Williams did not leave a detailed description of life at the school. Robert Graves, entering Charterhouse a few years later, did include such a description in his autobiography *Goodbye to All That* (1929, revised 1957). Graves appreciated the 'hard knocks and character training that public schools are advertised as providing' but goes on:

Photo 6: Charterhouse School.

Photo 7: Ralph at Charterhouse, 1890.

'From my first moment at Charterhouse I suffered an oppression of spirit that I hesitate to recall in its full intensity…The school consisted of about six hundred boys, whose chief interests were games and romantic friendships. Everyone despised school-work; the scholars were not concentrated in a single dormitory house as at Winchester or Eton, but divided among ten, and known as 'pro's'. Unless good at games…they always had a bad time'.[3]

Vaughan Williams seems not to have had such a difficult time at Charterhouse perhaps because of music; he joined the school choir and then the school orchestra as a violin player, later changing to the viola. He played the viola part in the slow movement of Beethoven's *First Symphony* which gave him some early insights into orchestration. Pupils joined the orchestra, Vaughan Williams said later with typical humour, because it: "Practised once a week in the time otherwise devoted to extra French, and was therefore very popular".[4] It was at Charterhouse that a one movement *Piano Trio in G* by R. Vaughan Williams was played on 5 August 1888, almost certainly the first public performance of a Vaughan Williams work. He remembered it later as 'distinctly reminiscent of Cesar Franck, a composer whose name I did not even know in those days, and whom I have since learned to dislike cordially'.[5]

While this might have been taken as a positive sign of the musical gifts of the teenage boy, part of his family retained a deep distrust of art in all its forms, particularly of music which was seen as barely respectable as a profession. Gwen Raverat recalled overhearing a conversation about 'that foolish young man, Ralph Vaughan Williams, who *would* go on working at music when he was so hopelessly bad at it'.[6] His Aunt Etty, Henrietta Litchfield (Charles Darwin's third daughter), was similarly dismissive, saying of Ralph's talent in a letter:

'He has been playing all his life, and for six months hard, and yet he can't play the simplest thing decently. They say it will simply break his heart if he is told that he is too bad to hope to make anything of it'.[7]

Fortunately for the future composer, his mother and his aunt, Emma Darwin, felt differently and it was his mother's influence, and her financial support, which enabled Vaughan Williams to seek a place at a London musical college rather than continuing to study at Charterhouse. Before continuing his studies he visited Munich and heard his first Wagner opera – *Die Walküre* – and had the 'feeling of recognition as of meeting an old friend'.[8]

Vaughan Williams entered the Royal College of Music (RCM), in South Kensington, for the first time on 25 September 1890. His principal subject for study was the organ; he added the piano in mid-1891 and harmony in December 1891. Working initially on Grade 5 Harmony with Dr F. E. Gladstone, after two terms he transferred to study Composition under Sir Hubert Parry. Of Parry, Vaughan Williams wrote in later years that:

'I was quite prepared to join with the other young students of the R.C.M. in worshipping at that shrine, and I think I can truly say that I have never been disloyal to it… and I hereby solemnly declare, keeping steadily in view the works of Byrd, Purcell, and Elgar, that *Blest Pair of Sirens* is my favourite piece of music written by an Englishman'.[9]

As a teacher, Vaughan Williams remembered Parry always seeking something 'characteristic' in his pupils' work, the character revealed in even the weakest of his students' compositions.

Vaughan Williams's first stint at the RCM was followed by his enrolling for a History degree at Trinity College, Cambridge in 1892, a few days before his twentieth birthday. He carried on preparing for his Bachelor of Music degree with lessons from Charles Wood and the organist Alan Gray. Vaughan Williams quickly became a member of the University Musical Club, whose purpose was to study chamber music and give private concerts every Saturday evening, sometimes conducted by Vaughan Williams. He was very fortunate in his friends at Cambridge. There was the organ scholar H. P. Allen, who would later become Director of the Royal College of Music and the historian George Trevelyan, who would go on to command a British Red Cross unit in Italy in the First World War. Another contemporary was his cousin Ralph Wedgwood, who became Chief Officer for the London and North Eastern Railway and even had a streamlined A4 Pacific steam engine, No. 60006, re-named after him in 1944; an earlier named engine had been destroyed in the Second World War. There was also Maurice Amos, who became a legal adviser to the Egyptian Government, and the philosopher G. E. Moore. There were reading parties on the Isle of Skye, in Penzance and at Seatoller in Borrowdale, and long walks. There was poetry too, with Bertrand Russell, another Cambridge man, introducing the group to Whitman and to Shakespeare – both would remain lifelong companions. Vaughan Williams's early exposure to the great writers, scholars and thinkers of his day was a valuable element in the shaping of his character and, more specifically, assisted him when selecting texts for his many choral works and songs over the years that followed.

After three years at Cambridge University, Vaughan Williams had gained both his History degree and by 1894 his B. Mus. Creditable achievements although, toward the end of his undergraduate studies, the doubts about Vaughan Williams's talent as a musician resurfaced. One of his teachers, Charles Wood, advised him against a musical career.[10]

With uncertainty being expressed in various quarters about his musical abilities, Vaughan Williams decided to return to the Royal College of Music for a further period of study and joined the College again on 13 June 1895. Now his principal subject was Composition. This time, as Parry had become Director of the College, he was taught by Charles Villiers Stanford, who was also teaching at Cambridge University. He was much harder to please. Vaughan Williams later recalled:

'Stanford was a great teacher, but I believe I was unteachable. I made the great mistake of trying to fight my teacher…The details of my work annoyed Stanford so much that we seldom arrived at the broader issues, and the lesson usually started with a conversation on these lines: "Damnably ugly, my boy. Why do you write such things?" "Because I like them" "But you can't like them, they're not music" "I shouldn't write them if I didn't like them". So the argument went on and there was no time left for any constructive criticism'.[11]

Meanwhile, also in 1895, Vaughan Williams had taken on an organist role at St Barnabas's Church in South Lambeth, London, his family believing that he might make a decent career as an organist. Vaughan Williams, however, said he never could play the organ but he did at least obtain some practical knowledge of music by training a choir and giving organ recitals.

His friendship at this period with Gustav Holst also proved vital to both students; they would retain a close and trusting relationship until Holst's death in 1934. Vaughan Williams left the Royal College of Music on 26 July 1896 and was awarded Associate of the Royal College of Music (ARCM) in April 1899.

In July 1897 Vaughan Williams decided to carry on deepening his knowledge about music and this time he judged that it might be best to study abroad, in Germany, for a fresh stimulus – and to hear Wagner's *Ring* cycle without cuts. Germany was a surprising choice as his music was already rather 'Teutonic', something Stanford had recognised when he urged Vaughan Williams to study opera in Italy. Ignoring Stanford's advice, he became a pupil of Max Bruch (1838-1920) in Berlin for several months, taking part in Master Classes on Musical Composition, with his first lesson on 6 November 1897. Vaughan Williams worked hard and enthusiastically, and Max Bruch proved a very encouraging and friendly teacher. Bruch, in turn, said that Vaughan Williams was a "very fine musician and talented composer".[12]

Also in 1897 Vaughan Williams began preparing for his doctorate in music from Cambridge University and finished the exercise in 1899; he was awarded the degree in 1901 and was very proud to be referred to thereafter as Dr R. Vaughan Williams. The University had laid down very strict criteria for the composition which had to be a choral work of between 40 and 60 minutes. These guidelines were carefully followed by Vaughan Williams who wrote what we now call *A Cambridge Mass*. The work shows a personality, inventiveness and ability to compose on a large scale which suggests, as early as 1897-99, the great composer he was to become.

Vaughan Williams married Adeline Fisher on 9 October 1897. She was born on 16 July 1870, the third daughter – and fifth child – to Herbert William Fisher (1825-1903) and Mary Fisher (née Jackson, 1841-1916). Adeline was a gifted pianist who would play the piano every night for her father and then play piano duets with her younger sister Cordelia. Adeline was also an accomplished cellist. She was reserved, intelligent and widely read; one of her favourite authors was Sir Walter Scott.

Photo 8: Ralph and Adeline in 1897 at Leith Hill Place.

The Fisher and Vaughan Williams families had been very close for decades and the Fishers took summer holidays in the Dorking area of Surrey. Adeline's elder sister, Florence, had married the historian and lawyer F. W. Maitland in 1886 and their home in Downing College, Cambridge was the centre of much music-making in the 1890s when Ralph was also studying at Cambridge University. Adeline would often stay with the Maitland family, enjoying chamber music – she on the cello with Ralph playing the viola. So it was little surprise when Ralph and Adeline became engaged in 1896. Adeline was beautiful in a cool, still, rather angular way, quite pre-Raphaelite. She looked the image of her cousin Virginia Woolf. The appeal to the romantic side of Ralph Vaughan Williams was obvious. In addition, Adeline's wry sense of humour, which could at times be quite sharp, would have delighted him. Vaughan Williams's early song *Rondel* (1896) ('Kissing her hair'), in its still beauty, rather captures his love for the young Adeline Fisher.

Vaughan Williams continued to consider a career as an organist and became, in January 1898, a Member of the Royal College of Organists; he obtained a Fellowship of the College, by examination, in July 1898. However, he resigned his post as an organist in the autumn of 1899 and allowed his membership subscription to the College to lapse the following year. He never returned to an organist role for the rest of his long life.

In 1898 Vaughan Williams began to focus more of his time on composition. He began writing works of some importance which contained examples of imaginative and accomplished scoring. These included the charming *Serenade for Small Orchestra* (1898), with a particularly impressive *Andantino*, and *The Garden of Proserpine* (1898-1899) to words by Swinburne.

The Garden of Proserpine deserves further analysis. It was composed at the same time as *A Cambridge Mass* and is set for soprano soloist, chorus and orchestra. Unusually, the work begins with a lengthy *adagio* before the chorus enters with 'Here, where the world is quiet'. The interplay of the soprano with the chorus is handled with confidence and the closing pages have a nobility and warmth which point forward to *A Sea Symphony*.

However, as Vaughan Williams approached his thirtieth birthday, he would have been only too aware of the uncertainty about his musical ability expressed by certain members of his family and a few of his teachers such as Charles Wood. He had also been affected by critical comments from Stanford. Vaughan Williams decided to seek lessons from Elgar in 1900 but he refused saying he was too busy. Against this background, it is hardly surprising that for a large part of his life Vaughan Williams had a sense of his own inadequacy. He would often make reference to what he perceived to be his amateurish technique, adding that: 'Over-scoring has always been one of my vices, and it arises, I am convinced, from the fact that I am not always sure of myself and have not the courage of my convictions'.[13] Later he felt the continuing need to have his work 'vetted' by various people including his close friend Gustav Holst and, later on, Sir Arthur Bliss and Roy Douglas, as if he did not quite trust his own judgement.

Such insecurity may have proved a serious impediment to a less determined character. However, Vaughan Williams remained focused on achieving his musical goals and continued, with Holst's encouragement, to work hard, to talk to other musicians, to think deeply and to 'struggle away' on his own.

By 1901 this seemed to be working. With the lovely *Linden Lea* and the strong, valedictory *Heroic Elegy and Triumphal Epilogue* behind him, Vaughan Williams was clearly growing in confidence.

At this time, he also had a useful ally in William Harris, who had assisted Vaughan Williams as a 16 year-old at St. Barnabas. He wrote in a *Memoir* of 29 July 1959:

> 'I was sitting with Frank Pownall (the much-beloved Registrar of the Royal College of Music) during the playing of Vaughan Williams's new composition (this was the *Heroic Elegy and Triumphal Epilogue* of 1901 performed at the R.C.M. on 5 March 1901 conducted by Stanford). Parry came over and sat beside us. "Fine, strong stuff, Hubert" said Pownall. "Yes", said Parry, "there's no shadow of doubt about *him*'.[14]

'Strong stuff', yes, but not yet characteristic Vaughan Williams. His compositional style was yet to fully assimilate the influence of modality which would follow his immersion in folk song, as well as in English 16th and 17th century polyphonic music, and this would come after December 1903.

Vaughan Williams's period of increasing maturity, from around 1903 to the beginning of the First World War, shows the composer struggling to find his unique voice, which had been suggested in works such as *The Garden of Proserpine* and *Linden Lea*. A cycle of settings by Dante Gabriel Rossetti, *The House of Life*, including the lovely 'Silent Noon', was composed in 1903. Vaughan Williams also began working on the *Songs of Travel* to words by Robert Louis Stevenson. The freshness of these settings, including the sturdy 'The Vagabond' and the lyrical 'Let Beauty Awake', shows that the composer's characteristic style was emerging.

Despite these encouraging works, Vaughan Williams remained, according to Sir George Dyson, "a very uncertain student groping for a musical language of his own".[15] Lacking the experience of having been a choral scholar, Vaughan Williams's stint as organist at St Barnabas Church in Lambeth from 1895 to 1899 undoubtedly helped him with the enormous task he took on in September 1904 when the Rev. Percy Dearmer called on him at his then home at 10 Barton Street, London with a proposal to edit a new hymn book. Vaughan Williams thought over the proposal for 24 hours before accepting the job. At St Barnabas Church he had heard and performed a good deal of Victorian hymns and other church music and didn't much like what he had experienced. This was his chance to improve things. As he said, most people only came across music when in church once a week so they might as well hear and sing good music when they get the chance. His editorial policy included adapting English folk songs as hymn tunes, reviving Tudor composers and removing many poor Victorian tunes. The job took Vaughan Williams much longer than he, or anyone else, expected and *The English Hymnal* was not published until 1906. One of the reasons it took so long was that Vaughan Williams was determined, as he put it:

> 'To do the work thoroughly, and that, besides being a compendium of all the tunes of worth that were already in use, the book should, in addition, be a thesaurus of all the finest hymn tunes in the world...'[16]

For Vaughan Williams, hymn tunes were an 'expression of the soul of the nation' and an important part of his attempt to establish an English national identity in music.[17] From 1904 to 1954 Vaughan Williams wrote around 20 original hymn tunes and arranged almost 200 others.

When Vaughan Williams included folk songs in his hymnals the basis for selection was, as he put it, that: "The only 'correct' music is that which is beautiful and noble".[18] By removing many sentimental Victorian hymns Vaughan Williams improved the general musical quality of the hymns; the musical taste of congregations was broadened by a deliberate policy of including English traditional melody. As a result, Vaughan Williams's nationalist musical agenda was developed and his own music would occasionally feature hymn tunes. This included the evocative use of the tune *York*, derived from the Scottish Psalter of 1615, during the opening bars of *The Pilgrim's Progress*. Equally notable was the incorporation of Tallis's *Third Mode Melody* (*English Hymnal* No. 92) in the beautiful and original *Fantasia on a Theme by Thomas Tallis* (1910). This Tallis theme was also included in Vaughan Williams's incidental music to *The Pilgrim's Progress* for a production at Reigate Priory as early as 1906.

Vaughan Williams contributed several original hymns to the *English Hymnal* such as the much-loved *Sine Nomine* ('For All the Saints') (*English Hymnal* No. 641) and *Down Ampney* ('Come Down, O Love Divine') (*English Hymnal* No. 152), both credited to 'Anon' in the first edition. Even today, these hymns remain among the most popular in church services.

Alongside Vaughan Williams's increasing focus on hymn tunes came a new fascination with English folk song. He had been introduced to Stainer and Bramley's *Christmas Carols Old and New* when he was almost 10 in 1882 and he especially remembered the beauty of the *Cherry Tree Carol*. His real awakening to folk song, as he recalled, came in 1898 when he was given a copy of *English County Songs* and lighted on the *Lazarus* tune. Vaughan Williams said, however, that he was still a 'Doubting Thomas', lacking first-hand evidence of the importance and relevance of folk song. This all changed on 4 December 1903 when, after lecturing on folk song, he heard *Bushes and Briars* sung by a labourer, Charles Potiphar, in Ingrave, Essex – see Illustration 1. He said: 'I was like a psychic researcher who had never seen a ghost. But soon the ghost walked'.[19] His education, as he put it, was complete.

Vaughan Williams now began exploring the English countryside in search of folk songs to collect, starting in his childhood neighbourhood of Leith Hill in Surrey. He was involved in the preservation of many of Britain's loveliest folk melodies. In 1912 alone, he arranged 14 songs collected by W. Percy Merrick and published as 'Folk Songs from Sussex' in Cecil Sharp's collection called *Folk Songs of England*. This included one of the most memorable folk songs of all – *The Unquiet Grave* ('How cold the wind doth blow') along with *The Seeds of*

Love and *Lovely Joan*, which would be incorporated as the middle section of the *Fantasia on 'Greensleeves'* in 1934.

Illustration 1: *Bushes and Briars* melody and text, 1903.

The Vaughan Williams family moved from 10 Barton Street in London to 13 Cheyne Walk, Chelsea on 3 November 1905, partly to be nearer to Adeline's mother who lived in Chelsea, and partly to have a wonderful view of the Thames. As a composer with a few works to his name and no other source of income except occasional conducting engagements, lecturing and writing articles, Vaughan Williams's move to a fine home in Chelsea, with an impressive top-floor study, was probably supported by his mother's assets – the Wedgwood family wealth.

Vaughan Williams's life at this time appeared settled, with concerts, writing articles, giving lectures, visiting friends and family, folk song collecting and composition occupying his time. Sadly, in the year following the family move to Cheyne Walk, Fred Maitland died on 19 December 1906 from pneumonia while staying in Las Palmas on Gran Canaria. Vaughan Williams went immediately to the island to bring back Adeline's sister, Florence, and their two children. When Vaughan Williams died in August 1958 he still had on his bookshelf the three-volume *Collected Papers of Frederic William Maitland*, edited by Adeline's brother H. A. L. Fisher in 1911.

Just before and then during his time in Cheyne Walk, Vaughan Williams's musical style would develop away from the early influence of Brahms and

Dvořák; the building blocks of a fresh style were in place. There was still the impact of the music and teaching of Parry and Stanford but added to this mix was English and Welsh hymnody, Tudor polyphony and increasingly the modal influence of English folk song. The modes provided different harmonic possibilities along with a freshness, colour and poetic atmosphere that created a new musical style. Although not yet the finished article, there is a freshness in the *Two Vocal Duets* (1904) and the expressive *Norfolk Rhapsody No. 1* (1906) which, even allowing for later revisions, can be seen as 'characteristic'.

Vaughan Williams was, however, still beset by insecurity and occasionally dried up completely, as he did in 1907. The problem on this occasion was the dominance of 'Teutonic' influences, especially Brahms, in his musical style. After composing *Toward the Unknown Region* in 1907, Vaughan Williams said he felt 'lumpy and stodgy' and 'had come to a dead end'.[20] As M. D. Calvocoressi put it:

> 'Vaughan Williams had recently come back from Germany and was planning to go to Paris in order to work for a while with some teacher who could help him acquire practical experience and technical ease. He had thought of going to Vincent d'Indy…Despite my great admiration for d'Indy, it occurred to me that considering Vaughan Williams's special object – which was, I understood, to cast off the cramping influence of strict technical training under a German master, d'Indy's class might not quite fulfil requirements…I had been witnessing the amazing results achieved by Ravel…so I did feel sure that he would be the very man for Vaughan Williams and said so'.[21]

Fortunately, Calvocoressi's recommendation was accepted and Vaughan Williams began a period of study with Ravel at the end of 1907, finishing in March 1908. Vaughan Williams became deeply devoted to Ravel, who he considered to be a great technician. Ravel was very much the teacher Vaughan Williams was looking for, identifying, as the composer put it: 'Exactly what I half felt in my mind I ought to do – but it just wanted saying'.[22] Vaughan Williams added that 10 years of lessons from Ravel would not teach him all that he wanted.

Photo 9: Maurice Ravel in 1908.

The remarkable *On Wenlock Edge* (1909) certainly shows the influence of Ravel, particularly in the fifth song, a haunting setting of Housman's *Bredon Hill* – 'In summertime on Bredon'. The influence is there, too, in the *String Quartet No.1 in G minor* (1908).

Compositions completed in 1909 and 1910 such as *The Wasps* (1909), whose Overture remains a concert favourite, the noble and life-affirming *A Sea Symphony* (1909), with words by Whitman, and the visionary *Fantasia on a Theme by Thomas Tallis* (1910) all confirmed Vaughan Williams's growing stature and maturity.

A Sea Symphony was conceived by Vaughan Williams in choral terms. The scale of the work is impressive, although not, perhaps, surprising given the breadth of earlier compositions such as *A Cambridge Mass* (1899). The text is taken from poems by Walt Whitman whose declamatory, rhetorical and inspirational verse resonated with a generation of English composers. Vaughan Williams chose words which drew the analogy between a voyage on the seas and a voyage of the soul, bound for where mariners have not yet dared to go.

The symphony uses a melodic phrase first heard with the words 'and on its limitless heaving breast, the ships' which Vaughan Williams had used in *The Solent* in 1902. This visionary motif seems to have had great meaning for the composer and he returned to it in the *Ninth Symphony* of 1956/57. Both composer and poet grapple with bold questions: 'Whither O mocking life?' and 'Wherefore unsatisfied soul?' It is remarkable that Vaughan Williams tackled such major concepts in this, his first symphony; it is even more remarkable how well he succeeded in this noble and eloquent work.

Photo 10: Vaughan Williams around 1910.

The Agadir crisis in 1911, which had convinced Churchill and other members of the Cabinet about Germany's aggressive intent to dominate the European continent, coincided with one of Vaughan Williams most important early works – the lyrical *Five Mystical Songs* to words by George Herbert.

With the gentle *Fantasia on Christmas Carols* (1912) and some folk song collections to his name, by his fortieth birthday in 1912 Vaughan Williams felt that he could secure a 'good income' as a composer. It was the first period in which he had been able to devote all his time to composition. His impressionistic and folk-coloured second symphony – *A London Symphony* – was completed by the end of 1913 and first performed in its original version on 27 March 1914. The idea of an orchestral symphony had been suggested to Vaughan Williams by his friend George Butterworth – of whom more to come. Although he was born in Gloucestershire and lived for many years in Surrey, Vaughan Williams was a Londoner at heart. His house in Chelsea was within an easy distance of the bustle of Piccadilly, the quiet of Bloomsbury and the colour of the Strand or Tothill Fields, near Vauxhall Bridge where there were dog fights, bull-baiting, fairgrounds and other more dubious attractions.

These contrasting impressions of London are evoked in *A London Symphony*. The work, which owes some of its descriptive power to H. G. Wells's novel *Tono-Bungay* (1909), begins with the city asleep with the harp and clarinet striking the half hour of the Westminster chimes. The first movement is all hustle and bustle. The slow movement beautifully evokes 'Bloomsbury Square on a November afternoon' and includes the lavender-seller's cry, thus linking the piece to the ballad-opera *Hugh the Drover* which also features this poignant song. The *Scherzo* is London at night, jaunty – even garish. The *Finale* opens with a note of unexpected anguish and continues with an elegiac march before the three-quarters of the Westminster chimes are heard to conclude the work quietly.

In 1912, Vaughan Williams was introduced to Sir Frank Benson and became involved in writing incidental music for a number of Shakespeare plays at Stratford in 1913, including *Henry V* and *Richard III*. He also conducted the small orchestra. He continued this fascination with the theatre by composing music for Maeterlinck's play *The Death of Tintagiles* and *The Blue Bird* in 1913.

There were two further works in the months preceding the declaration of war on 4 August 1914 which remain important in Vaughan Williams's list of compositions – the *Four Hymns* and *The Lark Ascending*. Set for tenor with piano and viola obbligato, or string orchestra and viola obbligato, the *Four Hymns* was Vaughan Williams's first anthology, setting different poems by Bishop Jeremy Taylor, Isaac Watts, Richard Crashaw and *O Gladsome Light* translated from the Greek by Robert Bridges. The cycle was dedicated to the tenor Steuart Wilson who gave the first performance on 26 May 1920. This intimate and ecstatic music, appropriate to poems of divine love and longing, was described by the composer as 'much in the same mood as the *Fantasia on a Theme by Thomas* Tallis (1910)'. The choice of essentially meditative, symbolic poetry allowed full expression to the mystical and contemplative side of Vaughan Williams's musical style. This would be further developed in later works, such as *Sancta Civitas* (1923-25) and *Flos campi* (1925), which are both covered in more detail later on. The obbligato viola has a prominent part in the *Four Hymns*, adding colour to the texture of the music, and reaffirming the personal importance of the viola to the composer. Vaughan Williams shows remarkable sensitivity to the meaning of the poems, the melody arising naturally from the text. Considerable skill is also shown in the flexibility of the voice part.

The popular romance *The Lark Ascending* for violin and orchestra was largely completed in 1914 and was inspired by George Meredith's words:

> He rises and begins to round,
> He drops the silver chain of sound.
> Of many links without a break,
> In chirrup, whistle, slur and shake…
> For singing till his heaven fills,
> 'Tis love of earth that he instils…

Vaughan Williams had, as we have seen, been learning the violin since the age of seven and many of his most memorable passages from later works feature the solo violin against a gentle choral or orchestral background. For example, Elihu's rapturous 'Dance of Youth and Beauty' from *Job* or that wonderful passage for solo violin heralding May morning at the opening of Act II of *Hugh the Drover*. There is a magical quality to *The Lark Ascending* which captivates from the hushed first bars as the solo violin begins a songful ascent to the skies.

From the shimmering haze of a summer's day to the indescribable horrors of war! How quickly circumstances and life itself can change. Just a few months after composing *The Lark Ascending*, Private Vaughan Williams, service number 2033, had enlisted as a wagon orderly in the Royal Army Medical Corps and was soon to be serving to the southwest of Vimy Ridge, near Arras in Northern France.

If Vaughan Williams had been killed in action in, say, 1916 his extant compositions would have ensured his special place in English musical history. Up to that point, these included the deeply spiritual *Fantasia on a Theme by Thomas Tallis*, the exquisite *The Lark Ascending*, his first two symphonies, successful choral works such as *Toward the Unknown Region* and the *Five Mystical Songs*, a number of moving and evocative song-cycles such as *On Wenlock Edge*, the *Songs of Travel* and the *Four Hymns* and certain timeless individual songs including *Linden Lea* and *Silent Noon*. To this must be added his editing of the *English Hymnal*, his original hymns and his folk song settings and collecting. He was also fundamental to the early success of the Leith Hill Musical Festival since its formation in 1905, training the local choirs and conducting concerts in the Festival itself.

Fortunately for us all he survived the war and was eventually able to add to his illustrious compositions once peace had returned. However, as the following chapters will show, this was only after he had endured long periods of great danger, uncertainty, hard work, challenges and sacrifice.

Illustration 2: Title page for *Linden Lea*, 1912 edition.

References

1 Ralph Vaughan Williams 'Musical Autobiography' in Hubert Foss *Ralph Vaughan Williams – A Study* (George Harrap, 1950) p. 19.

2 *ibid*, p. 21.

3 Robert Graves *Goodbye to All That*, Cassell and Co. Ltd, 1929 (revised 1957), p. 33.

4 Quoted in *The Carthusian*, December 1952 and reproduced in Ursula Vaughan Williams, *R.V.W. – A Biography*, Oxford University Press, 1964, p. 26.

5 Ralph Vaughan Williams in Hubert Foss, *op. cit.*, p. 21.

6 Gwen Raverat *Period Piece – A Cambridge Childhood*, Faber and Faber, 1952, p. 273.

7 *ibid*, p. 273.

8 Ralph Vaughan Williams in Hubert Foss, *op. cit.*, pp. 21-22.

9 Ralph Vaughan Williams in Hubert Foss, *op. cit.*, p. 22.

10 See Wilfrid Mellers *Vaughan Williams and the Vision of Albion*, Albion Music Ltd., 1997, p. 3.

11 Ursula Vaughan Williams, *op. cit.*, p. 44.

12 Letter from Vaughan Williams to Arthur Bliss, 27 April 1935, quoted in Hugh Cobbe (ed.) *Letters of Ralph Vaughan Williams*, Oxford University Press, 2008, p. 23.

13 Ralph Vaughan Williams in Hubert Foss, *op. cit.*, p. 38.

14 British Library *Collection of Ralph Vaughan Williams*, Ref. 1714/1/1 – 126.

15 *ibid*, Ref. 1714/1/10 – 59.

16 Ursula Vaughan Williams, *op. cit.*, p. 71.

17 See Ralph Vaughan Williams 'Some Conclusions' in *National Music and Other Essays*, Oxford University Press, 1986, p. 68.

18 See *English Hymnal*, Oxford University Press, 1906, p. viii.

19 British Library, *op. cit.*, Ref. 1714/5/3 – 40. See also Frank Dineen, *Ralph's People – The Ingrave Secret*, Albion Music Ltd., 2001.

20 Ralph Vaughan Williams in Hubert Foss, *op. cit.*, p. 34.

21 M. D. Calvocoressi *Musicians Gallery – Music and Ballet in Paris and London*, Faber and Faber, 1933, pp. 283-284.

22 Quoted in full in Stephen Connock *Toward the Sun Rising – Ralph Vaughan Williams Remembered*, Albion Music Ltd, 2018, p. 253.

2   1914-1916: From Chelsea Barracks to Le Havre

Vaughan Williams read *The Times* and may have noticed the article on 21 July 1914 that the diplomatic crisis following the assassination of Archduke Franz Ferdinand and his wife on the morning of 28 June 1914 was considered grave and was increasing in intensity. There remained hopes, at least in the British cabinet, that the conflict would remain localised to Austria and Serbia and that diplomatic efforts at the highest levels in Berlin, Vienna, Paris, Belgrade and St Petersburg would avoid escalating the conflict. By 27 July the crisis had deepened; Germany had hardened her obligations to Austria and questions about the overall balance of power in Europe were being openly discussed. Treaties and alliances were re-examined, especially the *entente* between Russia, France and Great Britain, and armies began to mobilise. Austria declared war on Serbia on 29 July and in London instructions were given for 'Precautionary Measures' to be taken prior to full mobilisation. Attention now turned to Belgium and Dutch neutrality, to Germany's territorial ambitions – for a greater 'place in the sun' – and to economic moves to prevent panic as people sought the safe haven of gold. Within days, Russia and Germany were formally at war and on 2 August, the Belgium Government rejected a German demand to allow German troops to cross Belgium in return for a treaty. News that sections of the German Army had violated the Belgium border reached the British Cabinet early on 4 August. An ultimatum from the British Government to Germany, seeking assurances about Belgium neutrality, was rejected. Accordingly, a state of war was declared between Great Britain and Germany with effect from 11 pm on 4 August 1914.[1]

Although aware of what was happening – Vaughan Williams speculated on 4 August that he might be unable to travel if trains were not working – the declaration of war had no immediate effect on his life. He continued working on his ballad-opera *Hugh the Drover*, focusing on an aria for Mary, with the line 'So dawns my last day of freedom', an irony that Vaughan Williams could not have appreciated at that time. Fortunately, the trains did allow Vaughan Williams and his wife to visit his mother in Margate on 5 August, staying for a week. Work also continued on the reconstruction of the full score of *A London Symphony* as the original had been lost in Germany. He showed a keen patriotic intent by joining the Special Constabulary, Chelsea Company in the summer of 1914 and had become a Sergeant by 29 August. He took his responsibilities seriously as shown by his ordering an inspection of all Special Constables at 13 Cheyne Walk on 2 September 1914 and issuing a Notice on 24 November to each one informing them of opportunities for rifle practice, what to do with cars carrying headlights and so forth.[2]

The British Army Expeditionary Force on mobilisation at the outbreak of war comprised around 160,000 troops. More men were needed and Lord Kitchener's first appeal for volunteers was issued on 7 August 1914 – the famous poster was not seen until 5 September 1914 on the front cover of *London Opinion*. The total number of soldiers Kitchener called for in the first month of the war was 100,000; in fact over 300,000 enlisted, enough to form 30 infantry divisions. The new recruits in 'Kitchener's Army' included many of Vaughan Williams's close musical friends such as George Butterworth, R. O. Morris (who married one of Adeline's sisters, Emmie, in February 1915), Francis Bevis Ellis and Geoffrey Toye. This group all joined the Duke of Cornwall's Light Infantry as privates. On 2 September they were drafted, along with hundreds of other recruits, to Bodmin in Cornwall. Just a few days later the group transferred to Aldershot for basic training. During the first week of October 1914, commissions were offered to Butterworth and five of his friends, with both Butterworth and Morris becoming second lieutenants in the 13th Battalion, Durham Light Infantry.[3]

Ivor Gurney and Arthur Bliss, who had both come under the influence of Vaughan Williams at the Royal College of Music, also sought to enlist in August 1914. Gurney was unsuccessful at first because of poor eyesight but managed to join the 2/5th Battalion, Gloucestershire Regiment, on 9 February 1915. Bliss enlisted on 13 August 1914 and secured a commission with the 13th (Service) Battalion, Royal Fusiliers. His brother, Kennard, joined the 134th Brigade, Royal Field Artillery, and was posted to France on 29 November 1915; sadly he was killed on 28 September 1916, hit by a heavy shrapnel burst. This was a terrible loss. He was admired by Arthur Bliss as the most gifted of all the family. Gordon Jacob, who would, in 1924, transcribe Vaughan Williams's *English Folk Songs Suite* for full orchestra, enlisted on 26 August 1914 in the Queen's Royal Regiment (West Surrey). He was taken prisoner in April 1917. As with Arthur Bliss, Gordon Jacob also lost an older brother, Anstey, who died in the *Battle of the Somme* on 18 September 1916 – he was not quite 23 years old. Other friends of Vaughan Williams had also enlisted, including Steuart Wilson who joined the King's Royal Rifle Corps. He was seriously wounded at Ypres in 1914 and again at High Wood in the Somme area in 1916. He lost both a lung and a kidney from these wounds yet, incredibly, was able to resume his singing career after the war.

Members of Vaughan Williams's family also enlisted. A cousin, Tom Harrison, joined the Navy and another cousin, on his mother's side, Josiah Wedgwood IV, a Liberal MP, joined the Royal Navy Volunteer Reserve. He fought in both Belgium and France in 1914 and was wounded in the Dardanelles campaign in

1915. Closer to home, Vaughan Williams's brother-in-law, Charles Fisher, was commissioned in the Royal Navy and served on *HMS Invincible*; he would lose his life in the *Battle of Jutland* in 1916. Another brother-in-law, Edmund Fisher, enlisted in the Royal Field Artillery and saw action in France in 1917-18. He was invalided home in 1918 with what was thought to be trench fever and died that year from peritonitis. A third brother-in-law, William Fisher, was a career Navy man – he first joined in 1888 – and also served in the *Battle of Jutland*. He survived the war and went on to become Commander-in-Chief of the Mediterranean Fleet.

W. Denis Browne, a young composer with the lovely *To Gratiana Singing and Dancing* (1913) to his name, had impressed Vaughan Williams in Cambridge. He was commissioned, with Rupert Brooke, in September 1914 to the Royal Naval Division. Tragically, both would be dead by mid-1915 – Rupert Brooke on 23 April from sepsis as a result of an infected mosquito bite while on board the French hospital ship *Duguay-Trouin* and Denis Browne on 4 June at Achi Baba overlooking the Gallipoli Peninsula in Turkey. Another musician from the Royal College of Music, E. J. Moeran, enlisted on 30 September 1914 with the 6th (Cyclist) Battalion, Norfolk Regiment as a despatch rider. By June 1917 he was commissioned as a Second Lieutenant with the West Yorkshire Regiment. He would be wounded in the head near Bullecourt, south of Arras, on 3 May 1917. This serious injury left Moeran with bullet fragments in the back of his head and this may have contributed to his death in Kenmare on 1 December 1950.

The poet Robert Graves had met Vaughan Williams in 1912 at Charterhouse where, as we have seen, Graves was an unhappy pupil. Vaughan Williams was visiting as a distinguished old boy. Graves joined the Royal Welch Fusiliers on 12 August 1914 and said at the time that: 'Joining up was the only honourable course of action'.[4] In October 1914, Graves was reading the Charterhouse casualty list which he described as 'awful'.[5] Vaughan Williams would have received the same list and this may have influenced his own thinking about enlisting. By the end of the war over 3,200 Charterhouse alumni had served in the Army and 687 (22%) had been killed.[6]

The actions of friends and family can be a powerful motivator for joining the Army, as the numerous 'Pals' battalions testify. Discussions between Vaughan Williams, George Butterworth and R. O. Morris in a dark and depressing London during a short but annoying delay in War Office procedures in early October 1914 would have focused on the war effort along with talk about progress on reconstructing *A London Symphony*. Butterworth spoke about how much he enjoyed his early field training, mainly because of his admiration for the men with whom he had to deal. Of these, 90% were miners in his platoon whom he described as: 'Physically strong, mentally alert and tremendously keen – everyone seemed so very much alive'.[7]

Vaughan Williams, however, was not a quick, adventurous or eager volunteer; there were two or three factors which made him reluctant to enlist immediately. Firstly his age; he was 42 in October 1914. The age limit for enlisting was 35 in 1914 and, even by January 1916, the Military Service Act restricted conscription of men from age 18 to just 41. This upper limit was not lifted to the age of 50 until April 1918. Secondly, he was married – and to a woman with increasing health problems. Becoming noticeable as early as 1909, by the beginning of the war Adeline's arthritis was limiting her mobility and she suffered increasing pain and discomfort. She was unable to leave her bed or chair without the aid of a walking stick. Add to these two personal factors the widespread view that the war would be over by Christmas, or shortly afterwards, and Vaughan Williams's delay in enlisting was understandable.

By this time, Vaughan Williams was a reasonably well-known composer in musical circles even if not quite a household name and he was writing music of real distinction such as *The Lark Ascending*. At his age he could have continued writing music and conducting as opportunities arose. The example of two fellow composers, Arnold Bax and Rutland Boughton, is instructive. At the outbreak of war in August 1914 Bax was 31 and Rutland Boughton 36. Neither chose to enlist. Bax was declared unfit for military service in September 1916 because of his 'nervous temperament' and this decision was reaffirmed in 1917 and again in 1918.[8] This was a similar diagnosis to that provided to Philip Heseltine (Peter Warlock) which also exempted him from military service in 1916. Bax was free to compose even if concerts were now less frequent. Bax's *Violin Sonata No. 2* appeared in 1915 and, in 1917, the *Symphonic Variations* alongside two of his finest works, *Tintagel* and *November Woods*. The level and quality of these compositions in the war years suggests what Vaughan Williams might have achieved if he had not enlisted. Between 1911 and 1914, Vaughan Williams composed or arranged around 40 works, not excluding folk song collections; it would be reasonable to assume he would have continued to produce another 40 works between 1915 and 1918. It is not, of course, as simple as counting potential works in these 'lost years'. As we will see in chapter 7 ('With rue my heart is laden') Vaughan Williams's wartime experiences inspired him to write music of power and eloquence, including the profound *Pastoral Symphony* which he began in 1916 and finished in 1921. The 'lost years' were certainly not wasted; instead these years at war deepened the composer's musical genius.

As for Rutland Boughton, he organised the first Glastonbury Festival in August 1914 and arranged another between 11 August and 28 August 1915. The main work of the 1915 festival was his own *The Immortal Hour* along with scenes from his *The Birth of Arthur*. With enthusiastic reviews, he went ahead with a third festival in 1916. However, as soon as this event was over Boughton received his Army call-up papers. He immediately lodged an appeal for exemption on grounds of the importance of his artistic endeavours, but this was rejected by the military authorities. Boughton was ordered to join the Cambridgeshire Regiment in September 1916 although he somehow avoided being posted overseas. Instead, he spent his service life mainly engaged as a Bandmaster in various home-based regiments including the 1st Suffolk Regiment, the King's Royal Rifles and the Royal Flying Corps.[9]

Boughton's attempt to avoid the call-up was publicly supported by George Bernard Shaw who evoked the importance of his work as a composer and organiser of the Glastonbury Festival. Shaw railed against the 'honest barbarism' of the Army in the *Western Daily Press* in the following terms:

'The vital point is that the citizens of Glastonbury can now hope to see their sons and daughters grow up as cultivated Englishmen and Englishwomen, with refined sense, cultivated intelligences, developed sympathies, and pleasures that are ennobling instead of degrading and destructive. It would be absurd to attempt to estimate Mr Boughton's value to his country in respect of this public work of his in pounds, shillings and pence, though in Germany he would be in the public service with a specially respected position and pension. His value as a soldier is in comparison absurdly negligible…yet the military authority declares contemptuously, not to say snobbishly, that Mr Boughton's work is 'not of the least national importance'.[10]

No doubt Sir Hubert Parry and others would have agreed with Shaw in respect of Ralph Vaughan Williams. Parry had written to Vaughan Williams on 19 January 1915 saying: 'You have already served your country in very notable and exceptional ways and are likely to do so again; and such folks should be shielded from risk rather than exposed to it'.[11] Parry added that he was going to raise the fact that Vaughan Williams had enlisted with one 'Major Darwin'. This was Major Leonard Darwin, son of the botanist Charles Darwin and a relative of Vaughan Williams on his mother's side. Nothing seems to have come from this intervention; more of this in the pages that follow.

Parry worried about other composers too. He wrote to Herbert Howells on 13 April 1917 saying:

'The thought of so many gifted boys being in danger, such as Gurney and Fox and Benjamin and even Vaughan Williams, is always present with me. This is what horrible senseless war means – and we can do nothing. To put our views, that such beings are capable of doing the world unique services, before the military authorities would surely appear to them absurd'.[12]

Howells avoided being called-up because of ill health; he was diagnosed with a thyroid gland disease linked to a heart condition and given just six months to live. Fortunately he was cured by experimental radium treatment and was 90 when he died in 1983.

High art or high military objectives as matters of national importance? At the end of 1914 Vaughan Williams would not have been impressed with arguments citing the unique importance of his work as a composer or with those seeking to 'shield' him from risk. In a letter to Holst in late June 1916, Vaughan Williams expressed his incredulity about Rutland Boughton's actions saying:

'Did you see that Rutland Boughton applied for exemption on the grounds that he was doing work of national importance at Glastonbury! I suppose I shall make you very angry with what I am going to say and I can't put it just as I mean – but I feel strongly that what you are doing at Thaxted is the real thing of which Boughton's vapourings at Glastonbury are the sham imitation…'[13]

To Vaughan Williams, there were wider issues: fighting a 'just cause', having a strong sense of public duty and demonstrating 'love of one's country' – in the best sense of this sentiment. News of the retreat of the British Army from Mons to Le Cateau during the *Battle of Mons* in late August 1914 was becoming more widely known, despite press censorship, and generated patriotic feelings. There was also the importance of supporting the large number of Vaughan Williams's friends and family who had already enlisted.

Therefore over Christmas 1914, following discussions with Adeline, he decided to sign-up and did so on New Year's Eve. With his public school education at Charterhouse and degrees from Cambridge University, including his Doctorate, Vaughan Williams might have sought a commission as an officer; almost all volunteers as junior officers in 1914 came from public schools. Instead he enlisted as a private in the Royal Army Medical Corps (RAMC). This says a good deal about Vaughan Williams's lack of interest in status and absence of vanity. Why the Royal Army Medical Corps? Belinda Norman-Butler, a student of Vaughan Williams in the 1920s, said: "He chose the Ambulance Service because he didn't want to fight, to kill or injure people. He wanted to save them instead".[14] Such an explanation seems unlikely given that Vaughan Williams went on to join the Royal Garrison Artillery in late 1917, serving with a heavy

60-pounder battery team – this was very much a fighting unit. Hugh Cobbe suggests that the drive to join the RAMC was 'partly due to the inspiration of Whitman, who went to the American Civil War and encountered all the horrors of it, later helping as a nurse in military hospitals in Washington…'[15] This is an interesting idea although the most likely explanation appears to be more prosaic – Vaughan Williams's age. As we have seen he had turned 42 just a few months earlier. The Army took a more relaxed view of age limitations when it came to recruiting ambulance orderlies. As one historian of the First World War put it:

> 'Many of the orderlies were middle-aged men, well over military age, who had volunteered for the hard and taxing work as medical orderlies in the Royal Army Medical Corps'.[16]

In addition, a less onerous level of physical fitness was demanded for the medical services compared with those being recruited to combatant units. The sculptor Francis Derwent Wood was also in his forties when war broke out – he was born a year before Vaughan Williams – and managed to sign-on with the RAMC. The poet, John Masefield (1878-1967) was 36 in 1914 and also joined the medical services as a hospital orderly; by December 1914 he was a corporal. David Edward Lindsay, the 27th Earl of Crawford, had enlisted as a private in the medical corps – he was, like Francis Derwent Wood, one year older than Vaughan Williams.

Vaughan Williams enlisted at the Duke of York's HQ, King's Road, Chelsea, a reasonable walk from his home at 13 Cheyne Walk, and was assigned to the 2/4th London Field Ambulance Territorial Force. This would ultimately be part of the Army's 179th Infantry Brigade within the 60th (London) Division, a 'New Army' force. A note on the structure of a British Army Infantry Division in 1915 is shown in Appendix 3 and a full list of the units in the 60th Division is shown in Appendix 4. Given the dreadful loss of life of British junior officers in the infantry in the First World War, estimated at just six weeks in the trenches during the Western Front's bloodiest phases, Vaughan Williams's choice of enlisting as a private in the RAMC may have saved his life.[17]

As Appendix 1 shows, Ralph Vaughan Williams was attested for service in the Regular Army as Private No. 2033 for a four year term on 31 December 1914. He undertook a medical examination that day at the Duke of York's HQ, Chelsea which showed his 'Declared Age' at 39 (reproduced at Appendix 2). It is unclear whether the Medical Officer, A. G. Atkinson, deliberately understated Vaughan Williams's age on the Medical History form, whether the composer said he was 39 rather than 42 or whether they were both involved in this minor conspiracy. The composer Havergal Brian definitely lied about his age when he enlisted with the Honourable Artillery Company in August 1914. He was well over 38 but declared his age as 34 and even prepared a false birth certificate to prove it![18]

Vaughan Williams's height was given as 6 feet 1 inches and his chest measurement at 39½ inches. With 6/6 vision in both eyes, his physical development was described as 'Good'. His next of kin was listed as Adeline Vaughan Williams of 13 Cheyne Walk, London and he was placed on the Married Roll. He was duly certified as fit for service in the 2/4th London Field Ambulance, Territorial Force that same day – 31 December 1914 – and, after 'swearing in', was able to stroll home in time for any muted New Year's Eve celebrations. Vaughan Williams was now a soldier in the British Army, joining another million new recruits in khaki service uniform. He would soon have his first encounter with puttees, the soldier's leg bindings, which – as we will see – he never learnt to master.

One anecdote about this recruiting procedure does not appear in the official records. Vaughan Williams's second wife, Ursula, recounted in her biography of her husband that: 'Although he was otherwise fit, the medical examiners discovered that he had flat feet, a serious handicap; but the CO who had seen him and been impressed by his appearance, found a way round the difficulty – he was made a wagon orderly, where this disability would be of no consequence'.[19] This was ironic as, at the time, the Ambulance had no wagons, horse-drawn or motorised – these would come later in 1915.

The 2/4th London Field Ambulance was typical of many such units being created over the country in the months after the declaration of war. The Army Medical Services had received Royal Corps status on 23 June 1898 and field ambulance medical units had been created following experiences in the South African War of 1899-1902. The Territorial and Reserve Forces Act of 1907 had established the Territorial Force (TF) and these formed the new RAMC units, including the one Vaughan Williams joined.[20] The RAMC deployed around 900 medical officers, 10,000 other ranks and 600 military nurses to France in the early weeks of the war.[21] This was not nearly enough, and severe personnel shortages continued. By 31 December 1915 there were 66,139 voluntary enlistments to the RAMC.[22]

The divisions of the 'New Armies' being formed for combat each included three field ambulances filled from the training centres of the RAMC. The Division to which Vaughan Williams was enlisted became the 60th (2/2 London Division), created in September 1914 as the 2nd London (Reserve) Division. The three field ambulances in the new division were the 2/4th, 2/5th and 2/6th with the 2/4th being formerly attached to the 179th Infantry Brigade in January 1916.[23]

Each Field Ambulance had around 240 personnel in total consisting of medical officers, stretcher-bearers, nursing orderlies, wagon orderlies, cooks and others.

Photo 11: Major T. B. Layton CO 2/4th London Field Ambulance.

The 2/4th London Field Ambulance was commanded by Major (later Lt.-Col.) Thomas B. Layton (1882-1964) from 4 October 1914 to July 1918 when the Ambulance was disbanded – see Photo 11. He had become a Fellow of the Royal College of Surgeons in 1909 and specialised in diseases of the ear and throat.[24] His Unit, which included Vaughan Williams, was billeted at Dorking in Surrey from Monday 4 January 1915. The Ambulance entrained at London's Victoria Station for the journey south. How ironic that Vaughan Williams would be based from 4 January to 11 February at 31 Mount Street in Dorking, not far from Westcott Road, and so close to his childhood home of Leith Hill Place. The new recruits drilled and drilled again before receiving some basic medical instructions including how to apply bandages – the 'Thomas Splint' would not feature until 1916. The men learnt stretcher drill, including how to lift and carry the sick and wounded. They were taught the most effective ways of stopping bleeding and how to apply field dressings.

As there were no horses or wagons, the Unit took part in numerous route marches. There was also stretcher drill on Box Hill and Ranmore Common. Vaughan Williams and his colleagues spent hours marching up and down Box Hill carrying heavily weighted stretchers. Despite proximity to Dorking, the Surrey countryside in 1915 was remarkably rural and remote – route marches of up to 20 miles a day could take place without seeing a town. Vaughan Williams managed the physical demands of soldiering better than most; he was naturally strong and reasonably fit from his long walks, with Holst and others, during the pre-war years.

One 'highlight' of this period at Dorking was an inspection by Lord Kitchener on 21 January 1915, when he was accompanied by the French Minister of War Alexandre Millerand. A. P. Ford of the 2/4th London Field Ambulance described what happened:

'We paraded at 4 am, in pitch darkness, bitterly cold, and having our greatcoats on and boot brushes in our haversacks to clean up with prior to the inspection. We marched and marched until we arrived at the parade venue, on Epsom Common. It was snowing slowly at first, but gathered strength so that in a few hours the troops were covered by a thick layer of snow which lay inches high on their caps and shoulders. The inspection actually took place about 8.30 am, although we had been there about two hours. We felt we might as well have stayed in our billets because Lord Kitchener appeared to be more interested in the combatant troops than the RAMC who did not seem to get even a glance…'[25]

Photo 12: Vaughan Williams in 1915 near Dorking.

Lord Kitchener was, perhaps, reflecting a widespread view that the military medical units, unarmed and lacking the training of combatants, were somehow an inferior branch of the regular Army although the *Official History of the Great War* says that the distinguished guests reserved their inspection to the London Scottish as this was the only unit fully equipped with efficient rifles.[26] In any event, perceptions about the Ambulance Service being a 'poor relation' to the infantry had changed by the end of 1918, especially as 6,873 personnel had died serving in the RAMC.[27]

Photo 13: Garth House Hospital, Dorking.

Vaughan Williams's Unit was now marching on average 15 miles each day. Field hospital experience was gained at the well-appointed Garth House, today a nursing home in south Dorking, along with a smaller house nearby that was redeveloped as an isolation hospital. The day started with route marches, kit inspections, drills of all kinds and lectures. While Vaughan Williams was fitting into a very different life in the Army, he had difficulty with kit inspections and his puttees were either too tight or too slack. Ursula Vaughan Williams relates:

> 'Much older than most of his fellows, unused to the order expected at kit inspections, finding difficulty in wearing his uniform correctly, in putting his puttees on straight and wearing his cap at the correct angle and in many other details of daily life, he found these minor afflictions called for elementary skills he had never needed before and had not got'.[28]

An Army colleague, the Rev. M. L. Playfoot, remembered Vaughan Williams's appearance in similar terms:

> 'Puttees wrinkled to his boots, tunic humped across his broad shoulders, and a naked leg of mutton in his hand'.[29]

With French losses alone exceeding 300,000 by early 1915[30] and fortified earthworks stretching from the North Sea to the Swiss frontier it was very clear that the war would not be over quickly. Barbed wire began to appear in large quantities around the trenches, support lines and reserve areas. Underground shelters in the forward lines could be over 30 feet deep. It would become increasingly likely that this would be a static war, a war of attrition, one with little opportunity for improvisation.

At the end of March 1915, a few weeks after the opening of the *Battle of Neuve Chapelle* on 10 March, the embryonic 60th Division moved by rail to Hertfordshire taking over the training district between St. Albans and Watford. This had been vacated by the departure for France of the first-line troops of the newly-formed 47th (London) Division. The 2/4th London Field Ambulance was based in Watford and Vaughan Williams took up residence in a rather dour terraced house at 76 Cassio Road. Here he received an affectionate letter from Maurice Ravel saying that he had managed, after eight months, to join the 13th Artillery Regiment while he was waiting to receive a nomination to join the French Air Force. This did not happen and, by June 1916, Ravel was on the Western Front in charge of a lorry.

The property in Cassio Road was very close to the West Hertfordshire Sports Ground where Watford Football Club played their matches prior to moving to Vicarage Road in 1922. Night operations were mounted in nearby Cassiobury Park involving the collection and treatment of the 'wounded' – another soldier who had been placed on the stretcher – see Photo 14. Training focused on stretcher-bearing and the loading and unloading of field ambulances.

The Division relocated again in May 1915, travelling by road to the quaint market town of Saffron Walden via Ware, Dunmow and Thaxted. Gustav Holst had rented a cottage at Monk Street, two miles south of Thaxted, in 1913 and this became Holst's family home until 1917. However, there is no evidence that Vaughan Williams was able to visit his friend at this time. Instead, Vaughan Williams was initially billeted under canvas in Audley End Park and, for part of the time, in the laundry of Audley End House before settling near the centre of Saffron Walden at 29 Bridge Street. This is an attractive (and now listed) small timber-framed cottage almost opposite *The Eight Bells*, a fine 16th century inn.

Photo 14: The 2/4th London Field Ambulance practising with the 'wounded', 1915.

Vaughan Williams was fed up with the increasing length of route marches; the Field Ambulance would occasionally trek over four days, sleeping out in farmyards and farm buildings. He wrote to E. J. Dent from Saffron Walden on 24 May 1915 saying:

'I expect you are doing much more for your King and Country than I am – indeed you can't be doing less'.[31]

The *War Diaries* for this period show the Ambulance engaged in lectures on map reading, camp sanitation, first aid, bandaging and handling fractures. Field activity was undertaken in August, with more work on the collection of the 'wounded'. In mid-August, 30 new recruits joined the Field Ambulance.

Vaughan Williams and his colleagues were still at Saffron Walden on 1 September 1915. The Commanding Officer of the 179th (London) Infantry Brigade, to which the 2/4th London Field Ambulance was attached, inspected the transport on 2 September. There was one ambulance wagon

Photo 15: Vaughan Williams (back row, far left) relaxing, 1915.

as shown in Photo 16. The men continued to practice the collection of the 'wounded', sometimes at night from makeshift trenches.

While at Saffron Walden a band was formed and led by Vaughan Williams. The instruments were bought with funds raised from canteen profits and from donations given by friends in the town. Photo 22 shows a picture of the band.

Photo 16: The only ambulance wagon in 1915, Saffron Walden.

Route marches continued, including to Ashdon on 8 September, where a Zeppelin passed near the camp without causing any disturbance. Littlebury was reached on 10 September. On 14 September, a makeshift dressing station was created at Hadstock. Next came a route march to Quendon on 23 September which was followed by an inspection by the GOC 60th (London) Division, the second such inspection in just two weeks. Soon, the Field Ambulance was in bivouac at Elmdon.

Every Sunday there were church parades and these would continue into France in 1916.

When possible, Vaughan Williams spent his free time playing Bach on the organ of the impressive medieval church of St. Mary the Virgin, very close to his billet at 29 Bridge Street in Saffron Walden. At this time he sketched a few organ works including the

Photo 17: RAMC motor and horse ambulances, 1915.

Three Preludes on Welsh Hymn Tunes, published in 1920, with the beautiful 'Rhosymedre' at its heart. *The Prelude and Fugue in C minor* also had its genesis at this time, though publication was held back until 1930.

While at Saffron Walden, Vaughan Williams wrote a letter to Clive Carey on 8 August 1915 in similarly frustrated terms to that sent to E. J. Dent back in May 1915:

> 'I suppose there is no chance of my being able to transfer to a unit like yours – there seems so little chance of our ever doing anything – have you ever heard any rumours as to our chances of our coming across the water – how are we looked upon – as a hopeless lot never to be made use of?
>
> I must tell you that I was sent up…to Guys (Hospital) for a month to try me 'prentice hands on the uncomplaining poor – the attendance at the surgery fell off eventually but I learnt a lot in the way of bandages, stitches, fomentations, operations, dissections & the rest'.[32]

Vaughan Williams was not alone in these feelings. The writer J. B. Priestley was a private in the Duke of Wellington's West Riding Regiment in 1915 and found the endless parades and exercises hard to endure. He wrote in his war memoir *Margin Released* (1962) that:

> 'Three of us decided that if the battalion were still in England in eight or ten weeks – I forget the date we agreed upon – then we would desert, to join up again at some depot where men were being sent out almost at once'.[33]

Seemingly endless route marches and lectures can cause such frustrations especially as the training seemed to bear little relationship to what was going on in France and elsewhere. Some even feared that the war might end before they made the front line. Siegfried Sassoon railed against the Army instructors who, with pencil and paper, 'Made arrangements for unhurried defence or blank-cartridged skirmishing in a land of field-day make-believe'.[34]

Photo 18: RVW in the RAMC in 1915.

Major Layton, CO 2/4th London Field Ambulance, echoed Vaughan Williams's comments about the Unit's chances of 'coming across the water' in a file note in the *War Diary* for 4 October 1915:

> 'There is unfortunately a feeling among officers, NCOs and men that no more Territorial Troops are going abroad and that we are to be used only for home defence. This results in many wanting to transfer'.[35]

It might seem strange that the men from the Royal Army Medical Corps, training in a pretty rural village in the English shires, wanted to get overseas to take part in wartime action, especially as between September and October 1915 the *Battle of Loos* alone had resulted in 8,000 British killed or wounded. Even if the extent of the casualties was not generally known, the troops understood enough to grasp that the war was not going well. Despite this increasing realisation, the men wanted to make a difference, to help save lives, to do their bit for their country. They had not signed up many months earlier to take part in numerous map reading classes or to attend interminable lectures on sanitation. However, the authorities did not feel the new Division was yet ready to face enemy action and, as we will see, it was to be another nine months before the 60th Division, and the 2/4th London Field Ambulance, were on their way to France.

Photo 19: Vaughan Williams (far left) on firewood fatigues, 1915.

If not France, then Bishop's Stortford. For a while, the routine for the men of the 2/4th London Field Ambulance continued unchanged, with lectures on bandaging on 5 October and drills in the fields near Much Hadham Road on 8 October. The wagon orderlies, including Vaughan Williams, joined the NCOs for a discussion on map reading on 11 October. The Unit was still in Saffron Walden in mid-October with route marches to Stebbing on 20 and 22 October and Braintree on 21 October. Finally, the 2/4th London Field Ambulance marched 12 miles south to Bishop's Stortford, travelling via the attractive villages of Newport and Quendon, on 26 October 1915. All the troops were accommodated in billets between 27 and 31 October. Householders were rewarded at the rate of nine pence a day for each soldier found a place to sleep.

Both Vaughan Williams and his new friend Pte. Harry Steggles were found a home at 19 Apton Road with Mrs Frances Machray. This house, long since demolished – the road now starts at No. 21 – was around a mile north east of Bishop's Stortford station. As Mrs Machray's daughter remembered:

> "When the billeting officer asked my mother whether she would take some soldiers she suggested he might send anyone who was interested in music. I remember her saying how the next day a soldier arrived announcing himself as 'Mr Williams'. We had two other soldiers who came at the same time, Pte. Steggles and Pte. Edwards".[36]

It was a happy period for Vaughan Williams. Mr Machray played the viola, his two sons the clarinet and trumpet and two daughters played the violin and piano. Sunday music-making became a much anticipated event, with Vaughan Williams also playing the viola borrowed from Mr Machray and teaching the family Morris and country dancing.

On 4 November, the Unit took part in Civil Defence practice, remaining three miles behind the main body of troops who were 'marching to London' as part of the exercise. In addition, an Ambulance Reception Hospital was formed on 4 November for the treatment of notifiable diseases involving men from the 179th Infantry Brigade, 60th Division HQ and Divisional personnel and staff from the Third Army HQ. The hospital had 16 medical NCOs and six nursing orderlies. In its first six weeks of operation there were 17 cases with treatment mainly for mumps and diphtheria.

Field work took place in Elsenham on 13 December 1915 and Christmas Eve was spent in the field in Much Hadham and in Buntingford.

Vaughan Williams stayed with the Machray family over a fine and cold Christmas 1915, enjoying civilian life while he could. As a bonus, 27 December was declared a holiday for the troops. His friendship with Harry

Photo 20: Pte. R. Vaughan Williams, 1915.

Steggles was very important to him. Although 20 years younger, Harry played the mouth organ with real ability which earned him the admiration of the older soldier-composer. As Harry put it in a *Memoir*[37] of 1959:

"Bob' as I knew him, for I couldn't call him Williams and R.V.W. seemed impertinent, and Bob it has been up to his death, became intrigued with my mouth-organ playing, especially the improvised notes; for it was the old fashioned 'suck, blow' instrument not the modern type of harmonica used by virtuosos today.

A very fit man really, apart from his flat feet, and until we were issued with ambulances, for he was appointed wagon-orderly; he would march miles with the rest of us. He slouched rather than marched and suffered a lot no doubt, but he never complained. I can see him now in my mind's eye – his huge frame bent forward, his pack perched on his back and wobbling as he marched either to singing or to mouth organ, no mean effort for a man of 42 years of age. He enjoyed life and on one occasion the unit went to church parade, Bob played the organ, I pumped for him. The tune? A popular song of those days *Make your mind up Maggie Mackenzie* duly disguised, as the troops moved reverently to their seats.

He used to say he would compose the real songs soldiers sang after the war, but he was afraid no one would publish them.

Most Army routine was deadly to him: saying it was soul destroying. Stretcher drill was his bête noire for he could never see any sense in it, neither could anyone else for that matter, except those that made the drill up. Of the Regimental March-Past, *Her bright smile haunts me still*, he said they gave all the good tunes to the Army with only this sentimental humbug being left to the RAMC.

Photo 21: The Unit at Saffron Walden. Vaughan Williams is in the middle of the second row.

Make no mistake and do not underrate him, he took his turn and more than his turn nobly and unflinching in all the Army had to offer in those days, from the lowest forms of fatigue duties, up to the transport of wounded from the front line, and was all for the prosecution of the war'.

While at Saffron Walden and Bishop's Stortford, the recently formed band of the 2/4th London Field Ambulance continued to

Photo 22: The 2/4th London Field Ambulance Band in Saffron Walden, 1915.
Vaughan Williams is standing at the back with cap askew.

perform occasional concerts, including a Christmas concert on 28 December 1915 preceded by dinner. As one private from the Unit remembered:

> 'We practised when we could, and made a small amount of progress. The fault was in no way due to our leader, R. Vaughan Williams, but was no doubt due to insufficient practice. Time could not be spared for such a sideline in those strenuous days…'[38]

Within the Division, rumours were rife about being posted overseas and draft after draft of men were called for and despatched to the 47th Division already fighting in France. British and French losses had been high in the *Battle of Artois* in May 1915. However, the prospect of going overseas again receded by the end of 1915 and the Division moved by train, via London, to a military camp near Warminster, Divisional HQ was located at Sutton Veny near to Warminster and Vaughan Williams was based at Camp 14, Sandhill Camp, Longbridge Deverill in Warminster.

Photo 23: The huts at Sutton Veny.

The Field Ambulance was billeted in Army huts and final touches were put to the unit's training on Salisbury Plain. The troops created a complete set of trenches, with dug-outs, communication and support trenches with each unit occupying these trenches for a couple of days and nights. Exercises were carried out on an ever-increasing scale.

By the spring of 1916, there were 70 Army divisions in Great Britain of which 24 were 'New Armies' such as the 60th Division. Many of these were waiting to be relocated to the Western Front. The Germans had begun bombarding Verdun on 21 February 1916. Extremely heavy French losses meant that British divisions were required to replace French battalions on certain sectors of the front line, including to the south of Vimy Ridge. It was, therefore, no surprise when mobilisation orders for the 60th Division, and the 2/4th London Field Ambulance, reached divisional HQ on Thursday 15 June 1916. A complete inspection took place on 17 June with stores not necessary for an overseas posting being moved aside. Horses were harnessed and wagons loaded. Newly arrived officers were given additional training in gas defence and all ranks had an inspection of gas helmets and field dressings on 20 June.

Photo 24: Vaughan Williams, with Harry Steggles standing on the left, on Salisbury Plain in early June 1916 a few weeks before leaving for France.

The move was to begin early on 22 June – Midsummer's Day – following a final inspection at 11.30 am on 21 June. As a colleague of Vaughan Williams, Private T. H. Lewis of the 2/4th London Field Ambulance, put it:

'In June 1916 there were various unmistakable signs of a move to destinations overseas. When gas-helmets were issued most of us thought at last we were "for it", and when the Army pay-books were allotted, the most hardened sceptics amongst us doubted no longer, and made their wills'.[39]

He continued:

'On the morning of our departure (22 June), 'réveillé' was sounded at 2 am and before it was daylight the Unit marched off for Warminster station…

There the sea crossing from Southampton (where we arrived after a circuitous train journey) was so peaceful as to drive away thoughts of enemy submarines. We were all feeling very cramped and tired the next morning at Le Havre owing to the extreme overcrowding on board ship'.[40]

Private Lewis was right to have been worried about enemy submarines. The Spanish composer Enrique Granados and his wife were lost at sea following a torpedo attach by a German submarine on 24 March 1916 when crossing the English Channel on board *SS Sussex*.

The *War Diary* for the 2/4th London Field Ambulance added to Pte. Lewis's account of the Unit's departure for France as follows:

22 June 1916

2.45 am	Breakfast
3.45 am	Parade
4.15 am	Roll call
5.20 am	Arrive at Warminster Station
6.23 am	All personnel and horses on the trains
6.30 am	Depart Warminster
9.10 am	Arrive at Southampton
11.15 am	All officers, wagons and horses on board S.S. Inventor
5.45 pm	All other personnel on board S.S. Connaught (see Illustration 3)

23 June 1916

| 7.50 am | Arrive at Le Havre |

After 18 months of service, endless route marches and lectures, along with rumours about whether the Ambulance would end up in France, Salonica, Mesopotamia or wherever, a fit and close-cropped Ralph Vaughan Williams had at least achieved his aim of an overseas posting. It would not be long before he could hear the unmistakable ocean-like roar of gunfire on the Somme battlefield.

Illustration 3: *SS Connaught*.

References

1   The finest analysis of the events leading to the declaration of war between Germany and Great Britain can be found in Simon Heffer *Staring at God – Britain in the Great War*, Penguin Books, 2019, pp. 1-88.

2   Hugh Cobbe *Letters of Ralph Vaughan Williams 1872-1958*, Oxford University Press, 2008, p. 106. For the reference to Mary's aria see the letter to Harold Child of 4 August 1914 in the online database of *Letters of Ralph Vaughan Williams*, edited by Hugh Cobbe, at VML 4924.

3   Michael Barlow *Whom the Gods Love – The Life and Music of George Butterworth*, Toccata Press, 1997, p. 127.

4   Robert Perceval Graves *Robert Graves – The Assault Heroic 1895-1926*, Weidenfeld and Nicolson, 1986, p. 110.

5   *ibid*. p. 117.

6   John Lewis-Stempel *Six Weeks – The Short and Gallant Life of the British Officer in the First World War*, Orion, 2010, p. 25.

7   George Butterworth *War Diary*, reprinted in Wayne Smith (ed.) *George Butterworth Memorial Volume*, YouCaxton Publications, 2015, p. 43.

8   Lewis Foreman *Bax – A Composer and his Times*, Boydell Press, 2007, p. 140.

9   Michael Hurd *Immortal Hour – The Life and Period of Rutland Boughton*, Routledge and Kegan Paul, 1962, pp. 66-67.

10 *ibid*, p. 65.

11 Ursula Vaughan Williams *R.V.W. – A Biography of Ralph Vaughan Williams*, Oxford University Press, 1964, p. 117. The letter is reproduced in full in Hugh Cobbe, *op. cit.*, p. 107.

12 Christopher Palmer *Herbert Howells – A Centenary Celebration*, Thames Publishing, 1992, p. 19. The composers mentioned are Ivor Gurney, Douglas Fox and Arthur Benjamin.

13 See the online database of *Letters of Ralph Vaughan Williams*, edited by Hugh Cobbe, at Letter Number VML 353.

14 See Stephen Connock *Toward the Sun Rising – Ralph Vaughan Williams Remembered*, Albion Music Ltd, 2018, p. 193.

15 Hugh Cobbe 'Ralph Vaughan Williams: not a pacifist but…' in the *Journal of the RVW Society*, June 2019, p. 12.

16 Lyn MacDonald *The Roses of No Man's Land*, Macmillan, 1980, p.111.

17 See John Lewis-Stempel *Six Weeks – The Short and Gallant Life of the British Officer in the First World War*, Orion, 2010, p. 5.

18 Kenneth Eastaugh *Havergal Brian – The Making of a Composer*, Harrap and Co., 1976, p. 188.

19 Ursula Vaughan Williams, *op. cit.*, p. 116.

20 See Timothy McCracken *Images of War – The Royal Army Medical Corps in the Great War*, Pen and Sword Books, 2017, p. 5.

21 Susan Cohen *Medical Services in the First World War*, Shire Publications, 2014, p. 11.

22 Timothy McCracken, *op. cit.*, p. 15.

23 For more information see Col. P. H. Dalbiac *History of the 60th Division*, Naval and Military Press, 1927, Appendix 1, p. 240.

24 For a fuller explanation of his career see Timothy McCracken, op.cit. p. 183.

25 A. P. Ford 'From Chelsea to Dorking' in *Tales of a Field Ambulance*, Borough Publishing, 1935, p. 17.

26 Col. Dalbiac, *op. cit.*, p. 28.

27 Timothy McCracken, op.cit. p. 174.

28 Ursula Vaughan Williams, *op. cit.*, pp. 117-118.

29 Quoted in the *Journal of the Ralph Vaughan Williams Society*, No. 3, July 1995, p. 15.

30 John Keegan *The First World War*, Hutchinson, 1999, p. 146.

31 Hugh Cobbe, *op. cit.*, p. 108.

32 Hugh Cobbe *Letters of Ralph Vaughan Williams*, online database number VWL 4833.

33 J. B. Priestley *Margin Released – A Writer's Reminiscences and Reflections*, Harper and Row, 1962, p. 94.

34 Siegfried Sassoon *The Complete Memoirs of George Sherston*, Faber and Faber, paperback edition, 1980, p. 286.

35 *War Diary 2/4th* London Field Ambulance 4 October 1915, WO 95/3029/1.

36 For more information see Stephen Connock, *op. cit.*, p. 316.

37 *ibid*, p. 312.

38 *Tales of a Field Ambulance* 1914-1918, *op. cit.*, p. 24.

39 *ibid*, p. 43.

40 *ibid*, p. 43.

3 1916: Private Vaughan Williams on the slopes of Vimy Ridge

The men of the 2/4th London Field Ambulance had to sit about on the quayside in Le Havre until 12 noon on 23 June 1916 before suitable overnight accommodation could be found; they finally arrived at their overnight Rest Camp at 3.40 pm. Given Vaughan Williams's love for *Henry V*, he would have been aware that the port of Harfleur was close by. Otherwise there was little to find attractive about the town at that time. The actor Basil Rathbone, then a Second Lieutenant with the 2nd Battalion, Liverpool Scottish, said:

> 'A miserable town, Le Havre. At least it seemed so to me in those days. There was little to do but to get into trouble. And there was plenty of trouble almost anywhere you cared to look for it'.[1]

Vaughan Williams and his colleagues were not reassured by what they saw at Le Havre – 'sombre-miened French women, decrepit looking French sentries, and a gang of sturdy and defiant-looking German prisoners'.[2] The women, perhaps understandably given what they had been through, mostly wore black.

Illustration 4: Primary rail routes from Le Havre.

The next day, 24 June 1916, the Ambulance departed from Le Havre at 4.11 pm in packed troop-goods-trains, often over 40 carriages long, reaching

Abbeville at 8.15 am the following morning. With a short break, they continued by train to the railhead at St Pol, arriving at 12.15 pm – see the rail routes shown in Illustration 4. All ranks were off the train by 1.30 pm. It was a hot day and the men watched an aerial fight taking place – their first glimpse of wartime combat. They then had a stiff march to Maizières, 16 miles west of Arras, reaching the village in late afternoon where the tired men were served dinner and slept for the first time in a local barn. Advance parties were sent forward to check on the status of various hospitals, including that in Haute-Avesnes. The 2/4th London Field Ambulance were to work in these hospitals, taking over from the retiring 1/2nd Highland Field Ambulance under the command of Colonel David Rorie.

At this point it might be helpful to describe the medical organisation of the Field Ambulance on the Western Front in 1916. The Army operated a casualty evacuation chain from the point of being wounded on or near the front line through six stages moving progressively rearward to comparative safety, as follows:

1   Removal of the wounded man by stretcher from the front line to a Regimental Aid Post (RAP) which might have been little more than a dug-out, or half dug-out, or bunker in a support trench, reinforced by sandbags. Here the soldier would be seen by regimental orderlies or, if he was lucky, by a regimental Medical Officer.

2   After practising a form of reverse triage, whereby the most seriously wounded were treated last – the aim being to get fitter men back to the front – the wounded soldier would be carried (the process was called 'the carry') by the RAMC stretcher-bearers to Collecting Posts (CPs) which might be situated in a reserve trench or somewhere a little away from the front line.

3   The injured soldier would then be taken, if necessary, from the Collecting Posts to an Advanced Dressing Station (ADS), where facilities were slightly better to tend to the wounded. The ADS might be in a cellar or natural cave enlarged by Army engineers. The transfer was usually by stretcher or, if the terrain allowed it, by motor ambulance. The ADS was normally the closest to the front line that a motor ambulance could manage. The 'walking wounded' would make their own way to the ADS, often following the motor ambulance.

4   If appropriate, the wounded man was then transported by motor or horse-drawn ambulance to a Main Dressing Station (MDS) where Medical Officers and nurses from the Field Ambulance could help these more seriously injured men. This transfer most often took place at night except in emergencies such as for serious abdominal wounds.

5   The next stage in the chain was a Casualty Clearing Station (CCS), patients being transported by motor transport or, occasionally, by light railways. Typically these hospitals would have seven Medical Officers in attendance and would be located near to railway lines for ease of transfer to ambulance trains. The wounded soldiers were at this stage the responsibility of the Motor Ambulance Convoy rather than the RAMC. These forward hospitals could treat abdominal or head injuries through surgery and could quickly deal with damaged limbs. Early surgical intervention generally offered the best hope of survival.

6   Finally, the seriously ill or wounded soldier would, if deemed appropriate, be taken by rail to a base hospital and from there, if necessary, by rail and hospital ship home to the UK. One constant thought among the soldiers on the Western Front was: "Do get me down to the Base!" – and then to Blighty.[3] Obvious care was needed when deciding to evacuate injured soldiers to the UK if the delay meant that an operation became impossible. Many lives were lost by such delays.[4]

These six stages were laid out in a diagram by the Commanding Officer of the 1/2nd Highland Field Ambulance, David Rorie, and are shown in Illustration 5.

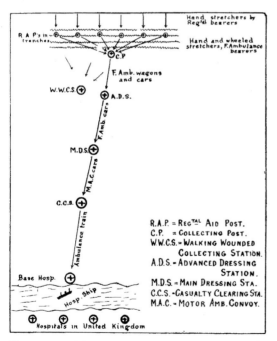

Illustration 5: The casualty evacuation chain, 1916.

There were flaws in this chain. The respective roles of Regimental Medical Officers and medical personnel in the Royal Army Medical Corps overlapped and were often confusing leading to uncertainty in the treatment of wounded soldiers. More importantly it was vital for many injured soldiers, particularly those suffering from abdominal or head wounds, to have an operation in antiseptic conditions as soon as possible. Such facilities were generally available only at the Casualty Clearing Station. Yet, as Illustration 5 shows, a patient was taken to an

Advanced Dressing Station and then transferred by motor ambulance to the Main Dressing Station. Here he was taken out of the ambulance and, in serious cases – and after inevitable delays – the soldier was put into another ambulance to reach the Casualty Clearing Station. As Hugh Bayly, a doctor serving in the Royal Army Medical Corps in 1916, put it:

> 'Out of one ambulance, delay, into another ambulance created much unnecessary waste of time before the Casualty Clearing Station was reached. If all lying cases had been sent straight back from picking-up point to the CCS, very many lives would have been saved and the field ambulance might have been of very great assistance in looking after walking wounded, adjusting the necessary splints and dressings, providing hot soup and cocoa, cigarettes and rest…'[5]

Vaughan Williams, responsible for taking the wounded soldiers out of one ambulance and then placing them in another, was to become well aware of the suffering created by such delays. However, rules were rules and, in the confusion of war, it was often hard to make a decision on the seriousness of an injury at the first picking-up point – best follow the evacuation chain and let others decide later. There were also too few ambulances to allow some to make a longer journey while others adhered to the evacuation chain.

From 26 June 1916 the Commanding Officer of the 2/4th London Field Ambulance, Major Layton, organised 'working parties' to visit each location in the evacuation chain on arrival at Maizières, including exploring the Casualty Clearing Station at Aubigny-en-Artois. Another exploratory group reported to the 1/2nd Highland Field Ambulance at Ecoivres where the Main Dressing Station was located.

All ranks finally arrived at Acq, their temporary holding point, at 8.40 pm on 2 July 1916. Cleaning of the camps, including the use of quicklime, began as these locations were in a bad state. From Acq, Major Layton next visited the Advanced Dressing Station at Aux Rietz (see Illustrations 7 and 9) on 3 July where he noted that: 'My men very pleased at last to be at work'.[6] Between 5 and 8 July, officers reconnoitred the evacuation lines for the wounded between Ecoivres, Aux Rietz, La Targette and Neuville St Vaast. On 10 July another advanced party concentrated on Ecoivres and equipment of the 2/4th London Field Ambulance was taken to the ADS at Aux Rietz.

The Field Ambulance as a whole, including Vaughan Williams, left Acq at 2.30 pm on 13 July, arriving at their base of Ecoivres, a small hamlet to the north east of Arras in the Vimy Ridge sector, at 3.10 pm that same day – it was a march of only a few miles. Ecoivres had little going for it then, as now. They found the Main Dressing Station: 'Full of sick and wounded, not yet attempted to be evacuated'.[7] It was the first time that their medical training would be called upon on a large scale. It would not be the last.

Photo 25; Vaughan Williams (far right) with Harry Steggles and the Motor Ambulance, Ecoivres, 1916.

The French had suffered horrific casualties in the sector of the Western Front north of Arras in 1915, with 150,000 dead or wounded. Both the sad but also inspiring French basilica and cemetery at Notre Dame de Lorette, near Souchez, and the large German cemetery at La Targette bear witness to the tragedy that unfolded here in the summer and autumn of 1915. The village of Neuville St Vaast was destroyed by June 1915 – little stood over five feet high in this desolate place (see Photo 26) and buried bodies were visible well into 1916. The French had secured what was left of Souchez on 28 September 1915 and could at last look up to Vimy Ridge.

During the first two weeks of March 1916 the French Tenth Army had progressively withdrawn from that part of the Front which ran through Arras, Vimy, Souchez and Lens, over 20 miles in total, and handed over responsibility to the 6th Corps of the British Third Army. The transfer allowed the French to concentrate on holding Verdun and took place without major incident. The *Battle of Verdun*

Photo 26: Neuville St Vaast in 1915.

began on 21 February 1916 and continued until 15 December 1916. It has been estimated that the battle caused over 700,000 French and German casualties. Strategically, the Germans had sought to open a new battle zone near Verdun, on the River Meuse, for reasons that the historian Sir John Keegan spelt out succinctly:

> 'The French, forced to fight in a crucial but narrowly constricted corner of the Western Front, would be compelled to feed reinforcements into a battle of attrition where material circumstances so favoured the Germans that defeat was inevitable. If the French gave up the struggle they would lose Verdun; if they persisted, they would lose their army'.[8]

In the meantime, the Artois sector remained relatively quiet, with both sides adopting a 'live and let live' policy.[9] This was shortly to change with devastating effect.

The 47th (London) Division came into the line on 16 March 1916 and the 46th (North Midland) Division, including the 1/4th and 1/5th Leicestershire Regiments, also arrived in the early days of that month. They found the trenches largely intact but very dirty, with the poor weather – alternating rain and snow, thaws and frost – severely damaging the trench system. Pneumonia and trench foot became common illnesses along with the continual threat of snipers and of mines exploding under the trenches. As Nigel Cave puts it in his *Battleground Europe* book on Arras and Vimy Ridge:

> 'The last three weeks of April and the first three of May witnessed a frenzy of underground fighting, mine and counter-mine, following each other with bewildering speed and stupefying effect'.[10]

Arras suffered extensive damage in this period, as shown in Photo 27.

Photo 27: Arras Cathedral and belfry, 1916.

A German attack on 21 May 1916 fundamentally changed the 'quiet' status of the sector, with fighting concentrated around Berthonval Wood, some four miles from Neuville St Vaast. The German objective was to prevent mines being blown under their positions. The ferocious artillery bombardment began at 5.30 pm and finished at 9.45 pm, with mines also being exploded under the British troops. The British were forced to retreat in the darkness with very severe losses. Hand to hand fighting continued before the Germans gained control of part of the British front line. A counter-attack failed with terrible consequences; the roll call of 23 May was awful – 2,475 British losses. General Haig contemplated a further counter-attack but with the *Battle of the Somme*, further south, only weeks away he decided, for strategic reasons, to let things stay as they were.

Into this devastated sector came Ralph Vaughan Williams and his colleagues within the 60th Division. They had just over two weeks to manage the handover from the 51st (Highland) Division, a transition which had to be completed by 6 am on 14 July 1916. The Division's area of responsibility focused on the locations that had seen such bitter fighting in late May 1916. It was centred on Ecoivres and the ruined village of Neuville-St.-Vaast, with Vimy to the northeast, Souchez to the north, Arras to the south, and Hermaville and Aubigny, with its vital railhead, forming the western boundary, as shown in Illustration 6. The battered and rather gaunt towers of Mont St Eloi formed a memorable landmark for the troops just a short distance from Ecoivres.

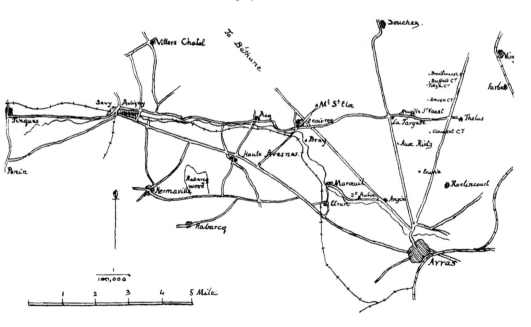

FRANCE. DIVISIONAL AREA.

Illustration 6: The area covered by the 60th Division in July 1916.

The handover from the Highland Ambulance occurred at high pressure, with the front line trenches subject to constant bombardment, as the Divisional troops were overlooked almost end to end by Vimy Ridge, at this time in the hands of the Germans. They well understood the strategic significance of this escarpment which had an elevation of 450 feet. The Highland Ambulance were scheduled to deploy in the Somme area to take part in the *Battle of the Somme* which had begun, with terrible loss of life, on 1 July 1916.

The 2/4th London Field Ambulance was specifically responsible for evacuating the sick and wounded from Regimental Aid Posts in the left and centre sectors, with relays of stretcher-bearers at Neuville St Vaast and at the forward end of what was named 'Territorial Trench'. The Advanced Dressing Station to which the casualties were first taken was located at the hamlet of Aux Rietz, on the Maroeuil to Neuville St Vaast road, near La Targette. The Main Dressing Station in Ecoivres occupied one of the few large buildings in the village.[11] As noted above, the hospital (Casualty Clearing Station) was in Aubigny, the location of which is shown in Illustration 6. Here the wounded soldiers would meet female nurses often for the first time – over 260 nurses died in the First World War, mainly from infectious diseases. Further details of the procedure for evacuating the wounded in the Neuville St Vaast area are included in Appendix 5.

Photo 28: The 2/4th London Field Ambulance at Ecoivres, 1916.
Vaughan Williams is in the back row, fourth from the right.

The men of the 2/4th London Field Ambulance would soon become very familiar with the roads and trenches around these villages on the south-western slopes of Vimy Ridge. Soon after arriving at Ecoivres they followed a guide who took them to the end of the Territorial Trench, which was nearly a mile in length and communicated directly with the front line. They met other soldiers whose faces were white and strained, their eyes red through lack of sleep, and explored the Collecting Posts near Neuville St Vaast.

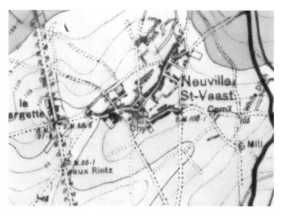

Illustration 7: Location of the Advanced Dressing Station at Aux Rietz, south of La Targette.

Others explored the Advanced Dressing Station at Aux Rietz, shown in Illustration 7, just south of La Targette on the Souchez-Arras road. This was a huge underground shelter, dug out by a previous Field Ambulance and soon to be improved by the troops of the 2/4th London Field Ambulance. This ADS was described in the following terms:

'The Advanced Dressing Station at Aux Rietz, near Neuville St Vaast, on the south end of the Vimy Ridge, was used to evacuate wounded from the famous Labyrinth. This post was largely extended and improved, and the sketch plan (below) shows a characteristic type of dug-out suited to RAMC requirements. It was a freely shelled locality, and the old Territorial Trench leading to it from Brunehaut Farm, near Maroeuil, was regularly attended to by enemy gunners. Ambulance cars only came up the Maroeuil-Neuville St Vaast road after night fell, as it was under observation; and cases reaching the ADS by daylight had to be kept there till dark, the cars being parked by day in a sandpit at the roadside on the other side of Maroeuil'.[12]

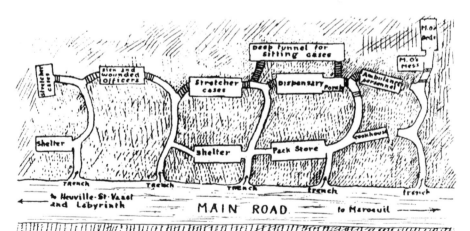

Illustration 8: Layout of the ADS at Aux Rietz.

The sketch plan at Illustration 8 is based on one produced by Major Layton of the 2/4th London Field Ambulance which, in turn, was derived from an illustration prepared by Colonel David Rorie, Commanding Officer of the 1/2nd Highland Field Ambulance. He organised this Advanced Dressing Station up to 13 July 1916 when the 2/4th London Field Ambulance took over.

Vaughan Williams, as a wagon orderly, was assigned the task of loading and unloading the wounded from a motor ambulance – the role of driver was taken by soldiers of the Army Service Corp (ASC) who were attached to the Field Ambulance. Generally, 10 such ASC drivers were allocated to each Field Ambulance.

Vaughan Williams was typically matter-of-fact about his job. He told Gustav Holst:

> 'I am very well and enjoy my work – all parades and such things cease. I am 'wagon orderly' and go up the line every night to bring back wounded and sick in a motor ambulance – all this takes place at night except an occasional day journey for urgent cases'.[13]

Bringing back the wounded by road night after night could be a nightmare for the injured soldier, the driver – and the orderlies. The primitive ambulance wagons (see Photo 16) would bump and jolt on the broken roads causing more pain and anguish for those being transported. To drive slowly caused less screaming and cursing from the wounded, but any delay in arriving at the MDS might itself be life-threatening. Slower speeds could also mean that the wagon could get stuck in the mud leaving everyone exposed.

On arrival at the dressing station, Vaughan Williams and another orderly would then have to retrieve the wounded from the back of the motor ambulance and carry them into a makeshift ward, or outside if the receiving tent was full, where the Medical Officer and supporting personnel could provide help. Hopefully, another dose of morphine might be available to ease the pain. Sadly, many died on the journey back to the dressing station. Orderlies became used to carrying men straight to a cordoned-off area, known as the 'death tent', where there was generally a chaplain waiting. Amid the chaos of war, this area was always unnervingly silent.

The wagon orderlies also had to deal with emotional and mental problems caused by warfare. 'Shell-shock' was not yet a term in common usage in 1916, although the palpitations, sleeplessness, nightmares, tremors, loss of speech, chest pains and tearfulness of those affected were real enough. Lack of empathy for such conditions remained widespread within the Army, equating the problems with cowardice. In early 1918, the composer and poet Ivor Gurney was diagnosed with shell-shock, or shell 'neurasthenia', defined as nervous exhaustion following a gas attack in the *Third Battle of Ypres* (Passchendaele) in August 1917.

Returning to the UK, he was hospitalised in Warrington and never recovered, ending up in an asylum in 1922. Suffering from delusions of being tormented by electricity, Gurney lingered on until Boxing Day of 1937, when he died, weighing only a little over seven stone.[14] One of his finest poems is this 'Song' from the 1917 collection *Severn and Somme*:

> *Only the wanderer*
>   *Knows England's graces,*
> *Or can anew see clear*
>   *Familiar faces.*
>
> *And who loves joy as he*
>   *That dwells in shadows?*
> *Do not forget me quite,*
>   *O Severn meadows.*

Photo 29: The twin towers of Mont St Eloi in World War 1.

Sadly, this most original and moving war poet and musician was to dwell in the shadows of his own mental problems for almost 20 years. He had longed to return to the Severn meadows but was not allowed to leave his asylum for fear he would take his own life.[15]

When dealing with serious physical or mental problems, Vaughan Williams and the driver manning the ambulance wagon would come up as near as possible to Neuville St Vaast before taking casualties to the MDS at Ecoivres. The looming twin towers of Mont St Eloi acted as a landmark when the moonlight allowed it, as shown in Photo 29.

In 'Notes on the Evacuation of the Wounded in the Neuville St Vaast area', the Commanding Officer, Major Layton, provided details of the whereabouts of the various locations in the chain and the degree of difficulty in evacuating the wounded. Sometimes the wounded had to be carried for over 2,000 yards on the shoulders rather than hands because of the numerous traverses. The resources allocated were less than that used by the Highland Field Ambulance and were as follows:

At the RAPs:	16 stretcher-bearers.
At the CPs:	2 sergeants, 1 lance corporal, 1 cook, 1 orderly and 21 stretcher-bearers.
At the ADS:	2 officers, 1 sergeant, 1 corporal, 8 nursing and general orderlies and 10 stretcher-bearers.

The drivers of the motor ambulances had particular difficulties with the cross roads at Aux Rietz and La Targette as two trolley lines converged onto an engineers' dump where, without any lights except for hurricane lamps in the hands of people moving about, ambulances could break down while turning or get stuck in disused French trenches.

More than half the casualties dealt with by the RAMC in the battles on the Western Front were caused by artillery fire, with firearms responsible for a third of all wounds.[16] The destructive force that was ever-present in the trenches or surrounding areas was the artillery shell, which we have seen with the death of Kennard Bliss from a shrapnel burst. As Jeremy Paxman put it in his Great Britain's Great War:

'A direct hit meant red-hot metal, rocks, earth, bricks, wood and body-parts flying everywhere…If whether you lived or died depended not on the outcome of a fight with an enemy soldier you could see but on the decisions of someone commanding an enormous weapon out of sight over the horizon, it produced a new kind of fear: totally incapable of retaliation or self-preservation as the shells rained down, the men were reduced from warriors to victims, and their response – perhaps the only response available to them – was a widespread fatalism'.[17]

The soldiers did not always see it this way. Robert Graves, an officer in the Royal Welch Fusiliers, wrote in 1916 that he found rifle-fire more trying than shellfire:

'The gunner, I knew, fired not at people but at map references…it seemed random somehow. But a rifle bullet, even when fired blindly, always seemed purposely aimed. And whereas we could normally hear a shell approaching, and take some sort of cover, the rifle-bullet gave no warning'.[18]

Vaughan Williams was active in the area around Neuville St Vaast, shown in Photo 26, which one member of the 2/4th London Field Ambulance described as follows:

> 'Nothing stood more than five feet high and we lived in cellars and dug-outs. Owing to the heavy losses sustained by the French in holding the position, we were surrounded by buried bodies, and these were troublesome on damp, sluggish nights. There were rats by the million. They used to run by the duckboards head to tail. Here I saw the start and finish of a trench raid, which passed from silence, the sudden crack of bombs, followed by rifle-fire, field artillery, 60-pounders and finally the heavies'.[19]

Another stretcher-bearer from Vaughan Williams's unit, Private C. Chitty, added that tea and bread were served alongside torn and shattered bodies which were wrapped in clotted, bloodstained blankets. He went on:

> 'The sickening putrefying smell is ever present, and the air hums with lustrous bluebottle flies. Thus, direct from home, we receive initiation into the savagery of war, and seek to gulp down before those poor insensate forms which but the night before had been as we'.[20]

The driver, along with Vaughan Williams and the team of wagon orderlies, would wait at the ADS with the motor ambulances at the end of the shell-riven road from Ecoivres that bypassed Mont St Eloi towards the Aux Rietz-La Targette crossroads, close to what was left of Neuville St Vaast – see the trench system shown at Illustration 9.

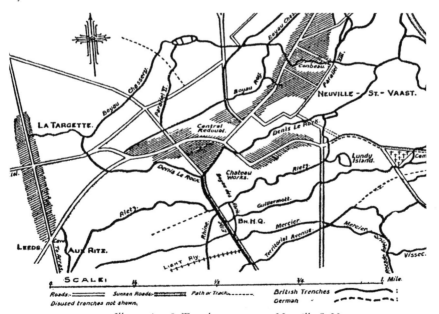

Illustration 9: Trench system near Neuville St Vaast.

The stretcher-bearers would carry the wounded to the ADS along waterlogged duckboards within the trenches, with 'walking cases' stumbling along behind. There was little lighting except perhaps the flash of a torch in front or some illumination from the Very lights. Occasional bullets whined overhead. Private C. Young of the 2/4th London Field Ambulance recalled:

'We are too wet and miserable for speech; we are automatons wound up and propelled by one fixed idea, the necessity of struggling forward. The form on the stretcher makes not a sound; the wet, the jolts, the shakings seem to have no effect on him. An injection of morphine has drawn the veil'.[21]

Eventually the 'Halfway House' was reached – not a house at all but just a pile of ruins – and another team of stretcher-bearers would take the wounded man to the underground ADS at Aux Rietz. After medical assessment some would be passed over to the wagon orderlies, which included Vaughan Williams, for the night journey back to the MDS at Ecoivres.

Siegfried Sassoon described what happened in an underground dressing station: [22]

They set him quietly down: I think he tried
To grin…moaned…moved his head from side to side.

He gripped the stretcher; stiffened; glared, and screamed,
'Oh put my leg down, doctor, do!' (He'd got
A bullet in his ankle; and he'd been shot
Horribly through the guts). The surgeon seemed
So kind and gentle, saying, above that crying,
'You must keep still'. But he was dying…dying.

The future poet laureate, John Masefield, also captured what it was like collecting the wounded and carrying them to hospital:

'One had been lying out for four days on the battlefield, without tending or food, one had a leg smashed to pieces, and another had been blown by a shell and had bits of rope in his face and no eyes and no nose, and his knee broken and his wrist…'[23]

Despite the dangers, Vaughan Williams was fortunate in that his duties were generally outside the trench system. He was able to see the sky and to use the looming towers of Mont St Eloi towers for guidance. Significant danger arose when the wagons were asked to travel closer to the front line at Neuville St Vaast. This was ordered to relieve the physical strain on the stretcher-bearers. Many of the casualties that the wagon orderlies had to transport were very seriously injured. Private C. R. Wellum of the 2/4th London Field Ambulance described one incident involving a platoon of Yorkshire Hussars:

'It was about 5.30 pm and a score of these men were in the tiled forecourt above their cellar when, before they had time to think, a German shell dropped and burst among them…We dashed across with stretchers. Of the score or so men there, one was killed outright and about a dozen or more wounded. We carried across on stretchers those that could not walk and bandaged some on the spot and others back in our dug-out. One man was wounded in twenty-three places. Having completed the dressings we despatched them down to the MDS.'[24]

Another stretcher-bearer from Vaughan Williams's Unit remembered:

'Among the sick and wounded who passed through our hands was to be seen much of the pathos and tragedy of war. I recall one fine-looking lad who had lost his three chums. They had been blown to pieces in a mine or shell explosion while he himself had completely lost his reason. He was so quiet, gentle, and amenable and it was pathetic to hear him implore us to allow him to go out and gather three wild flowers in memory of his three lost friends'.[25]

The road back to Ecoivres was dangerous and it was a great relief to see the towers of Mont St Eloi and to know the ambulance wagon was very near to the MDS. One of Vaughan Williams's colleagues remembered a tender moment amid the desolation:

'The far-off blue horizon melted into a misty golden sky, while the ruined tower of Saint Eloi, solitary and grand, crowned a nearer slope. All the foreground and the fields as far as the eye could reach were beautiful with flowering plants, poppies, marguerites, the yellow tansy and others far too numerous to specify…'[26]

When not engaged on transporting the wounded from the ADS at Aux Rietz to Ecoivres, there were endless rounds of 'fatigues' (the ironic Army term for extra duties) for the wagon orderlies, including whitewashing buildings and looking after the horses. One private in the 2/4th London Field Ambulance put it this way:

'The greater part of the day was devoted to strenuous work, for even if there were no wounded to be carried there were always sandbags to be filled, dug-outs to be strengthened and gutters to be made. The intensive digging was valuable as a means of keeping the unit fit'.[27]

Photo 30: The front of the building that housed the MDS at Ecoivres in 1999.

Nobody was allowed to go outside the Brigade area but there was solace in visiting the local *estaminet*, a run-down café in the village of Mont St Eloi, overlooking the towers. Amid all this desolation there was music too. Private C. R. Wellum relates:

'Later, matters improved and R. Vaughan Williams got a choir together. The choir was first formed by Vaughan Williams at Saffron Walden and we practised at all available opportunities wherever we were, Bishop Stortford, Sutton Veny, etc. We took a box of music abroad with us and that box gave us some very happy evenings. It went through France and on to Salonica with us. On rare occasions when enough of us could be got together we gave concerts'.[28]

Mining and counter-mining went on from the first days of the 60th Division taking over the Arras to Souchez section of the front. The whole line was riddled beneath the surface by mine galleries – old and new. Vaughan Williams had been at Ecoivres for less than a month when the Germans blew a mine on the night of 26 July 1916 under an old crater known as 'Duffield'. Two mines were blown by the British that night including a huge crater, 120 yards across from east to west, called 'Tidza' which led to fierce fighting near the lip of the crater. In addition, from 15 to 22 August, the Divisional Artillery maintained a series of concentrated bombardments on certain sectors of the enemy's line.[29]

Photo 31: Captain Francis Bevis Ellis.

Systematic raiding of the German trenches by 60th Division Infantry Units began in August 1916. An exceptionally large crater was formed just in front of the 179th (Infantry) Brigade's sector on 11 August leading to significant crater fighting in the waterlogged terrain.

Vaughan Williams still found the time to write to Gustav Holst on 21 October 1916. After commenting that he had: 'longed to be home in many ways during the last month', he added:

'I sometimes dread coming back to normal life with so many gaps – especially of course George Butterworth – he left most of his MS to me – and now I hear that Ellis is killed – out of those 7 who joined up together in August 1914 only 3 are left'.[30]

'Ellis' here refers to Francis Bevis Ellis rather than his brother Roland Ellis, both of whom had enlisted with Butterworth in the autumn of 1914. Captain Bevis Ellis, a composer and concert promoter, was with the 10th Northumberland Fusiliers and was killed on 25 September 1916. He is buried in Miraumont, some ten miles north-east of Albert.

His Majesty the King passed along the road north of the Main Dressing Station at Ecoivres on 9 August 1916. As Major Layton noted:

'All patients were sitting on the bank above the road…expecting that he would inspect our Dressing Station on the way back but he did not do so'.[31]

The Unit would have recalled, with irony, Lord Kitchener's inspection (or lack of) over 18 months earlier while they stood in the snow near Dorking. That would have felt like a lifetime ago.

Photo 32: The church at Ecoivres.

Night by night, work revolved around evacuating the wounded along the road between Ecoivres, Mont St Eloi and La Targette. The 17th Corp Light Railway helped plan the laying of light tracks in evacuation trenches around Neuville St Vaast to ease carrying the wounded. A decision was made on 24 August to go ahead with this work. Much cleaning and re-cleaning of the huts for the wounded took place and both the ADS and the MDS were considerably expanded.

On 25 August Major Layton visited the Commanding Officer of 179th Infantry Brigade to see if he needed any further medical assistance. The CO of the 2/4th London Field Ambulance was firmly put in his place and was told that he 'did not think that I ought to have known of a proposed raid'.[32] The raid involved a working party trying to capture a German prisoner for questioning. The gap between the RAMC and the Infantry seemed as wide as ever.

There were rumours, usually picked up in the latrines, that the Division would be redeployed to the Somme where the battle was still being fought. After the catastrophe of the initial attack, which had left 20,000 British dead and another 40,000 wounded on 1 July 1916 alone, the battlefield had become one of attrition which ultimately would claim an astonishing 1.2 million dead or wounded on both sides. Tanks were deployed for the first time in the war in September 1916. The allied offensive on the Somme officially ended on 18 November 1916.

Before then, on 20 October 1916, an Allied conference of ministers and senior military advisers had taken place in Boulogne. The main subject for discussion was the role of Allied forces in Greece and Macedonia. The French proposed sending reinforcements to Salonica and, on 26 October, Sir Douglas Haig, Commander of the British Expeditionary Force (BEF) on the Western Front, was ordered to send one division from France to Salonica. He chose the 60th Division as the troops in this division were, as the *Official History of the Great War – Military Operations France and Belgium, 1916*, put it: 'Fresh, well-trained and at full strength'.[33] Britain reserved the right to withdraw the 60th Division in the spring of 1917 if necessary and the move was conditional on the French forces in Greece also being increased in strength.[34] Allied Army commanders thought these extra resources, deployed wisely in local offensive action, might lead to nothing less than the break-up of the Bulgarian Army.

The 60th Division was to be relieved by the 3rd Canadian Division and a Major Bazin of the Canadian Field Ambulance begun preparation to assume the duties of the 2/4th London Field Ambulance on 21 October 1916. At 7.40 am on 24

October the Ambulance left Ecoivres arriving, via Acq and Berles, at Monts-en-Ternois at 3 pm on the same day; it was a journey of around five miles. The men of the 60th Division, including the 2/4th London Field Ambulance, next relocated ten miles south to Fortel-en-Artois, arriving on 28 October. The soldiers still thought they would be sent to join the fighting in the Somme battlefield. Most patients with the Ambulance were evacuated to hospitals in Doullens and Fortel and the Unit's motor ambulances were transferred to the 56th Division.

Another move on 30 October involved the troops marching 11 miles to Prouville, a commune in the Somme department. Uncertainty about the final destination was resolved on 1 November 1916 when the Commander of the British Expeditionary Force (BEF), General Haig, confirmed to the officers of the 60th Division that they would be proceeding to Salonica. This was quickly communicated to all units. Major Layton laid out detailed plans for the evacuation of the remaining wounded soldiers of the 179th Infantry Brigade on 2 November, confirming to Battalion Commanding Officers that the march south would begin on 3 November. The troops, including Vaughan Williams, were informed on 3 and 4 November 1916 that their destination was to be Greece.[35] The soldiers now arrived at their holding destination of Eaucourt-sur-Somme, a march of around 17 miles from Prouville.

Given the slaughter still taking place on the Somme, this would prove to be a fortuitous redeployment for Ralph Vaughan Williams and his colleagues – albeit one, as we shall see, with continuing dangers.

References

1   Basil Rathbone *In and Out of Character*, Limelight Editions, 1956. p. 9.

2   *Tales of a Field Ambulance*, Borough Publishing, 1935, p. 43.

3   This is adapted from Niall Cherry 'The RAMC on the Somme, 1916' in *Stand To! The Journal of the Western Front Association*, April 2002, p. 37.

4   For more information see Kevin Brown *Fighting Fit – Health, Medicine and War in the Twentieth Century*, The History Press, 2008, p. 48.

5   Hugh Bayly *A Medical Officer in Khaki – The Story of a Doctor in the First World War*, 1935 and now published as a Kindle Edition, 2017, location 745.

6   2/4th London Field Ambulance *War Diary*, WO 95/3029/2, p. 6.

7   *ibid*, p. 6.

8   John Keegan *The First World War*, Hutchinson, 1998, p. 302.

9   Alain Jacques (ed.) *Somewhere on the Western Front, Arras 1914-1918*, Leclerc, 2003, p. 44.

10 For more information on the fighting in this sector see Nigel Cave *Vimy Ridge – Arras*, Battleground Europe series, Leo Cooper, 1996, p. 33 and p. 46.

11 See Col. P. H. Dalbiac *History of the 60th Division*, George Allen and Unwin, 1927, p. 46.

12 Col. David Rorie *A Medico's Luck in the War*, Naval and Military Press, 1929, p. 78.

13 Ursula Vaughan Williams *R.V.W. – A Biography of Ralph Vaughan Williams*, Oxford University Press, 1964, p. 120.

14 For more information see Michael Hurd *The Ordeal of Ivor Gurney*, Oxford University Press, 1978, p. 169.

15 For a poignant account of Gurney's mental state at this time see Helen Thomas's recollections in the Royal College of Music magazine for 1960 quoted in Michael Hurd *The Ordeal of Ivor Gurney*, Oxford University Press, 1978, pp. 167-169.

16 Susan Cohen *Medical Services in the First World War*, Shire Publications, 2014, p. 23.

17 Jeremy Paxman *Great Britain's Great War*, Penguin Group, 2013. P. 117.

18 Robert Graves *Goodbye to All That*, Cassell and Co. Ltd., 1957 edition, p. 84.

19 *Tales of a Field Ambulance, op. cit.*, p. 47.

20 *ibid*, p. 51.

21 *ibid*, p. 62.

22 Siegfried Sassoon Diaries 1915-1918, Faber and Faber, 1983, p. 173. These extracts are reproduced with the kind permission of the Barbara Levy Agency.

23 Letter dated 10 March 1915 quoted in Philip W. Errington (ed.) *John Masefield's Great War*, Pen and Sword Books, 2007, pp. 6-7.

24 *Tales of a Field Ambulance, op. cit.*, p. 68.

25 *ibid*, p. 71.

26 *ibid*, p. 51.

27 *ibid*, p. 73.

28 *ibid*, p. 74.

29 Col. P. H. Dalbiac, *op. cit.*, p. 49.

30 Ursula Vaughan Williams and Imogen Holst (eds.) *Heirs and Rebels – Letters written to each other and occasional writings on music by Ralph Vaughan Williams and Gustav Holst*, Oxford University Press, 1959, p. 45.

31 Royal Army Medical Corps *War Diary*, WO 95/3029/2.

32 *ibid*, p. 13.

33 Captain Wilfrid Miles *History of the Great War: Military Operations France and Belgium 1916*, Imperial War Museum, 1938, p. 460.

34 Cyril Falls *Official History of the Great War; Military Operations – Macedonia, Volume 1*, The Naval and Military Press, 1932, p. 202.

35 See Dalbiac, *op. cit.*, p. 64.

4 1916-1917: The Salonica Front

The assassination of Archduke Franz Ferdinand and his wife, Sophie, in Sarajevo on 28 June 1914 was the incident that ultimately led to the outbreak of the First World War. However, so high were the military, political, personal and colonial stakes in mid-1914 that, together with the web of treaties, *ententes* and alliances that existed, war may have been inevitable even without the drastic action taken by 19-year-old Gavrilo Princip. Austria's decision to invade Serbia after Franz Ferdinand's assassination derived from longstanding grievances against their difficult neighbour; Princip gave Austria-Hungary a reason to act decisively.

There were many complex unsolved issues in the Balkans. Bulgaria and Serbia had border disputes arising from the Second Balkan War of 1913. Further south, King Constantine of Greece was married to the Kaiser's sister and personally favoured Germany, while his Prime Minister, Eleftherios Venizelos, supported the Allied cause. Both Greece and neighbouring Bulgaria had remained neutral in August 1914 even though Britain and France sought to forge alliances; Germany and Austria had similar objectives. British military planners hoped that naval success in the Dardanelles might persuade both Greece and Bulgaria to join the *Entente* but failure in Gallipoli ended that particular aspiration. Bulgaria had secured a large loan from Germany on 2 February 1915 and allowed German weapons through her territory heading for Turkey in March of the same year. It was therefore of little surprise when Bulgaria signed a pact with Germany and Austria on 17 July 1915, securing promises of land in return. This was followed by four formal treaties on 6

September 1915 as part of which it was agreed that Bulgaria would attack Serbia within 30 days. The attack duly took place on 7 October 1915, securing Skopje in Macedonia on 21 October 1915. Against this background, the Greek Prime

Photo 33: A Bulgarian infantry attack at Monastir.

Minister allowed an Anglo-French force to land in Salonica in October 1915 and the Allies became involved, rather belatedly, in fighting in Macedonia against Bulgarian forces at Strumica. A new front, called the 'Salonica Front', was formed.[1]

The Central Powers took Monastir, an important strategic centre in Northern Macedonia, on 21 November 1915 before a long period of attrition began. The stalemate arose mainly because of the difficult weather conditions in the Macedonian winter – wind, rain and snow in the mountainous terrain was tough on the Allied troops in particular.

By mid-1916, General Maurice Sarrail, the Allied Commander on the Salonica Front, decided that Monastir (also known as Bitola) should be the focus of a new offensive with the objective of opening an Allied route into Serbia. On 12 September 1916, French, Serbian and Russian troops were sent into action against heavily fortified Bulgarian positions west of the River Vardar. Casualties were high.

However, on 19 November 1916 Monastir fell to the Allies. The British objective during this battle was to exert pressure on the Bulgarians in the Struma Valley and around Doiran and Lake Doiran. At this time, General George Milne, who led the British forces, was forced to focus attention further south after Venizelos had arrived in Salonica on 9 October 1916 and established a provisional Greek Government supportive of the Allies. While this might have seemed a helpful strategic move, military planners thought it might lead to tactical problems if the Royalist Greek forces, who were supporting Germany, used Venizelos's actions as a reason to mount an attack on the Allies in Greece. To prevent such an outcome, French, Italian and the British 60th Division were to be redeployed to Salonica. As part of the initial skirmishes, the 179th (Infantry) Brigade, which included the 2/4th London Field Ambulance and Ralph Vaughan Williams, was asked to hold the Katerini Pass – see Illustration 11.[2]

Little of these vital geo-political considerations would have meant much to the troops of the 60th Division who were still in northern France. By 4 November 1916 Vaughan Williams and the soldiers of the 2/4th London Field Ambulance had concentrated in Eaucourt-sur-Somme, near Abbeville. Major Layton found a chateau in Épange which was suitable for sick patients; the owner allowed the Field Ambulance to occupy it on the condition that no infectious cases were admitted. As the Ambulance was now officially 'at rest', the historian in Vaughan Williams might have explored the ruins of the 12th century Eaucourt Castle ('Château d'Eaucourt'), on the right bank of the River Somme, or he may have had enough of ruins, medieval or otherwise, by late 1916.

Alternatively, Vaughan Williams and Harry Steggles could have made the short trip to Abbeville, a town that had not been occupied by German troops, even though it had been shelled. In late 1916, it was relatively peaceful; there were even shops – the novelty of looking in shop-windows reminded the soldiers of home – and a café that served omelettes and coffee, luxuries indeed in the Somme region at that time. On 7 November 1916 an impromptu concert was given by the band of the 2/4th London Field Ambulance, presumably led by Pte. R. Vaughan Williams. Such concerts lifted the spirits of the soldiers, helped by extra rations of rum and whisky.

Final preparations were made for the journey southwest to Marseille, with lighter wagons taking precedence for the expected conditions in Greece and Macedonia. Patients were transferred from Épange to hospitals in Abbeville and Étaples. Unusually, Vaughan Williams was himself ill with what was described as 'PUO' (a 'fever of unknown origin'), probably the short form of trench fever which was common among medical orderlies at that time and largely caused by lice. He was ill enough to be admitted to hospital on 10 November 1916 and discharged four days later, just in time to join his colleagues for the journey to Marseilles.

On 14 November 1916, the Ambulance marched the seven miles or so from Eaucourt-sur-Somme to Longpré where they caught the train for the first leg of the journey. Entrainment of the troops took place late on 14 November with the men herded together, 40 to a carriage. Moving at a stately ten miles per hour, the 2/4th London Field Ambulance arrived at Mâcon on 16 November at 2.30 am. Back on the train, the journey took the men to Vienne, 25 miles from Lyon, and then on to Pierrette, finally arriving at Marseilles at 12.35 am on 17 November 1916. French soldiers were posted around the camp with orders to shoot on sight anyone endeavouring to get out to explore the dubious pleasures of Marseille, where there were women of 'easy affections', although three officers were allowed into the town.[3] It was a very cold night; the local camp was muddy and unpleasant so the men were taken out for a four-hour route march just to keep warm. On Sunday 19 November equipment was loaded onto wagons and the Unit duly arrived at the quayside at 2.15 pm to embark on *HMT Transylvania*. Even Dracula would have hated the 11-day journey the 2/4th London Field Ambulance endured before they arrived at Salonica on 30 November 1916.

The problems began with rough weather on the first night. The men had to cling to any fixed object they could find and this resulted in large numbers becoming ill with seasickness. The mess rooms were very dirty and the food was:

'So bad as to be uneatable by many of us and was often tossed out through the portholes, while tea, coffee and soup were so indistinguishable one from another that we often didn't know which had been served out. Many of us felt so starved that night after night we were thankful to purchase from the ship's stewards, at the price of 1s. per bowl, debris from the officers' tables – chicken legs, puddings, jellies and any odds and ends dumped together indiscriminately into basins from the sale of which the stewards must have reaped a generous harvest'.[4]

Vaughan Williams, who had little time for the officers of the 2/4th London Field Ambulance, would have been livid at this further evidence of the enormous gulf between officers and men.

While the weather improved, there was the threat of German submarines, a serious worry despite the presence of Royal Navy ships as a deterrent. That the Mediterranean was a dangerous sea was confirmed when the *Transylvania* itself was sunk by a German submarine on 4 May 1917 with the loss of over 400 lives. On board, inoculations for cholera and typhoid went ahead although it was decided against vaccinations for smallpox. Malaria would have been a real and ongoing danger to Vaughan Williams and his colleagues; in 1916 alone over 3,000 malaria-stricken British soldiers were admitted to Casualty Clearing Stations on the Struma front in Greece.[5] Sanitary and anti-malarial campaigns remained a constant feature of military life in Greece and Macedonia, a location called 'the land of dirt and flies' by one of Vaughan Williams's colleagues, Pte. E. C. Beavis.[6]

The ship arrived at Malta at 10.45 am on 22 November and remained there all day and well into 23 November. As a consequence, the on-board hospital became full of men with raised temperatures due to the lack of ventilation on the stationary ship. The option of landing and re-embarking around 3,000 men for exercise was judged impractical. The ship moved at last but only from St Albion's Bay to Grand Harbour, Valetta, arriving there at noon on 24 November 1916. Again, it was officers only who were allowed ashore. Just five years earlier, Ursula Lock – the future Ursula Vaughan Williams – had been born in this capital city of Malta. By 25 November a strong gale meant that the ship still could not sail for Salonica. There was a diarrhoea epidemic on board arising from infected tinned meat and peas. Finally the ship left Valetta harbour at 10 am on 27 November. A second batch of cholera inoculations began and one hot bath was made available to all ranks. It was a most welcome development.

After a circuitous journey to avoid submarines, the ship finally arrived at Salonica at 11 am on 30 November 1916. The view of Salonica from the harbour impressed the soldiers. However, with no one to meet the 2/4th London Field Ambulance, the Unit made its own way to Summer Hill Camp at Dudular, near Urchantar, seven miles north west of Salonica, without seeing much of the town.

Illustration 10: Camp Dudular, near Salonica.

The camp was located in a barren, open plain near Diavata, where the ground sloped gradually to the sea – see Illustration 10. Everything was very dry with layers of dust and grit which the slightest breeze forced into the soldier's faces. It gave the wags of the Ambulance a chance to repeat the slogan: 'Are we not full of grit?' Vaughan Williams hated it. When he found out that Holst was staying in the same camp as a musical educator for Allied troops in late 1918, he told Holst that it was a 'God-forsaken place'.[7] The men were quickly introduced to the 'Vardar Blast', a strong gale that swept down the valley of the River Vardar.

Divisional HQ, under Major-General E. S. Bulfin, landed at Salonica over a week later on 8 December 1916. The Division joined the British Expeditionary Force, forming part of the 'Allied Army of the Orient', which consisted of French, British, Italian, Serbian and Russian contingents under the command of the French General Maurice Sarrail. The British forces alone numbered six divisions with over 100,000 troops. They were responsible for the right sector of the line, from the River Struma west to Lake Doiran and then onto the River Vardar – see Illustration 11.

It was difficult terrain. This part of Greece consists of bleak, mountainous highlands and huge alluvial plains, interspersed with lakes, including the Doiran. Wheeled traffic found this landscape very tough even in fine weather – and the weather, as we shall see, was often atrocious. The 'Vardar Blast' would blow for four or five days with unrelenting fury followed by periods of bitterly cold and wet conditions.

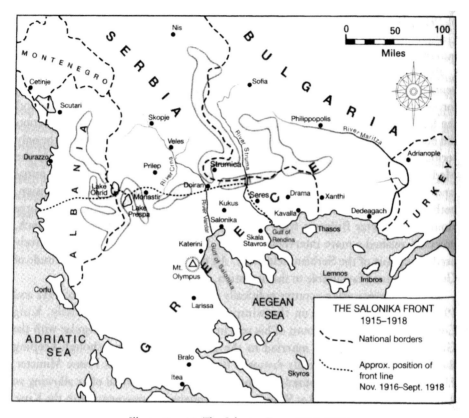

Illustration 11: The Salonika Front 1915-1918.

On 11 December 1916 the 179th (Infantry) Brigade with the 2/4th London Field Ambulance arrived at the quay in Salonica at 6 am. The men of the Field Ambulance departed at 11.30 am in small paddle steamers heading toward Mount Olympus. They landed at Vromeri Beach, a small fishing village near Katerini, to the north of Olympus on the Gulf of Salonica. The jetty at Vromeri Beach had been washed away in an earlier storm so that the men had to wade ashore fully clothed through deep water. This was no problem for the tall Ralph Vaughan Williams but others suffered. The men created a human chain of over 70 yards to bring supplies to land. After sleeping on the beach they marched the following morning just a few miles to Katerini itself. Unfortunately, the boat with most of the Ambulance's equipment and the men's packs was sent back to Salonica by mistake on 12 December leaving the soldiers with only what they had on their backs.

On 15 December 1916, a rear dressing station was created at Lone Tree Tumulus, three miles from Katerini near the village of Stypi. The Main Dressing Station (MDS) was located in Katerini itself, housed in an old building which was previously the municipal offices. It still showed traces of bullet marks from earlier Balkan wars. The MDS served British forces as well as injured civilians. Katerini lay in the centre of a wide plain bounded by the west shore of the Gulf of Salonica; Mount Olympus formed the opposite boundary. The town had a population of around 7,000, swollen by Greek refugees escaping war zones further north. While the houses were extremely clean, with whitewashed walls, the area beyond the properties was very dirty. Major Layton explored the area on arrival in the town and became stuck up to his knees in quicksand; he had to be pulled to safety by two stretcher-bearers.

The strategic purpose of this position was to protect the right flank of the Allied Army from Bulgarian forces as well as any hostile moves by the main Greek army which, as we have seen, had pro-German sympathies. No other British troops had been to this part of the country although there was a small French garrison.

The main Brigade transport section then joined the Ambulance by travelling overland from Salonica, a journey of over 100 miles.[8]

The early priority for the 2/4th London Field Ambulance was sanitation. The risk of catching typhoid fever and malaria was very real. Major Layton had spoken to local doctors who informed him that between 40 and 50 civilian deaths had occurred in 1916 alone from typhoid fever due to polluted water. The Commanding Officer of the 2/4th London Field Ambulance took the view that the troops faced far greater danger from sanitation issues than from a brigade of enemy artillery on the surrounding hills. On 17 December 1916 he issued instructions that all refuse must be incinerated and that 'promiscuous defecation must be rigorously suppressed'.[9] When some of the soldiers accused the local Greek villagers of creating the problem. Major Layton dealt with this complaint, with a rare note of humour, in a circular to all troops dated 2 January 1917:

> 'It is a common thing for me to be told that the fouling of the ground is chiefly due to the Greek inhabitants. I do not believe that this is so. Even if the Greeks of this town are in the habit of reading the *Daily Mail*, I am confident that they do not take in the *Passing Show* and *Punch* or own pages from a copy of a Training Manual, and I am certain they do not have letters from Plumstead which begin "Dear Brother"; yet all these documents I have found this morning near the town in close proximity to masses of faeces'.[10]

Illustration 12: Mount Olympus at nightfall.

Troops were forbidden to use water from the local wells for drinking, cooking or washing. Deep trench fly-proof latrines were constructed.

Amid the sanitation worries and the unforgiving terrain, there was always Mount Olympus. Vaughan Williams's friend Harry Steggles said:

'The one redeeming feature of Katerini was Mount Olympus, which always looked to me like a big homemade cake with plenty of caster sugar on top. The various views of this lovely mountain were simply gorgeous. Our Ambulance took quarters in some old municipal buildings and I, with R.V.W., had a bell tent on the small triangular green by the beech trees… R.V.W. and I visited a café one evening…It was a queer place, smelling of wine and coffee, the whole show having the appearance of a sort of Oriental-Shoreditch affair. The Greeks danced there one night and R.V.W. performed some miracles with pencil and paper writing music'.[11]

Even more memorable for the troops was singing Christmas carols from Sussex and Herefordshire on a bright and clear morning of Christmas Day 1916, within sight of the snow-capped Mount Olympus. It was the unit's first Christmas abroad and Harry Steggles added:

'I cannot leave Katerini without commenting on our wonderful Christmas. R.V.W. got our choral society going, and they sang carols under the shadows of Olympus for the first time in history, I'll warrant. Ernie Allen's sweet voice singing *Good King Wenceslas* was worth going out there to hear. Our COs efforts on behalf of our Christmas dinner were greatly appreciated, together with the pudding. Vaughan Williams and I spent our day in the bell tent, winding up with Samos wine, which was very nice'.[12]

The Christmas pudding had been sent to the Unit by the *Daily Telegraph*.

This was a period of relative peace for the troops which, alas, was not to last. The Unit left Katerini on 28 December heading for Kolokuri, just a few miles across the River Pelikas. The new camp was subject to very high winds and it was with some relief that the Ambulance returned to Katerini a week later.

As the 179th (Infantry) Brigade was scattered over considerable distances, the sick and wounded had to be carried on the backs of mules to the MDS at Katerini. They proved to be temperamental animals for the orderlies who had to saddle and lead them.

The daily routine for Vaughan Williams and his colleagues was laid out by Major Layton as follows:

Réveillé	6.30 am
Breakfast	7.45 am
Fall in	8.30 am
Orderly Room	8.45 am
Dinner	1.00 pm
Tea	5.00 pm
In billet	8.00 pm
Lights out	9.00 pm

Illustration 13: Eastern end of Lake Doiran, Salonica Front.

Men not involved in hospital duties were required to attend to latrines, incinerators and cleaning up the grounds before breakfast.

Tragically, many died during the winter treks around Katerini when the weather was atrocious with blinding snowstorms. Living in the bivouac tents was tough going for the men, especially those of the build of Vaughan Williams. Touching the supporting sticks of the tent might cause an instant collapse, and dressing or undressing could only be managed while lying on your back. With rain and snow, it was impossible to remain dry. Vaughan Williams and Harry Steggles shared such a 'bivvy', an area slightly smaller than a double bed. One notable characteristic of Vaughan Williams was that he would share the discomforts endured by others with stoic humour and good grace.

The Division received orders at the end of February 1917 to take over the section of the front line between the River Vardar and Lake Doiran as the Allies refocused on the Bulgarian army through a new spring offensive. General Milne proposed an attack at Doiran, important strategically because of its location at the head of the Kosturino Pass. One of the main books on the war in Macedonia, *Under the Devil's Eye – The British Military Experience in Macedonia 1915-1918*, said of this offensive:

> 'The area to the west of Lake Doiran that Milne planned to attack is a defender's dream, being a tangled mass of hills cut by numerous ravines. Certain natural features dominate the area and these were incorporated into the Bulgarian's defensive scheme. The most imposing of these is Pip Ridge, which rises to a height of 2,000 feet and is so narrow as to only offer an attacking frontage of 50 yards. Each of its six peaks was defended by a redoubt from which heavy fire could be concentrated on any attacking formation'.[13]

The 60th Division was required to support the main attack through diversionary manoeuvres between the River Vardar and Lake Doiran, a distance of some eight miles. The Division held the left flank of the Front, with the more experienced troops of the 22nd and 26th Division leading the offence in what became known as the *Battle of Doiran*.

Vaughan Williams let his wife know he was near Lake Doiran by sending her a note with a musical scale in the Dorian mode – it was most unlikely that the Army censors would have understood this message. Leaving on 10 March, the 179th (Infantry) Brigade arrived at Lake Doiran on 18 March 1917. The weather throughout the move was awful; rain and sleet storms alternating with snow blizzards. The journey to Karasouli, now called Polykastro, was described by the members of the Field Ambulance as 'our worst experience', and another called it 'the most horrible torture we had to endure during our war service'. He went on:

Illustration 14: The MDS at Kalinova.

'The 'Ides of March' when we marched up to Karasouli seemed to us our worst experience. It was the last stage of a week's continuous trek. We were drenched to the skin; there were long halts, but we could not rest our aching shoulders; we moved forward but a few yards at a time; our feet were sodden and weary; and we knew, worst of all, that there were miles yet before us'.[14]

Each member of the Field Ambulance had to carry a rolled blanket and mackintosh sheet on his back, with waterproof cape above it, along with a holdall, towel, pair of socks, cap and brush in his haversack and a few days' rations, box respirator, steel helmet and a water bottle. Quite a load, between 70 and 100 lbs., especially when walking against the 'Vardar' wind.

The 2/4th London Field Ambulance set up another Main Dressing Station at Kalinova, where it arrived in a blinding snowstorm and with the Vardar wind blowing with terrific violence. This dressing station was totally unlike its equivalent at Ecoivres, being a 'tumble-down sort of building'. Kalinova was located to the south west of Lake Doiran, not far from Iriniko. The Advanced Dressing Stations were at Clichy ravine and Bekirli ford. There was hardly any sign of a village for miles around, neither were there any local inhabitants. Life at Kalinova was isolated and humdrum.

The Ambulance evacuated the wounded from this wild countryside, making the journey sometimes three times a night from the MDS at Kalinova (see Illustration 14) to the Clichy ravine, in the side of a gorge near the front line trenches, and back. The wounded were often evacuated during enemy air raids. The mountainous terrain, bad conditions of the roads and the flooded rivers made the transport of the sick and wounded extremely hazardous.

The Bulgarians had begun a bombardment of the British front on 17 March 1917, concentrating on the area between Lake Doiran and the Vardar. Gas shells were used on the front held by the 22nd Division. On 30 March an enemy aircraft shot down the observation balloon near Kalinova. Thankfully, both observers in the balloon were able to parachute to safety. This success motivated other enemy planes to attempt to shoot down a second observation balloon. Defences held and one of the German aircraft was, in turn, shot down.

Such bursts of action were accompanied by long periods of stalemate. The 179th (Infantry) Brigade was relatively uninvolved during this *Battle of Doiran*. The men of the 2/4th London Field Ambulance were required to dig drainage trenches and deep latrines at the Main Dressing Station, a task which Vaughan Williams undertook with some fortitude. In addition, much time and energy was spent making a large red cross about 100 feet long on the ground using stones. This effort proved too much for the increasingly bored Vaughan Williams whose energy and spirit were draining away. As Harry Steggles put in much later:

> 'Salonica was too dilatory for him. He went on mosquito squad work, which consisted of filling in puddles to prevent mosquitos breeding; he thought this useful in an abstract way. But what caused him the most anguish was to sit down and wash red bricks, which were laid on the ground to form a red cross as protection from German planes. He swore one day, saying: "I will do anything to contribute to the war, but this I will not do".[15]

Vaughan Williams then made the momentous decision to move on. On 27 March 1917 he applied for a Temporary Commission as an officer – this important application is explored in detail in the following chapter.

Meanwhile, two Bulgarian raids on transport and ammunition dumps occurred in the first week of April 1917 on sectors held by the 179th (Infantry) Brigade, leading to three killed and nine wounded before the raid ceased. Relative calm prevailed for the remainder of the stay on the Salonica Front.

Photo 34: Vaughan Williams's band in Katerini, near Salonica, 1917.

Whenever possible Vaughan Williams would form a band to give occasional concerts. As we have seen, this practice had begun in England and would continue through Ecoivres to Salonica and then to the Western Front again in the spring and summer of 1918, even as the Germans began their last great offensive.

A further attack against Bulgarian defences in the Doiran area was planned for early May 1917. Troops of the 179th (Infantry) Brigade, including the 2/4th London Field Ambulance, were involved in subsidiary attacks on five hills near Doiran. Fortunately, these were secured without enemy engagements as the enemy had abandoned its outposts. Bulgarian shelling of the newly-held position on 9 May slowed progress, although no further attempts were made to push the British troops back. British losses in the attack of 8-9 May totalled 1,861 of which all but 118 had been borne by the 26th Division.[16] Fate had again looked kindly on Vaughan Williams and his colleagues.

The British Government had decided at a conference held in Paris on 4 and 5 May 1917 that it was their intention to withdraw one infantry division from Macedonia along with two cavalry brigades. The destination of these troops was to be Egypt where the Army was hopeful of better results.[17] Macedonia was becoming, in the eyes of the military planners, an isolated theatre of war and the War Cabinet in London was advised on 29 July 1917 that 'The Salonica forces will never materially contribute to winning the war'.[18] David Lloyd George, the Prime Minister, continued to favour offensives on the Salonica Front which he felt would be more successful against Germany's weaker allies than more attrition on the Western Front.

By late May, rumours began circulating within the Field Ambulance of a possible move to Egypt. With the hot season approaching and the risks of malaria increasing, the men were ready to leave Greece. On 1 June 1917 the 60th Division received orders that it had been selected to return to Salonica to prepare for a transfer to Egypt. It handed over its sector of the Salonica Front to the 26th Division. The 179th (Infantry) Brigade held its position until 5 June 1917, under renewed enemy shelling, before marching back to Urchantar, near Camp Dudular, where they awaited embarkation for Egypt. Lack of shipping meant that for the next month the troops had to wait for transport to become available. Finally, they boarded the troopship *Menominée*, and arrived in Alexandria on 9 July 1917.

Vaughan Williams, however, for the first time since January 1915, was not with his colleagues of the 2/4th London Field Ambulance. His application for promotion had been approved by his Commanding Officer, Major Layton, by the Brigadier-General of the 60th Division and by the War Office in London. On 16 June 1917 he embarked for England to prepare for life as an officer. Despite often cursing those in command, he was preparing to become one of them. His caustic parting words while still in Salonica were: "My regret at leaving is that I shall cease to be a man on becoming an officer…"[19]

Harry Steggles always maintained in later years that Vaughan Williams regretted his decision to become an officer. He missed the shared experiences of being with his comrades, however different were their pre-war backgrounds. David Jones put it best in *In Parenthesis*:

'My companions in the war were mostly Londoners with an admixture of Welshmen…Together they bore in their bodies the genuine tradition of the Island of Britain…It was curious to know them harnessed together, and together caught in the toils of 'good order and military discipline'; to see them shape together in the remains of an antique regimental tradition; to see them react to the few things that united us – the same jargon, the same prejudice against 'other arms' and against the Staff, the same discomforts, the same grievances, the same maims, the same deep fears, the same pathetic jokes…'[20]

The same jokes, the same stories. There was the transport driver who was usually slow in getting up but came out of his tent at the double one morning when he discovered a six-foot snake sharing his blanket. There was the occasion when orders came to dig-out a swimming pool at Kalinova only to be told to dismantle it as soon as it was finished because it might pollute the stream from which mules drank below the camp. For the Unit, these were happy days:

Happy Days. Happy Days.
When you wake and find the tent a perfect maze.
Someone's gone and put your vest in
His disgusting dirty mess tin,
Then the goat looks in the doorway.
Happy Days.[21]

It was this camaraderie which sustained the troops through tough times; now heading for training as an officer-cadet this was what Vaughan Williams would miss.

References

1 For more information see Martin Gilbert *The First World War*, Weidenfeld and Nicolson, 1994, in particular the chapter 'War on every front'.

2 See Alan Wakefield and Simon Moody *Under the Devil's Eye – The British Military Experience in Macedonia 1915-1918*, Pen and Sword Military, 2017, pp. 3-6 and p. 61.

3 *Tales of a Field Ambulance*, Borough Publishing, 1935, p. 76.

4 *ibid*, p. 79.

5 Captain A. J. Mann *The Salonika Front*, A. & C. Black Ltd., 1920, p.145.

6 *Tales of a Field Ambulance, op. cit.*, p. 81.

7 Michael Short *Gustav Holst – The Man and his Music*, Oxford University Press, 1990, p. 166.

8 Col. P. H. Dalbiac *History of the 60th Division*, George Allen and Unwin, 1927, p. 69.

9 See *War Diary* for 2/4th London Field Ambulance, National Archives, WO 95/4927, December 1916.

10 'Sanitation' included in *War Diary, ibid*, Volume IV, January 1917.

11 *Tales of a Field Ambulance, op. cit.*, p. 90.

12 *ibid*, p. 91.

13 Alan Wakefield and Simon Moody, *op. cit.*, p. 66.

14 *Tales of a Field Ambulance, op. cit.*, p. 108.

15 See Harry Steggles 'Tribute to Vaughan Williams' reproduced in Stephen Connock *Toward the Sun Rising – Ralph Vaughan Williams Remembered*, Albion Music Ltd., 2018, p. 315.

16 Alan Wakefield and Simon Moody, *op. cit.*, p. 97.

17 Captain Cyril Falls *Official History of The Great War – Macedonia, Volume 2*, The Naval and Military Press, 1934, p. v.

18 *ibid*, p. 3.

19 Ursula Vaughan Williams *R.V.W. – A Biography of Ralph Vaughan Williams*, Oxford University Press, 1964, p. 125. Ursula quotes this as being: "My only regret at leaving is that I shall cease to be a man and become an officer" and this is also the quote confirmed by Harry Steggles. However James Day in his *Vaughan Williams*, Master Musicians Series, J. M. Dent and Sons, 1961, p. 34 gives a more caustic version of 'cease to be a man on becoming an officer'. This version sounds more characteristic and is preferred in this book.

20 David Jones *In Parenthesis*, Faber and Faber paperback edition, 2018, p. xii.

21 *Tales of a Field Personnel, op. cit.*, p. 277.

5 1917-1919: Becoming a 'one-pipper' – 2/Lt. R. Vaughan Williams

The decision by Vaughan Williams to apply for a commission in March 1917 coincided with the British Army being increasingly short of officers and NCOs as casualties among these ranks had been significantly higher through 1916 and into early 1917. Instructions went out to find men in the ranks who, through experience, education or training might be appropriate for a Temporary Commission, or 'Temporary Gentleman' as Vaughan Williams might have put it. With his public school education at Charterhouse, a first degree and a doctorate from Cambridge University and other qualifications, along with 18 months service in the ranks, Vaughan Williams would have stood out, intellectually as well as physically, from his comrades in the 2/4th London Field Ambulance. He could still have chosen to remain with his friends in the Ambulance and head for Egypt. He did not, instead applying for admission to an Officer Cadet Unit with, in the words of the official form he completed, 'A view to appointment to a Temporary Commission in the Regular Army for the period of the war'. The first page of his application form is shown at Appendix 6.

Photo 35: Sir Francis Darwin.

Vaughan Williams needed to provide two references as to his 'moral character during the past four years' and he nominated both Sir Francis Darwin and his brother-in-law the Right Hon. H. A. L. Fisher, Minister of Education and a member of the Cabinet in Lloyd George's coalition Government.

A botanist and son of Charles Darwin, Sir Francis ('Frank') Darwin (1848-1925) was related to Vaughan Williams on his mother's side and had also, in 1913, married Florence, the eldest sister of Vaughan Williams's wife Adeline. As noted above, Florence was a widower following the death of Frederick Maitland in 1906.

H. A. L. Fisher (1865-1940) was one of Adeline Vaughan Williams's elder brothers. He was President of the Board of Education, having been offered the role in December 1916.[1] The officer who had to endorse Vaughan Williams's application, the Brigadier-General of the 60th Division, was suitably impressed. Having reviewed the recommendation by Major Thomas Layton, the Officer Commanding the 2/4th London Field Ambulance, that Vaughan Williams be granted a commission, the Brigadier-General noted, on the application form dated 1 April 1917, that Vaughan Williams had:

Photo 36: H. A. L. Fisher in 1940.

'A very good education. I think he would make a good Royal Garrison Artillery officer. He is 44 years of age and too old for the Royal Field Artillery as a subaltern. I recommend that he be sent to a cadet school'.

As part of the procedure for promotion, a medical examination by Major Layton was undertaken in Katerini on 29 March and Vaughan Williams was declared fit. His application for a commission could now be forwarded to the War Office. In less than a month, on 29 April 1917, the War Office sent a telegram to Vaughan Williams which stated:

'Recommended for admission to an Artillery Officer's Cadet Unit. Proceed to Base to await passage to England. Authority – War Office'.

Were there deeper reasons other than boredom and worries about malaria that prompted Vaughan Williams to apply for a commission after more than 18 months as a private? We know he had not found the RAMC officers congenial, feeling that the gulf between officers and men was very great both on the basis of rank and by medical qualifications.[2] His second wife and biographer, Ursula Vaughan Williams, suggested that: 'Someone in authority arranged for him to be sent back to England'.[3]

This 'someone in authority' in the War Office in London suggests that the unit dealing with applications for a 'Temporary Commission' was, like the Brigadier-General, impressed with Vaughan Williams's credentials – after all, how many privates in the British Army in 1917 had a doctorate from Cambridge and a brother-in-law in Lloyd George's Cabinet? The War Office would have taken Vaughan Williams's references seriously and made the arrangements for

Vaughan Williams to return to London. Herbert Fisher would not, in all probability, have become personally involved although a quiet word from him to various colleagues in the Cabinet, such as Lord Milner, cannot be ruled out. Fisher had certainly kept in touch with his family during the war, notably with Virginia Woolf (née Stephen), who was a first cousin. At one such meeting between Herbert Fisher and Virginia on Tuesday 15 October 1918 her diary entry relates the following fascinating comment:

> "We've won the war today" he said, at once. "I saw Milner this morning, & he says we shall have peace by Christmas. The Germans have made up their minds they can't fight a retreat".[4]

Fisher went on to refer to the *Second Battle of the Marne* from 15 July to early August 1918 as the decisive French and British counter-attack which led him to this bold, and largely correct, judgement about the course of the war. These comments came only five days after Field Marshal Haig (he had been promoted in early 1917) had met the French Marshal Ferdinand Foch when they had discussed, in conditions of the strictest secrecy, the possible terms for an armistice with Germany. That Herbert Fisher was willing to share such insights with his cousin showed the trust in family that existed for the Fishers – and the Vaughan Williamses. On 26 February 1918, while on leave in London, Vaughan Williams was talking to his brother-in-law about raising funds for English opera and gave Fisher's home address to E. J. Dent, saying: 'Now is the time to strike!'[5]

Having friends with 'pull' in high places was certainly useful then, as now. Rupert Brooke had secured a commission in the Royal Naval Division on 15 September 1914 following the intervention of his close friend Eddie Marsh, who was Private Secretary to Winston Churchill, then First Lord of the Admiralty, a role Marsh had held since 1905. Churchill had promised such a commission to Brooke a few weeks earlier. Marsh told Rupert Brooke he would recommend this commission for both Brooke and his composer friend W. Denis Browne, saying he would do this: 'For all I'm worth. I can make play with Winston having promised you an appointment'.[6] Marsh succeeded; no official form, examination or interview were required. Brooke had lunch with Churchill on 23 September 1914 and Rupert Brooke recalled the conversation:

> 'Winston was very cheerful at lunch, and said one thing which is exciting, but a *dead* secret. You mustn't *breathe* it. That is, that it's his game to hold the Northern ports – Dunkirk to Havre – at all costs. So if there's a raid on *any* of them, at any moment, we shall be flung across to help the French reservists. So we may go to camp on Saturday, and be under fire in France on Monday! I'm afraid the odds are against it, though'.[7]

Whatever or whoever was behind Vaughan Williams's decision to apply for a commission, he left Salonica for the UK on 16 June 1917, having spent 210 days in Greece, as shown on the Military History Sheet at Appendix 7.[8]

Vaughan Williams was asked to report to the War Office rather than continue duties at the RAMC training camp in Blackpool. Though his 'Statement of Service' suggests he was posted to Blackpool on 12 July 1917 there is no evidence that he went to the RAMC base in this seaside resort. He was, in fact, staying with Bruce Richmond, the journalist and editor, at 6 Phene Street in London – his wife was away from home – and he wrote a letter from there on 25 July to the Carnegie Trust regarding publication of *A London Symphony*. Ursula Vaughan Williams, in her biography of her husband, states that he had been sent to London to report to the War Office rather than having to go to Blackpool. She relates that Vaughan Williams's name had been put before an elderly officer who, having fallen from his horse, uttered the repeated exhortation to those about him: "You must do something about Vaughan Williams".[9]

On 27 July 1917, Vaughan Williams was notified of his admission to 2 Royal Garrison Artillery (RGA) Officer Cadet School at Maresfield Park and ordered to report there on 1 August 1917 – see Illustration 15.

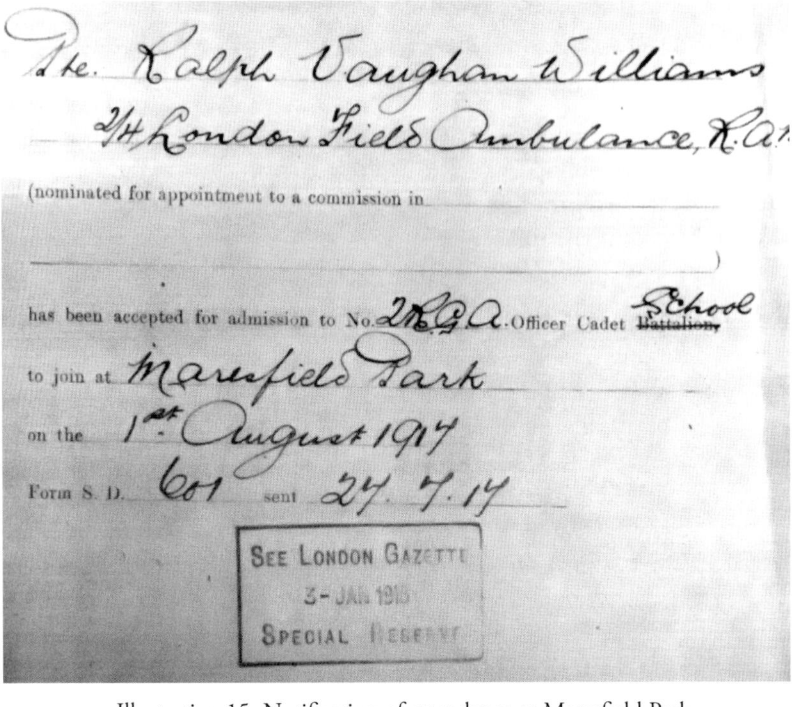

Pte. Ralph Vaughan Williams
2/4 London Field Ambulance, R.A.M.C.
(nominated for appointment to a commission in
)
has been accepted for admission to No. 2 R.G.A. Officer Cadet ~~Battalion~~ School
to join at Maresfield Park
on the 1st August 1917
Form S. D. 601 sent 27. 7. 17

SEE LONDON GAZETTE
3-JAN 1918
SPECIAL RESERVE

Illustration 15: Notification of attendance at Maresfield Park.

The War Office was following up the suggestion of the Brigadier-General of the 60th Division, referred to earlier, who had recommended a Royal Garrison Artillery cadet role for Vaughan Williams on 1 April 1917. The RGA was formed in 1899 to man the guns in British forts and coastal defences. By the First World War it had grown to be the technical and professional custodian of the Army's heavy batteries. It was very much a fighting unit and Vaughan Williams would have known as soon as he received that War Office telegram on 27 April that he would likely be returned to active service, probably in Northern France. In a letter to Cecil Sharp of 28 December 1917 he said:

> 'I came back from Salonica…to try my hand at another trade – Artillery – I wondered if I was crazy to start an absolutely new subject at my age'.[10]

The Royal Garrison Artillery was felt to be less exposed than a front-line infantry division or the Royal Field Artillery and therefore more suitable for a 44-year-old. To an extent this was true: with a range of over 15,000 yards by 1918, the heavy battery units were usually many miles behind enemy lines. Danger remained from attacks, or counter-attacks, by German long-range artillery or, less likely but possible, from rapid offensives by German infantry of the sort that did, indeed, occur on 21 March 1918 as part of the German *Spring Offensive*. Enemy aircraft attacks, too, were an increasing risk. The probability of Vaughan Williams being caught up in one of the fiercest battles of the war in the spring of 1918 would presumably have seemed most unlikely to either the Brigadier-General of the 60th Division or the War Office personnel when they considered and ultimately approved his application in April 1917.

It was, of course, well known that officers generally, and especially Artillery officers, were vulnerable. John Lewis-Stempel in his book *Six Weeks* (2010) estimated that the average time a British Army junior officer survived during the Western Front's bloodiest phases was six weeks.[11] The poet Edward Thomas had joined the Royal Garrison Artillery in June 1916. He went on to serve with the 244th Siege Battery and, to underline the dangers that would face Vaughan Williams in 1918, the poet was killed by shellfire while manning an observation post on Easter Monday 1917 on the first day of the *Battle of Arras*.[12] Edward Thomas's poem *Adlestrop* would gain a posthumous poignancy, for the poet would never again see the station or village:

> *And willows, willow-herb, and grass,*
> *And meadowsweet, and haycocks dry,*
> *No whit less still and lonely fair*
> *Than the high cloudlets in the sky.*

Photo 37: Adlestrop Station – sadly now closed.

2/Lt. Patrick Hadley, who would go on to compose the beautiful *The Trees So High* in 1931, was a gunner in the Royal Field Artillery, 162nd Brigade, in 1918 and was seriously wounded – his right leg had to be amputated below the knee. Another musician, the horn player and composer Adolphe Goossens, the brother of Eugene and Léon, had joined the Artists Rifles in 1915 and was quickly commissioned as an officer. Leading a platoon in the Somme in August 1916, his sergeant had boasted that "he had never brought back an officer alive". This proved prophetic as Goossens died of wounds and gas gangrene on 17 August 1916 after the 20-year-old had led his men 'over the top'. He is buried in the Military Cemetery at Puchevillers, north-east of Amiens.[13]

In early August 1917 Vaughan Williams would not have been aware that Thomas Armstrong, the composer and conductor, Dennis Arundell, actor and producer, and H. C. Colles, music critic and editor of *Grove*, were officers in the Royal Garrison Artillery at this time. Thomas Armstrong later recalled how he saw a fellow soldier in France without a jacket and sitting on an upturned bucket milking a cow – this was Ralph Vaughan Williams! Lt. Dennis Arundell was invalided home after being gassed in early 1918. He would survive the war and, in 1954, gave Vaughan Williams the satisfaction of producing a remarkable performance of *The Pilgrim's Progress* in Cambridge with the young John Noble as Pilgrim. Captain Colles served with the RGA in Macedonia and was awarded a medal by the Greek Government for his role in training the Greek artillery in the use of British guns.

For Vaughan Williams events now moved quickly. He wrote to Gustav Holst on 4 August 1917 as follows:

'I wish we could have met again – but I was bunged off here in a hurry – so I'm in it now – though we don't really start work until Monday – no leave until the middle of the course – about two months – it seems a fairly free and easy place at present – but a good deal of stupid ceremonial – *white gloves* (on ceremonial parades) (N.B. I believe there is a war on)'.[14]

The 3,000 acre site at Maresfield Park, in what is now East Sussex, had been seized by the crown in 1914 (the owner was a German, Prince Munster of Derneberg) and used as an Army training camp from October 1914. The Royal Garrison Artillery set up a Cadet School in the park in 1917. In August of that year a gun pit was constructed in the grounds, with sandbag gun emplacements and trenches nearby.[15]

Despite the officer shortages, standards of entry and training were taken very seriously with practical tests and exam papers on subjects like 'Military Law and Military Organisation', 'Higher Mathematics', which included trigonometry, and the 'Chemistry of Explosives'. In addition, much time was spent on mounting, dismounting and transporting guns. This was a complicated business especially in relation to the siege artillery which involved levers, pulleys, cradles and so forth. The Royal Garrison Artillery Training Manual (1914) on 'Sheers and Derricks' alone ran to over 150 pages. If you failed the exams you were R.T.U. – 'Returned to Unit'. Success led to a notice on a pass list stating that: 'The following cadets will be gazetted and will report to…' with a location specified. Appendix 6 shows the London Gazette stamp for Vaughan Williams's entry to the 'Special Reserve'.

Photo 38: Maresfield Park main building.

Joseph Mason was a colleague of Vaughan Williams at Maresfield Park and later recalled 7 am parades consisting of brisk marches along the local country roads of Sussex and added:

'Our first course parade was taken by the staff Regimental Sergeant-Major (RSM). We were a mixed body of about 70 young men, the majority in our twenties, a few older, and a few youngsters in their late teens, from public school. A comparatively small number of us had, even in 1917, served overseas!

I remember clearly my first impression of a big bronzed, rugged-looking man, somewhat 'over twenty', a little ungainly, and not, in any accepted sense of the term, a smart, spruced-up looking soldier, especially for an officer cadet. Yet he was impressively striking: his hair cropped in the military style, cap a little askew, powerful determined face, his broad shoulders rather stooping, and slightly lop-sided, his feet enclosed in large-sized army boots; all denoting purposeful strength built on firm foundations.

Photo 39: Vaughan Williams in the Royal Garrison Artillery, 1917.

Reports circulated that this 'old man' was in his 'mid-forties', had been a private in the RAMC in Palestine[16] and, in his desire and determination to serve in a combatant role, had got himself accepted and posted as an officer cadet in the Royal Garrison Artillery, the heavy branch of the Royal Artillery.

He answered his name to the RSM in correct form, "Here, Sir" in a quick, cultured, firm voice.

Our first parades, at 7.00 am, consisted generally of a brisk march, with some doubling[17] along the country roads near Maresfield Park. Ralph seemed literally to hurl himself forward, as if impelled by some fierce determination to 'get there', though doubling, for a man of his age and build, would be no easy exercise.

We left Maresfield Park at the end of November 1917 and were posted in two groups to refresher and firing courses, Ralph going to Lydd (I think)[18] and I to Cooden, near Bexhill'.[19]

Joseph Mason referred to many of the officer-cadets being in their 20s with a few in their 'late teens' and this illustrates the considerable age disparity between Vaughan Williams and his fellow cadets. As a result, Vaughan Williams could have become a 'father' to his younger colleagues but this was unlikely. Although courteous and kind, with a keen sense of humour, he was rather formal, reserved and, heaven forbid, untidy for such a role. Sport was a key unifier between the subalterns and other ranks and Vaughan Williams disliked most sports including football and cricket. Cultural differences, too, were likely to have been considerable. Dennis Wheatley was just 18 when he was training at Maresfield Park in 1915 and became an officer at that age. He and other cadets were keen, idealistic and excited by what they were heading for – and largely ignorant of the realities of war. Vaughan Williams had already spent 18 months in action in France and Greece and knew first-hand the horror, suffering, pain, boredom and confusion of war. He most likely kept his own counsel.

Vaughan Williams was certainly not the oldest subaltern in the Army. Richard Blair, George Orwell's father, decided in 1917 – at the age of 60 – to become an officer and was, to everyone's surprise, accepted. He was assigned to the 51st India Labour Company in Marseilles and was thought to be the oldest subaltern in the Army.[20] At least because of their age and experience, officers such as Richard Blair and Ralph Vaughan Williams might have been more adept at handling troops compared to many of the 18 or 19 year-olds, straight out of public school, who were training alongside them. They certainly had an air of authority. Second Lieutenant Frederick Hoy, of the 48th Field Artillery Brigade, wrote referring to the role of 'the most humble of all ranks, the 2nd Lieutenant' in a letter to his daughters as follows:

> 'He had to go where his men had to go. He was the man who simply dare not show any funk. He it was who must be with his men on raids and attacks, advances and retreats, frontline jobs and reserve, working parties and ration carrying…He must be ready at all times to advise, bully, sympathise, laugh or cry with them all. Stern in the face of danger or trouble and always remembering the proud title of the British Officer – gentleman – which in spite of many sneers was applied with truth to the majority of those men and boys from all stations of life who accepted the responsibility of trying to lead men in the greatest of all wars'.[21]

Fred Hoy was another artillery officer who was seriously wounded while on observation duty. On 18 September 1918 a bullet went through his left shoulder; it was a close call but he survived and was invalided out of the Army in 1919.

While leadership of men might have been easier for Vaughan Williams, given his natural authority, age and experience, he still had to learn about artillery techniques. Artillery warfare had made tremendous advances since 1914. More use was made of aerial observations (from balloons or aeroplanes) providing measurements for firing with increasing accuracy. These techniques were used alongside information provided by ground observers on special patrols. 'Sound ranging' was also becoming more common and this involved determining the location of hostile batteries from the sounds of its guns firing. Use was made of stop watches or microphones to gauge enemy heavy gun locations. Sydney Hall, a gunner with 242 Siege Battery, described the factors that had to be taken into account in accurately preparing both range and line of the heavy artillery for firing, including the force and direction of the wind, the wear of the gun, air temperature, barometric reading, weight of the shell and type of fuse. The calculations were rendered more complex by the lack of standardisation in shells and fuses. The range obtained in yards had to be converted into degrees and minutes for the Gun Captain to set the firing parameters on his clinometer – a typical field clinometer is shown in Illustration 16.[22]

Illustration 16: A field clinometer from 1917.

These subjects were being studied by Vaughan Williams who concentrated on the transport and firing of six-inch howitzers. This required all his formidable powers of concentration and capacity for hard work. In secret, he rented a room with another cadet, John Tindall Robertson, outside the grounds of the cadet school where they could find some measure of privacy. Tindall Robertson recalled his role with Vaughan Williams in a letter of 1958:

'I did my best to help him both with his work and in seeing that he got his equipment and so on right for parades. He was not one for whom the proper arrangement of straps and buckles, and all those things on which the sergeant-major is so keen, came easily. Neither was it easy for him, then in middle age, to learn and retain all the miscellaneous information which was pumped into us. But he achieved it by dogged perseverance and toil'.[23]

With Harry Steggles now in Egypt and Palestine, Vaughan Williams was fortunate to find another colleague willing to help him out with his uniform and equipment.

Vaughan Williams spent just a few weeks at Lydd in November 1917. This town is just to the north of Dungeness, which is at the most southerly point in Kent, on the Romney Marshes. It was known as a military location prior to the First World War. By 1917, there was an Army Training Camp, military barracks for the Royal Garrison Artillery, where Vaughan Williams was based, and a School for Siege Artillery. The nearby firing area, on the vast expanse of shingle heading to Dungeness, was called Lydd Ranges and was connected to the main site by a long narrow-gauge railway. Here Vaughan Williams learnt more about the science and practice of gunnery using six-inch howitzers for practice. This included the use of map coordinates for greater accuracy in long distance firing and mastering the use of the field clinometer. For training at Lydd, the gun-crew typically consisted of ten men although in the field this could be as few as five or six men. There was also a constant shortage of shells for training purposes, with a limit of three live rounds per gun-crew.

Photo 40: The Royal Garrison Artillery camp at Lydd, 1916.

Edward Thomas had also transferred to Lydd, on 3 December 1916, to complete his training. He found the trigonometry needed for artillery calculations very difficult. The camp at Lydd, part of it being known as 'Tin Town' or 'Hut Town' for the cheap metal huts the Army had erected, was a desolate place. Edward Thomas appreciated the shingle flats with the village's 'beautiful' church tower commanding the marshes in all directions.[24] The church was at least useful as an aiming point for the artillery. Officers were able to stay in 'Brick Town', a step up on the tin huts, although Vaughan Williams, as a cadet, found himself in Hut Town.

It was extremely cold during Vaughan Williams's brief stint at Lydd and the cadets had to undertake physical exercises in their shirtsleeves in a blizzard. Vaughan Williams succeeded in his passing-out

Photo 41: RGA training at Lydd.

examinations, despite the difficulties of trigonometry, and was duly discharged as a private 'As a consequence of being appointed to a Commission in the Royal Garrison Artillery' on 23 December 1917. The appointment was effective from 24 December 1917 and notification appeared in the *London Gazette* on 3 January 1918. Like E. J. Moeran and Paddy Hadley, he was now a 'one-pipper', a Second Lieutenant with a regimental 'pip' on his shoulder and one star on his cuffs. He received a stiff parchment containing His Majesty's Commission stating:

> To our Trusty and well beloved Ralph Vaughan Williams. Greetings.
>
> We, reposing especial Trust and Confidence in your Loyalty, Courage and Good Conduct, do by these Presents Constitute and Appoint you to be an Officer in Our Land Forces from the twenty-fourth day of December 1917. You are therefore carefully and diligently to discharge your duty as such in the Rank of 2nd Lieutenant…and you are at all times to exercise and well discipline in Arms both the inferior Officers and Men serving under you and use your best endeavours to keep them in good Order and Discipline…
>
> Given at Our Court, at Saint James's, the twenty-third day of December 1917 in the Eighth Year of Our Reign.
>
> By His Majesty's Command.
> Ralph Vaughan Williams
> 2nd Lieutenant
> Land Forces.[25]

There is no record of what Vaughan Williams thought of the term 'inferior Officers and Men', nor is there any evidence that he kept this parchment with its Royal Seal and reproduction of the King's signature.

At least the pay was better, not that this probably mattered to Vaughan Williams. Typically, a second lieutenant would receive £192 a year which, with

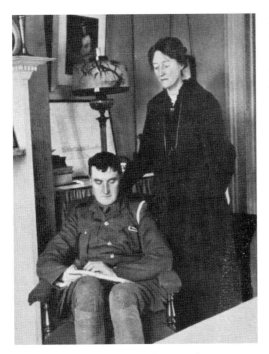

field allowances, might increase to £250 per year, amounting to around £13,000 in equivalent value today. Nearly all the officers were paid through an account at Cox & Co of 16 Charing Cross, London (later part of Lloyds Banking Group) and had their own chequebook. The branch in London was open all day every day during the First World War to allow officers on leave from the Front to cash cheques up to a limit of £5.

Vaughan Williams had returned to his home at 13 Cheyne Walk in London for Christmas leave when Photo 42 was taken. Cheyne Walk, with its views over the River Thames, must have seemed calm and restorative to the composer after the 'Vardar' winds of Salonica. He might have

Photo 42: 2/Lt. Vaughan Williams and Adeline when on leave, Cheyne Walk, late 1917 or early 1918.

remembered that Dante Gabriel Rossetti had lived at number 16 and Bertrand Russell, his friend from Cambridge University days, at number 14. He would have enjoyed domestic quiet, to bathe, to think about music and, most importantly, to sleep in a decent bed.

Vaughan Williams also spent some time in late December at 22 Marina, St. Leonards-on-Sea, in Kent, visiting family. He was reading Cecil Sharp's book *Eight Folk Songs from the Southern Appalachians* (1917) and said that he had no idea exactly what the Army would do with him next.[26] A short spell in February 1918 at the RGA Officer's Reinforcement Depot at Bordon Camp, south of Basingstoke in Hampshire, where he roomed with Tindall Robertson again in St Lucia Barracks, led to rumours about an overseas posting and there was speculation that it would be back to Salonica. Vaughan Williams immediately applied for inclusion – not the first time he had approached the adjutant looking for an overseas posting.[27] Clearly Vaughan Williams was ready for a combatant role, 'being up for it again'. Something of his sense of national duty, his character and his courage can be seen in this keenness for another overseas deployment.

After embarkation leave, Vaughan Williams said goodbye to his wife, Adeline, on Friday 1 March 1918 and headed for Southampton yet again. She would have been stoic about this leave-taking, for she was very much of a class that would only show a 'stiff upper lip'; it was in such poor taste to demonstrate emotion. In this she was not alone. Max Plowman, in his elegiac memoir *A Subaltern on the Somme*, mentions saying goodbye to his young wife at Charing Cross Station in London on his way to the Somme battlefield, noting: 'She does not touch my arm, we know the etiquette'.[28]

Nevertheless, Vaughan Williams would very likely have felt a sense of regret to be leaving his wife given her increasing disability. At the age of 48, ill-health and family worries had diminished the gentle beauty of her youth. She continued to wear black dresses, as shown in Photo 42, as a mark of respect following the death of one brother, Arthur Fisher, in 1902 and another, Charles Fisher, in the *Battle of Jutland* in 1916. This sad habit was further reinforced following the death of a third brother, Hervey Fisher, in 1921 – of which more later.

Carrying his personal baggage with a theoretical allowance of up to 35 lbs. in total – with a full pack this was often exceeded – Vaughan Williams travelled to Le Havre with a better idea of what he was going to find compared to his first visit there with the 2/4th London Field Ambulance on that mid-summer's day of June 1916. He was duly assigned to 141 Heavy Battery, 86th Brigade, Royal Garrison Artillery within, at that stage of the war, the 29th Division. This Battery would often switch command to, for example, the 3rd Canadian Division, the 32nd Division, 34th Division or the 36th Division over the course of the next nine months.

After a few days in base camp at Le Havre, he was sent by train to Rouen for refresher training. This 40-mile trip could take over seven hours by train; soldiers would sometimes get off the train and walk alongside it! Rouen is located on the river Seine, about 40 miles due east on the road to Amiens, and Vaughan Williams could have watched the hospital ships on the Seine heading for Le Havre, packed with wounded soldiers heading home. This would have reminded him of his days at the other end of the casualty evacuation chain at Ecoivres and Neuville St Vaast. Alternatively, he could have explored the attractive cathedral or the old quarters of the town. Probably, he had dinner in the Grand Hôtel de la Poste which supplied the finest meals in Rouen at the time and which was frequented by all British officers passing through on their way to the Western Front.

The 86th Brigade was a gunnery unit assigned in 1917 to the Second Army – this would change to the Third Army by March 1918 and the Brigade would also assist the Counter Battery Office of the 2nd Anzac Corps. By early 1918, the Brigade comprised the following sections:

- 86th Brigade HQ staff
- 324 Siege Battery (6-inch Howitzers) (initially under command of the 39th Brigade)
- 203 Siege Battery (6-inch Howitzers)
- 141 Heavy Battery
- 1/1 Wessex Heavy Battery [29]

'Heavy artillery' in the First World War included the 60-pounder guns weighing 4 tons and drawn by teams of horses. Anything heavier was described as 'siege artillery' and these guns were generally dismantled before being transported and then rebuilt at the firing platform. Understandably, the Army preferred the mobility of the heavy artillery until toward the end of the war when the destructive force of the siege artillery was more fully appreciated. Vaughan Williams's brigade included both heavy and siege artillery units.

Photo 43: A Heavy Battery of the RGA towing 60-pounder guns in Northern France.

The breech-loading 60-pounder guns emerged in 1905. In 1914, they had a range of 10,000 yards and, by 1918, as we have already noted, this had been extended to 15,000 yards – or over eight miles. This range was, however, exceeded by 30% on average by German heavy artillery. The Germans also had a 35 cm. (over 13 inch) gun with a range of almost 40 miles! During the First World War, the British 60-pounder guns were only deployed in 'Heavy Batteries' and these units were generally under Divisional command. There were 32 heavy batteries in the British Army in 1914 and this had expanded to 117 by 1918.

The 60-pounder guns had long muzzles that were elevated upwards from the horizontal position. They were deployed in attacking and destroying enemy artillery ('counter-battery fire') as well as destroying trenches, dumps, bunkers, stores or transport infrastructure behind enemy lines. Each gun weighed around 4,480 lbs but, with its carriage, weighed closer to 10,000 lbs. It was 14 feet long when fully extended, with a recoil of 4½ feet. The 60-pounder was provided with either amatol-filled high explosive shells or shrapnel shells to the ratio of 30% high explosive to 70% shrapnel.[30] Usually, the shrapnel shells consisted of hundreds of lead balls designed to explode in mid-air. Chemical, smoke and gas shells could also be used with the 60-pounder guns. The gas shells would leave a lingering aroma around the gun battery, a rather sickly sweet smell. Gas and smoke bombs were more capricious – who knew whether the wind direction might change?

A Heavy Battery within the Royal Garrison Artillery typically had four to six guns needing a team of six to eight horses to tow each gun. Allowing for rotation, a Battery might have around 80 heavy horses, along with an Ammunition Column of a further 72 heavy horses and others associated with the staff of Battery Headquarters, including riding horses. Leading the Battery were five to eight officers and 180 other ranks.

60 POUNDER MOVING UP IN SUPPORT

Photo 44: A 60-pounder gun moving up in support.

Horses were essential on the Western Front because of the difficult terrain. As Gordon Corrigan puts it:

'The field artillery had to be able to support the infantry, get its guns to a position from where it could fire at the enemy, and move forward once the infantry moved to the limit of the gun's range. As this movement was nearly always either off roads or along roads already damaged by shelling, the guns had to be mobile over any terrain…Only horses would do…Horses could get through all but the worst ground, were faster than traction engines and less liable to break down'.[31]

The Army's horse establishment had increased from 25,000 to 165,000 in just two weeks during August 1914 alone. This would not be nearly enough and, overall, a further 428,608 horses and 275,097 mules were purchased and shipped to the UK from U.S.A. and Canada.[32] Siegfried Sassoon remembered inspecting the heavy draught horses one afternoon in France:

'The horses, attached to their appropriate vehicles and shining in their summer coats, looked a picture of sleekness and strength. They were of all sorts and sizes but their power and compactness was uniform. The horse-hood of England was there with every buckle of its harness brightened'.[33]

2/Lt. Huntly Gordon had a similar role to Vaughan Williams but in the Royal Field Artillery and in 1917 was based just south of Ypres. He remembered that:

'The horses here are a rather scratch lot, and it is surprising to see so many American mules. They are well spoken of as being hardier and less excitable under fire than horses; and, though they are more particular about their drinking water, they can do well on less than the standard ration of 8 lbs. oats and 8 lbs. chaff. I am told they rarely give trouble provided you don't face them and pull at them'.[34]

What, therefore, was to be Vaughan Williams's role day-to-day in the 86th Brigade, RGA? A glimpse of his job can be detected from a letter he wrote to Gustav Holst in mid-1918:

'The war has brought me strange jobs – can you imagine me in charge of 200 horses!! That's my job at present – I was dumped down on it straight away, and before I had time to find out which were horses and which were wagons I found myself in the middle of a retreat – as a matter of fact we had a very easy time over this – only one horse killed so we were lucky'.[35]

Vaughan Williams was responsible for the Horse Lines, looking after the horses and mules for transporting guns and ammunition wagons to the relevant gun position or to a new location. He would have sergeants, lance-corporals and a team of soldiers for this purpose, with resources depending on the number of guns and ammunition being transported. Wagon-lines on the move might consist of 20 limbered wagons along with very basic general service (GS) wagons carrying supplies.

Moving guns and ammunition had to be managed at night to avoid German observation of unusual movement, especially by aeroplanes. This could be a nightmare – constant shelling meant that the maps bore little relation to the actual terrain, and blockages could easily occur if roads became impassable. The long wagons, drawn by a six-horse team, found it very hard to make turns on narrow damaged roads. A driver would ride on each near-side horse, controlling the off-side horse as well. Gun flashes and explosions in the half-dark were continuous, making the horses, mules – and men – jumpy. In the event of an enemy artillery barrage, men and horses had to immediately seek cover, generally by moving into another field or wood, or simply behind a hedge, hopefully well off the line of fire.

On arrival at the gun position, the limbered wagons would pull up as close as possible and the shells would be passed rapidly from hand to hand between the wagons and the guns. The team may rest near the gun pits, in makeshift billets, or begin the homeward trip. Vaughan Williams and his NCOs needed to remain calm, however agitated they were feeling inwardly. Shelling at night was particularly frightening as bursts always seemed much closer than was apparent the next morning.

Of the gun teams, the lead driver and horses needed to be outstanding. Feeding the horses, too, was a major challenge as they would eat over 10 times as much as the average soldier. Huntly Gordon recalled what was required of someone in Vaughan Williams's role:

'Life at the wagon-lines… is very busy. Nearly 200 horses in the battery have to be fed and watered twice daily, groomed when possible, and the forage fetched for them from dumps or railhead. Rations for about 180 men have to be fetched and allotted, and the gunner's share taken up to the guns, with mail and stores, and ammunition. Watering is done at special centralised water-points to which it is pumped in pipe-lines, the ditch water being too polluted for use. It takes some time to take the horses to the water-point and back twice daily'.[36]

The future novelist Dennis Wheatley also had a very similar job to Vaughan Williams except that, like Huntly Gordon, he served in the Royal Field Artillery. Wheatley mentions his 'purgatory with horses' in the following terms:

'Apart from wasting countless hours walking up and down while they were groomed they had to be watered and fed three times daily…There was never a truer saying than, 'You can take a horse to the water but you can't make it drink'. Lovers of horses should try standing in front of a thirty-foot long canvas trough while the 140-odd horses of a Battery are brought down in pairs to be watered'.[37]

Train loads of horses would arrive at regular intervals and had to be sorted out – some for the officers, some for NCOs, others to pull gun or limber teams with 'heavies' to draw the ammunition wagons. Many horses had never been ridden or worked in harness before and a few proved unmanageable. Hundreds had to be shot, too, often suffering from exposure to the bitter cold or to poisonous gas.

Vaughan Williams was a 'ranker' – someone promoted from the ranks – and one of the jobs he would probably have disliked was censoring letters. Each letter and postcard had to bear the signature of an officer. He may not have looked at the names on the letters so as to keep things impersonal although for many subalterns it was a way to find out personal details about the men in their platoon which could be helpful in times of stress.

Then there was managing the dipping of the horses to protect against skin infections such as mange. It was not an easy job persuading large horses to sheep-dip into a trench perhaps five or six feet deep. Horses had to be inspected daily for wounds and sickness; keeping them, and their harnesses, clean in the muddy conditions that often prevailed in northern France, could take hours each day. Finally, horses and mules had to be safely tethered, generally in the open as secure stables were hard to come by in the ruins of 1918. All this was more onerous for Vaughan Williams than for other subalterns on the Horse Lines. Unlike Delius, he was not a natural horseman – he said that the appearance of one horse seemed much like another to him. When possible, he preferred to move around by bicycle if he could get his hands on one.

As to the guns, Vaughan Williams admitted that he had been trained at Maresfield Park entirely on six-inch howitzers. These had a shorter muzzle and the recoil was more limited than for the 60-pounders. Vaughan Williams found it ironic that all his training in England had been on weapons that he would not be using – thus the purpose of a period of refresher training at Rouen on his arrival in France in March 1918. We do not know if Vaughan Williams took part in any gunnery duties at the battery positions such as supervising the loading of the guns, working out the positions of enemy artillery or calculating range and line – the science of gunnery that he had been taught at Maresfield Park and at Lydd. Similarly, there is no evidence that he took part in reconnaissance duties at the exposed Observation Posts attached to each battery. It seems reasonable to assume he remained one of the subalterns responsible for the Horse Lines throughout his deployment with 141 Heavy Battery, 86th Brigade, from March to December 1918.

Vaughan Williams's period of training in Rouen meant that he could not join his colleagues in the Battery until the third week of March or, perhaps, very early in April 1918. The exact date of his joining 141 Heavy Battery remains unclear. He would probably have had quite a job tracking down the unit south of Arras in the confusion of the 'Kaiser's Battle' raging at that time. The first part of his journey from Rouen would have been by train to Doullens, then he would have had to march or hitch a ride to his unit. It was rare to find transport organised, even for junior officers.

The 86th Brigade, Royal Garrison Artillery, had been deployed in Noordpeene, near St. Omer, in late summer of 1917 where it was 'in rest' for three weeks. The Brigade returned to its old lines in Vierstraat, Belgium, in early September 1917 and working parties established a battery position south east of Ypres. By late December 1917 the 86th Brigade had taken over the battery position, wagon lines, guns, equipment and stores of the 132 Heavy Battery near Mercatel, four miles south of Arras. The New Year began with a salvo from all the batteries. The 141 Heavy Battery moved to the St Léger camp to the south west of Mercatel just a few miles from the German front line. The Brigade formed at Beauval, in the Somme region, on 9 January 1918 before moving by train on 30 January to Mercatel. The range of the 60-pounders meant, as we have seen, that they could be placed between five and over eight miles back from the front line where no deep gun pits or in-depth concealment were needed – although enemy aircraft always presented potential danger.

Heavy snowstorms in early March 1918 meant that fighting was spasmodic with harassing fire being carried out by 141 Heavy Battery toward Hendecourt Road and, on 7 March, in the direction of Hendecourt itself where enemy transport was destroyed and a hostile battery was silenced. The Brigade had moved from Mercatel to Boisleux-Saint-Marc on 2 March, the transfer being completed by 12 noon. Gradually, but noticeably, the fighting was intensifying. On 13 March all batteries fired 336 rounds of harassing fire and 1,337 rounds counter-preparation in anticipation of a hostile attack. In addition, 266 gas shells were fired by 141 Heavy Battery and 1/1 Wessex Heavy Battery on selected points. Hostile activity continued from 14 to 17 March 1918.

Military planners were aware that a serious enemy offensive was possible in the spring of 1918. As early as 3 December 1917 Field Marshall Sir Douglas Haig had notified Army commanders that:

> 'The general situation on the Russian and Italian fronts, combined with the paucity of reinforcements which we are likely to receive, will in all probability necessitate our adopting a defensive attitude for the next few months. We must be prepared to meet a strong and sustained hostile offensive'.[38]

This was easier said than done. 'Back lines' had not been maintained in late 1917 and into 1918. Dug-outs were in decay, signal lines had been cut, there were no deeply-buried signal systems and the protective wire was slight. There had seemed little need to focus on the upkeep of such things if offensive actions could be sustained. Training in defence was also inadequate, especially in the conduct of a retreat which might last several days, or even weeks. The troops too were exhausted after the *Battle of Cambrai*, which marked the first large-scale, effective use of tanks in warfare. It was recognised by the War Office that a period of leave for the soldiers was a matter of urgent necessity.

By early January 1918, Haig referred to the Germans seeking to deliver a 'knock-out blow'.[39]

It was noted by British and French intelligence that the enemy's strength in France and Belgium had increased to 171 divisions (it would soon be 187 divisions) with 126 field and 100 heavy German batteries, and several Austrian.[40] It was increasingly clear that the attack would focus on the Western Front and not in Italy and that the offensive would be timed before the incoming American Army could take part in any numbers. But where and precisely when would the attack occur?

The debate continued with an increasing sense of urgency and, inevitably, conflicting personalities and politics added to the uncertainties of the military situation on the ground. There were many pressing questions. When would the USA have an effective Army in the field? Should the forces fighting in Italy be strengthened? Would the Germans seek to capture Paris or the Channel ports? This last question caused more anxiety than any other. An attack on Paris would seriously affect French morale; yet the Germans occupying the Channel ports would be disastrous for Britain, impeding the crucial seaborne traffic on which England depended.

On 3 February 1918, it was agreed by British military planners that the main German attack would likely take place on the front of the Fifth and Third Armies with the capture of Amiens as a key enemy objective. The relevant areas are shown in Illustration 17. The head of the Intelligence Section of the British Army General Staff, Brigadier-General John Charteris, said on 16 February:

> 'The enemy will attack; he will attack soon; he will attack on the Western Front'.[41]

All signs pointed to a severe attack against the British in the area south of Arras held by the Third Army – which is where Ralph Vaughan Williams was heading. According to information obtained from prisoners the high ground above Croisilles was to be an early objective of the Germans. The German commander, General Erich Ludendorff, intended to win the war by a single decisive operation and would later write that the German 17th Army:

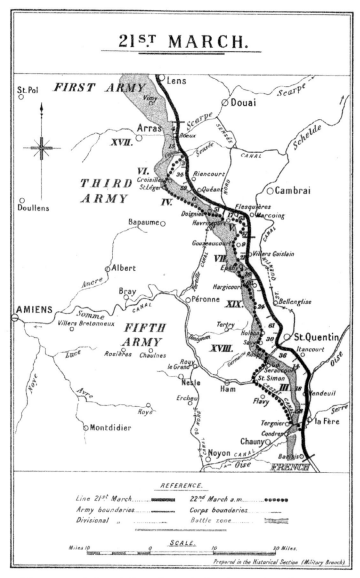

Illustration 17: British Army forces deployed on 21 March 1918.

'Attacked on the last days of March in the direction of Arras, making its principal effort on the north bank of the Scarpe. It was to capture the decisive heights east and north of Arras; the next day the 6th Army was to prolong the attack from about Lens and carry the high ground in the area. I attached the greatest importance to both these attacks'.[42]

With Russia out of the war following the signing of the Brest-Litovsk Treaty on 3 March 1918 the German military effort could be concentrated on the Western Front. As historian Sir Martin Gilbert put it:

'On March 9, the Germans began, with a series of artillery bombardments, the preliminary phase of what was to be their largest, and most essential gamble of the war: a massive offensive against the British and French forces on the Western Front. Hitherto the main military initiatives on the Western Front had been taken by the Allied powers: on the Somme, at Ypres (Passchendaele) and at Cambrai. Each of these offensives had broken themselves against superior German fortifications and defence lines. Now it was the Germans who were going to try to break through the line of the trenches. They had one overriding concern, that their victory should be secured before the mass of American troops, unbattered by battle, reached the war zone'.[43]

On 18 March, a German pilot was brought down and he revealed that an attack was planned for either 20 or 21 March 1918. However, poor weather hampered Germany's offensive intent. Allied planners asked themselves: would the first attack be the main effort or a preparatory one? In the event, the main German offensive was launched on 21 March 1918. The German attacks, code-named *Mars* and, further south, *Michael*, began at 4.40 am with the enemy launching an exceptionally heavy barrage on the British trench systems. The *War Diary* for the 86th Brigade said:

'The enemy gave us a quiet night until at 5.10 am he put down an exceptionally heavy barrage on our trench system, the intensity of fire being quite unprecedented. The batteries in the Brigade opened fire immediately in reply to SOS signals and continued firing throughout the day'.[44]

The 86th Brigade, now under the jurisdiction of the Third Army, had been trained to open artillery fire within three minutes of receiving an SOS signal, preferably sooner. SOS in this context meant 'Support or Suppression' and was invoked when Allied infantry were under attack, or such an attack was imminent. Such messages were communicated by field telegraphs or, if the wires were cut, by rockets and coloured flares. However, visual signalling became impossible on 21 March owing to thick fog and even the pigeons, many of which were gassed, failed to get through. Communications by wire were cut at 5.30 am which led to a system of runners being deployed between the batteries; sometimes the runners would arrive at the same moment as the enemy. Indeed, many Allied troops did not know a serious attack had begun until the enemy was upon them. Not before time, communications were re-established at

10.30 am. The gunners of 141 Heavy Battery shot down an enemy plane using their Lewis gun.

All the batteries of the 86th Brigade were heavily shelled during 21 March and were much troubled by enemy aircraft flying at very low altitudes. The 90th Heavy Artillery Brigade, RGA was also deployed with the Third Army near Arras and Captain Arthur Behrend wrote of the events at dawn on 21 March 1918 as follows:

'I awoke with a tremendous start, conscious of noise…so intense that it seemed as if hundreds of devils were dancing in my brain…Everything seemed to be vibrating, the ground, my dug-out, my bed…By Jove! The great Bosch offensive must have begun…Big stuff was now falling all around us thick and fast and I wondered how much longer it would be before my shack would get a direct hit. The concussion was so intense that it was impossible to light the candle. Suddenly the door blew off its hinges…The fascinating smell of high explosives and ravaged earth bewildered me'.[45]

Gunner Hall was with the 81st Siege Battery in Bapaume, just over nine miles to the north of where Vaughan Williams was heading. On 21 March 1918 he wrote in his diary:

'In the afternoon the battle intensified and respites became fewer. The enemy had the exact range of our guns and it seemed only a matter of time before we would be wiped out. At 2 pm No. 1 gun received a direct hit…I saw one familiar landmark after another fall into enemy hands. At 6 pm the range was dropped to its lowest level, 1,500 yards, which meant that the enemy were less than half a mile away'.[46]

Finally a ceasefire was ordered at 9.30 pm. Having been under remarkably heavy bombardment, orders came through for the rear section of 141 Heavy Battery to withdraw from the St Léger camp and take up position at Boiry-Becquerelle, a few miles to the north and east and nearer to Mercatel. Siegfried Sassoon observed of Mercatel in 1917 that it was: 'A place which offered no shelter except the humanity of its name'.[47]

The extent of the German advance westward across the British lines in just seven days is shown in Illustration 18.

That opening day of the battle, 21 March 1918, is officially the second worst day of losses in British military history, with more than 38,000 casualties. In terms of numbers, it follows only the first day of *Battle of the Somme*, 1 July 1916, in which the British Army sustained 57,000 casualties, the bloodiest day

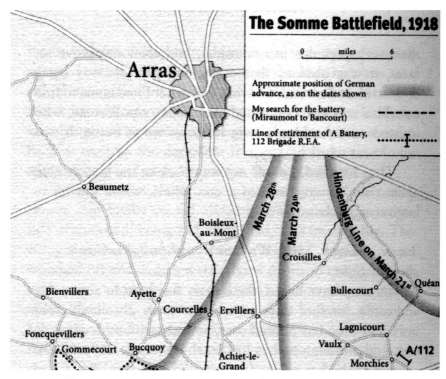

Illustration 18: The German advance south of Arras in March 1918.

in its history. The 1918 *Spring Offensive*, also known as the Kaiser's Battle or the Ludendorff Offensive, saw the German artillery unleash, on 21 March, a remarkable 1.16 million shells in just five hours. By the end of the day the figure had reached over 3.5 million shells.[48] The Germans drove the British and French back across the River Aisne and on 24 March crossed the Somme and captured Bapaume. The Fifth Army line along the Somme was broken by the Germans on 26 March 1918.

Pandemonium raged across wide stretches of the Allied front. During the retreats, guns were taken in any order, horses were terrified and would break away even from their tremendous loads. Heavy artillery behind the lines had serious casualties, often blown to fragments by the German bombing. Incredibly, 45,000 British and French soldiers were taken prisoner[49] and it has been estimated that in the five days between 21 and 26 March 1918, the British Expeditionary Force lost nearly 75,000 men.[50]

By morning on 22 March 1918 the question in everyone's mind was: what was the enemy doing? No one knew if the Germans would soon overrun their

Photo 45: Vaughan Williams in front of a 60-pounder, 1918.

position or if they would be subject to a direct hit from enemy field or heavy artillery. In London, there was talk of the British forces retreating to the Channel ports. The Germans were also keen to march to the coast between Calais and Dunkirk and, to achieve this aim, prepared a new offensive at Armentières, near Béthune, on the River Lys. Within three weeks, more than 30,000 German and 20,000 Allied soldiers had been killed – but the German drive to the coast was halted.[51] The *Battle of the Lys* was one important turning point, although German advances continued and by 1 June 1918 their army was only 40 miles from Paris. German long-range shells rained on and around Paris from 23 March.

Given the ferocity of the German *Spring Offensive*, Vaughan Williams was exposed to greater danger on the Western Front south of Arras than during either of his periods of RAMC service in France, at Ecoivres, or in Greece near Salonica. This was all the more acute because German artillery tactics involved concentrating on their opposite numbers in the British artillery gun lines.

Under ferocious enemy bombardment the 86th Brigade, RGA was forced to withdraw its HQ on at least three occasions.[52] The unit pulled out of St Léger on 21 March, in the face of an infantry attack by the German 6th Bavarian Division, relocating to a reserve position at Hendecourt by 23 March. That this retreat was not far enough was demonstrated by a further withdrawal which took the HQ to Ficheux by 6 pm on 25 March. Amid unbearable suspense, and under constant shellfire, they were on the move again, digging in on 26 March further northwest, near a quarry outside of Simencourt and still in the district of Arras. Throughout these withdrawals, 141 Heavy Battery continued shelling German positions near Wancourt, Héninel and Croisilles. Yet another retreat took place on 30 March when a new HQ was opened at Fermont (today Capelle-Fermont), to the north of Simencourt. Pulling out of a firing location is always an artillery nightmare – the guns get stuck in the mud of newly-formed craters, the horses are uncertain, communications are patchy at best, belongings are scattered and there is always the same two linked questions: will we get away safely or, if not, when will the enemy overrun our position? Every five minutes' delay in retreating might jeopardise the chances of removing the heavy artillery to relative safety.

The men of the 141 Heavy Battery were also retreating, pulling out of the battery position in Hénin Valley on 22 March 1918 to a new more northerly location near Boiry-Becquerelle in the rear portion of the Battle Zone. Drivers of the Battery had to return to their old position, under intense enemy fire, to retrieve ammunition. The 60-pounders of the Battery then concentrated firing on Croisilles. For days, counter-battery firing continued with great intensity. By early April 1918 the 141 Heavy Battery was still in action firing, on 1 April alone, 500 rounds toward Neuville-Vitasse, south-east of Arras. Another SOS called by the infantry at 6.55 am led to heavy bombardment of the area around Bullecourt.

Those who witnessed these retreats describe them in stark terms, hearing the noise of rifle-fire growing ominously nearer accompanied by constant and dreadful cries of 'Get out! Get out! The Germans are coming!' In late March 1918 Dennis Wheatley was retreating from the German advance near Ham, south of Péronne in the Somme district of northern France. He recalled:

> 'There was no mistaking the way as Ham was burning and the sky above it was a lurid glow. Never shall I forget the sight the town presented when we reached it. The bombardment had ceased, presumably because the enemy was now moving his artillery forward; but our troops and vehicles were streaming into the town from every road leading to what had been our Front that morning…The British Fifth Army had been completely routed and this was a remnant of it, every man concerned only with one thought – to escape death or being made a prisoner'.[53]

Further confusion in this retreat was caused by rumours of German troops dressed in captured British uniforms whose job it was to spread panic in the retreating Allied lines. The horses also suffered terribly in this advance. They would scream with fright and kick out savagely in attempts to break free of their wagons. Many were wounded and had to be shot. There is no record in the 86th Brigade RGA *War Diary* that the battery lost guns, horses or convoys of ammunition – in which case Vaughan Williams and his colleagues were extremely fortunate.

By late evening on 26 March 1918, relative stability prevailed and Allied reinforcements began to appear. The German advance in the region had been halted near Albert with enemy forces unable to enter Amiens. However, a new advance brought the Germans to within heavy artillery range of this major city and its important railhead which began to be shelled daily. Most of its inhabitants had fled leaving the streets empty. Military commanders made it clear that British and French troops needed to protect Amiens and further reinforcements must be found. German military planners, in turn, appreciated that the capture of Amiens would potentially split British and French forces; Allied troops, including Ralph Vaughan Williams, would be involved in defending Amiens for months to come.

One of the few first-hand references to Vaughan Williams in this period of intense fighting comes from W. A. Marshall who was a subaltern in the First World War and joined Vaughan Williams south of Arras. He recalled:

'I first set eyes on Vaughan Williams in 1918, in April I think, at the battery horse-lines whither I had been sent down from the guns for a short spell of duty. The battery was 141 Heavy Artillery, Royal Garrison Artillery i.e. 60-pounder guns. It was during the retreat which began on 21 March 1918, when the gun position was near Fontaine-les-Croisilles, some miles south of Arras and north of Bullecourt. We had retired twice and, when I first met Vaughan Williams, the guns were in position behind a wood, 'Athens Wood', I think. I remember the Guards passing us in open order with fixed bayonets. Vaughan Williams had not been with us for long and was in charge at the Horse-Lines – not a cushy job by any means, especially at that time'.[54]

Photo 46: This British large-calibre gun was destroyed during shelling near Fontaine-les-Croisilles, 1918.

Marshall's comment about 'two retreats' is telling and demonstrates that Vaughan Williams was caught up in the later stages of the German *Spring Offensive* – something he also confided to Gustav Holst in the letter quoted earlier on page 101.

On 28 March the German offensive continued north of the Somme in a further effort to break the British front. Vaughan Williams was fighting in the area east of Doullens protected by the Third Army. W. A. Marshall was right to remember the Guards passing through, as the Guards Division was responsible for the front line around Ficheux, Neuville-Vitesse and Mercatel, south of Arras, as shown in Illustration 19:

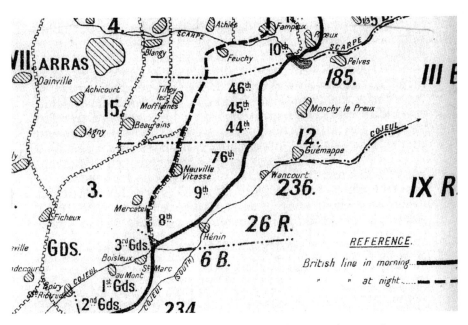

Illustration 19: The Guards Divisions hold the line around Mercatel.

The 1st and 3rd Guards Brigades alone lost 28 officers and 653 other ranks in the short period between 21 and 31 March 1918;[55] on 22 March they were left confronting the German advance around Croisilles when the enemy found a gap between the British 3rd Division and 34th Division.[56]

The Allied position improved and the Germans were repelled on 28 March by the combined firepower of artillery guns, machine guns and rifles. The German infantry was becoming exhausted, having fought for eight days. The British forces, in turn, were helped by the absence of fog.

There was a lull in fighting in the first few days of April although artillery and air activity continued. By 5 April, the Guards Division in front of the 86th Brigade, RGA reported 1,958 killed, wounded or missing.[57]

It was not only the Guards Division that suffered awful losses; between 21 and 26 March, British casualties included 2,500 officers and over 72,000 other ranks.[58] In addition, between 21 May and 5 April 1918 the German offensive had cost 177,739 casualties overall.[59] The troops badly needed rest and reinforcements. The heavy artillery, too, was nearly 2,000 guns short of what was deemed necessary, especially as a new enemy offensive was anticipated. Few doubted that German offensive operations would resume, but where would they strike? Various contingencies were explored and a favoured option among British military planners was another attack between the British and French lines near Amiens – very much in the territory occupied by the 86th Brigade, Royal Garrison Artillery – and Ralph Vaughan Williams.

German bombardments of the area south of Arras continued, partly as a diversionary tactic, although this was not known at the time. The enemy fired a smoke barrage on 4 April leading to much confusion. Over 100 rounds of gas shells were fired by the British 60-pounders of Vaughan Williams's Unit on two hostile batteries near Wancourt. By 7 April, considerable aerial activity was adding to the dangers which seemed to suggest that the Albert-Arras area was a prime German objective. 141 Heavy Battery fired 90 rounds of counter-battery on 8 April and a pattern of night time bombing continued throughout April. As the *War Diary* put it in an entry on 23 April:

> 'During the night 141 Heavy Battery took a section up to within 1,800 yards of the frontline and fired 160 rounds…The guns were withdrawn before daybreak'.[60]

General Haig then issued his famous rallying call to all ranks of the British Forces in France, including Ralph Vaughan Williams. This 'Special Order of the Day' was dated Thursday 11 April and said:

> 'Three weeks ago today the enemy began his terrific attacks against us on a 50-mile front. His objects are to separate us from the French, to take the Channel ports, and destroy the British Army.

> In spite of throwing already 106 Divisions into the battle and enduring the most reckless sacrifice of human life, he has as yet made little progress towards his goal…

> There is no other course open to us but to fight it out! Every position must be held to the last man: there must be no retirement. With our backs to the

wall, and believing in the justice of our cause, each one of us must fight on to the end. The safety of our homes and the Freedom of Mankind alike depend upon the conduct of each one of us at this critical moment.'

There is no record of what Vaughan Williams thought of this rhetoric involving a fight to the end, to the last man. In any event, the daily work of his Heavy Battery continued. Hostile shelling occurred during the night of 24 April, with Allied responses increasingly hampered by poor visibility. By the end of April, the batteries in the 86th Brigade had expended 24,000 rounds of ammunition. The German soldier, Ernst Jünger, described what it was like to be on the receiving end of such a bombardment from the British forces:

'Twenty yards behind us, clumps of earth whirled up out of a white cloud and smacked into the boughs. The crash echoed through the woods. Stricken eyes looked at each other, bodies pressed themselves into the ground with a humbling sensation of powerlessness to do anything else. Explosion followed explosion. Choking gases drifted through the undergrowth, smoke obscured the treetops, trees and branches came crashing to the ground, screams. We leaped up and ran blindly…'[61]

Night harassing operations continued into May. This was a period of continuing uncertainty for the Allies and it would still be many weeks before the American Army could make a real difference. For the 86th Brigade, Royal Garrison Artillery, targets on 1 May were roads, shelters, tracks, water-points, railways and enemy HQs in and around the village of Wancourt. The next day, the 60-pounders assisted the 2nd Canadian Division in a successful raid. An 'annihilating order' on 6 May saw an escalation of the bombing with a special focus on railways and tramways. By 15 May heavy explosive, shrapnel and gas (lethal) shells were all fired. The Germans replied in kind and the cry of the soldiers could be heard above the artillery din when the gas shells were fired: "Gas attack! Gas attack! Gas! Gas!" Wilfred Owen captured the effects of a gas attack in his moving poem *Dulce et Decorum est*:

Gas! Gas! Quick, boys! – An ecstasy of fumbling,
Fitting the clumsy helmets just in time;
But someone still was yelling out and stumbling
And flound'ring like a man in fire or lime…
Dim, through the misty panes and thick green light,
As under a green sea, I saw him drowning…

While the short-term effects of a gas attack could be devastating, the long-term problems – endless coughing and partial blindness – were equally ghastly.

With the batteries of the 86th Brigade firing a total of 17,700 shells on the German lines in May 1918, French and British military planners remained unsure about the whereabouts of the next main German attack, with options ranging from the Ypres area of Flanders to Verdun. However, during the early hours of 27 May the enemy focused intense fire on the sector of the front line between Montdidier and Reims, with Soissons at the centre of the offensive, and this soon became the *Battle of the Aisne*. The German assault began at 1 am and covered 24 miles of the Allied front. The concentration of artillery fire, trench mortars and gas was formidable; astonishingly it was rated even greater than that of 21 March 1918. Fortunately for Ralph Vaughan Williams and his colleagues, this overwhelming assault was taking place over 80 miles south of their location. Offensive action did continue in Vaughan Williams's sector but without the intensity of the Aisne battleground.

For the 86th Brigade, RGA, June began with the usual harassing fire which was maintained throughout the night, supported by balloon and aeroplane observations. Another 'annihilating fire' order was issued on 8 June as a consequence of heavy enemy bombardments on the left of the Brigade's sector. Raids by the 32nd and 2nd Canadian Divisions on 22 June were again supported by the Batteries.[62] The total ammunition fired by the 86th Brigade in June amounted to 20,565 rounds.

By late June, the German army was war-weary and influenza had taken a heavy toll with between 1,000 and 2,000 stricken personnel in each enemy division.[63] As a result, German army morale was deteriorating. British military intelligence observed that the Germans had ceased to dig fresh latrines or even to remove and bury their dead.[64]

The rising superiority of Allied forces in material, morale and manpower, including American troops totalling over one million by May 1918 on the Western Front alone, led to a realisation among senior commanders that a turning point in the war had been reached. A Conference at Chateau Bombon, in the Seine-et-Marne department some 30 miles south-east of Paris, on 24 July 1918 discussed moving from a general defensive attitude to one of attack. Various counter-offensive options were discussed. Priorities were freeing three vital railway lines, including Paris-Amiens, as well as relieving Amiens itself. General Haig noted in a report to his Army commanders that the Germans might make successive withdrawals to previously prepared positions and that it would be necessary for the British Army to follow the enemy across already devastated areas as well as to attack selected locations.[65]

By July 1918, the soldiers in 141 Heavy Battery had been engaged in intense artillery fire, day and night, for over two months. The length of night-time harassing fire was particularly demanding. There had been casualties – on 30 June alone one officer was injured and a private seriously wounded. The early days of July saw vigorous harassing fire continuing. Six more casualties in Vaughan Williams's Brigade were reported on 6 July with one soldier subsequently dying.

Throughout this sustained military onslaught Vaughan Williams became known and respected for remaining calm under pressure. As his batman, A. J. Moore, remembered:

'Lt. Vaughan Williams had the respect of the whole Battery as a kind, firm and considerate officer. In wartime, with heavy guns, powerful horses and all the work of dealing with the equipment necessary to the Battery, tempers can easily get frayed. With him this rarely happened'.[66]

A. J. Moore, a theology student before the war who was to become a Canon, was invaluable to Vaughan Williams. He cleaned his kit, cooked his food and carried his personal belongings and, most importantly, tidied him up for parade. Vaughan Williams, as we have seen from his early life at Leith Hill Place, was used to servants and always treated them with courtesy and good manners.

After this period of intense bombardments, the 86th Brigade came out of action at 8 pm on 22 July 1918, moving on 23 July to a reserve area behind the lines at Pommera, 20 miles south-west of Arras on the road to Abbeville. Vaughan Williams and the 141 Heavy Brigade were relocated on 22 July 1918 to Warlincourt-lès-Pas, just a little to the east of Pommera and still in the Arras district. Between 23 and 29 July the Brigade was in reserve where they carried out intensive training for what the *War Diary* called 'moving war'. Clearly this was in anticipation of a German retreat, following General Haig's suggestions, and the Brigade anticipated following closely behind the advancing Allied troops.

First, however, it was necessary to relieve both Amiens and Albert and to recover ground between the Avre and the Somme. Soon Vaughan Williams and his colleagues were to take part in one of the major Allied offensives in 1918 – the *Battle of Amiens*. This battle was planned in conditions of strict secrecy with a 'Keep Your Mouths Shut' notice being issued to all ranks, including Vaughan Williams. Amiens itself had been evacuated since March 1918. Allied artillery fire had continued in July, giving the impression that 'normal conditions' prevailed, to avoid alerting the Germans to the build-up of men, guns and tanks. The main gun park was established at Pont Remy, 22 miles north-west of Amiens with an advanced park, including the 60-pounders, formed at Longueau, southeast of Amiens – see Illustration 20. It was here that the 86th

Brigade, RGA arrived during the night of 31 July 1918, with the move completed by daybreak. On 30 July, Vaughan Williams's Unit had moved in great secrecy from Warlincourt to Fieffes, near Montrelet, before moving to Longueau, closer to Amiens, by 10 pm that night.

In total, 13 Heavy Brigades were deployed to this zone together with four siege batteries, with the leading Fourth Army being reinforced by artillery drawn from the First, Second and Third Armies – amounting to 684 heavy guns and 1,386 field guns. Over 500 tanks also joined the offensive.[67]

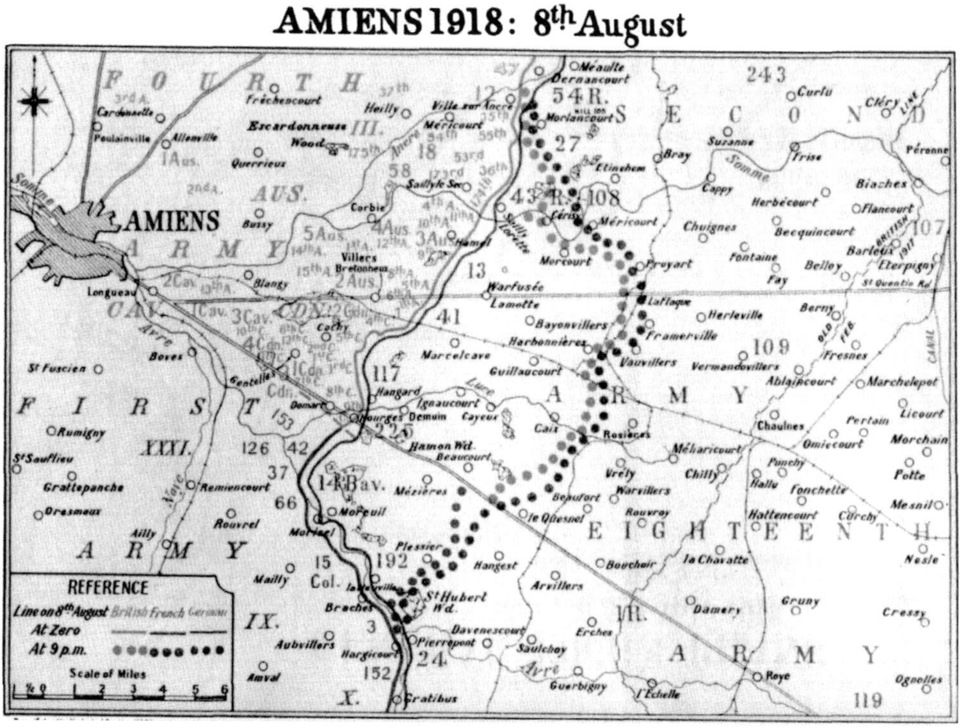

Illustration 20: Map showing the British, French and German lines on 8 August 1918 near Amiens.

With preparations continuing in great secrecy, Army Command fixed Zero Day for 8 August with Zero Hour at 4.20 am – over an hour before sunrise – when a third of the batteries would open fire to neutralise enemy artillery through a 'creeping barrage', with the pace fixed at three minutes for the first 100 yards, five minutes for the second and so on. The remaining guns would bombard every known battery position along with such places as were considered suitable as assembly places for German reserves. A protective barrage was also to be maintained in front of the old Amiens defence line until 'Zero-plus-four-hours' when all barrages were to cease.[68] Vaughan Williams's Unit was to concentrate on bombing locations in the vicinity of Parvillers-le Quesnoy, Gruny, Liancourt-Fosse and, further east, Fresnoy-le-Grand.

On the night of 8 August the Germans seemed to suspect nothing and no counter-preparations of any kind disturbed the British and French plans. Vaughan Williams's Brigade was now part of the 3rd Canadian Division, along with six field artillery brigades. As Zero Hour approached the mist grew thicker which helped to cover the launching of the attack. After intense fighting initial objectives had been achieved and by 11 am on 8 August the heavy batteries were no longer in action. This was because the infantry advance had been so rapid that, even with muzzles cocked up to the highest elevation, there was a serious risk of Allied casualties. The Germans facing the Canadian 3rd Division had lost their entire artillery by 10 am.[69] Over seven miles were gained on the first day of the battle and an estimated 30,000 German prisoners were captured – see Photo 47. Some Germans had shown white flags only to open fire when the Canadian forces approached to receive their surrender.

The 86th Brigade, RGA advanced eastward on 9 August to allow artillery to be fired over the advancing troops. The villages of Folies, Warvillers and Bouchoir were targeted as fresh objectives with 400 rounds being fired. On 10 August, the Brigade came under the orders of the British 32nd Division with the Batteries ordered to positions near Beaufort. 1,600 rounds were fired overnight on 10 August and a further 1,000 rounds on 11 August.

The battle was effectively over by late evening on 11 August 1918 and Amiens was saved. The British alone had captured 439 German officers and 18,061 other ranks along with 240 guns. British casualties were about 20,000 for the four days of the battle.[70]. As the *Official History of the Great War* put it:

> 'The moral effect of the Allied victory was far greater than the material; for the first time both the German High Command and the men in the ranks admitted a defeat and that the greatest defeat in the war. And they never in the coming days were able to shake off the impression of the inevitableness of final collapse'.[71]

Now the Batteries of the 86th Brigade, RGA moved to positions near to Warvillers, just north of Folies – areas that they had only recently bombarded. The focus of military planning became an advance on Albert, halfway between Amiens and Bapaume. There was strong evidence that the Germans were becoming more and more demoralised and therefore the Allies needed to press on, to allow the enemy no rest. Considerable advances were made in the second week of August. For example, to the north and east of Albert, iconic locations such as Monument Wood and Mametz were recaptured on 24-26 August[72] and the Australian Corps advanced along the Somme towards Péronne.

With orders given for attacks along the Western Front between 17 and 24 August, the batteries of the 86th Brigade fired 18,846 rounds as part of the *Battle of the Hundred Days* which had begun on 8 August 1918. The shells concentrated on harassing fire, aeroplane

Photo 47: German prisoners captured during the *Battle of Amiens.*

counter-battery shoots and on hostile batteries. The Brigade *War Diary* of 25 August noted that the Germans were often out of range due to the 'further rapid retreat of the enemy'.

The Brigade, with Ralph Vaughan Williams, was now on the move following the retreating Germans. They arrived at Rosières-en-Santerre on 25 August and the Batteries took up a position further east at Omiécourt on 26 August. From this position, harassing fire resumed. Acting on requests from the French artillery, the Batteries bombarded Villecourt while also coming under intense enemy shellfire and from machine gun fire from two German aeroplanes. Villecourt was again hit on 3 September. Over 5,000 rounds were fired between 27 and 31 August 1918.

The whole Brigade now concentrated in or around Bayonvillers, three miles or so to the east of Amiens, where the exhausted men took a well-earned break from 6 to 16 September 1918.

During this break, military planners considered the best use of resources of the Second Army, to which the 86th Brigade, RGA had now returned. By 2 September, French, British and Belgium commanders considered that Flanders represented the most likely area for an offensive given the paucity of German troops in the area, their exhaustion and lack of reserves. As the *Official History* put it:

'In view of the evident speeding up of the German retirement, it seemed probable that the Second Army and the Belgium Army could at small cost occupy the high ground east of Ypres; besides the advantages which would accrue by the unexpected extension of the Allied offensive to the north of the Lys, the line thus captured would afford an excellent jumping-off position for later operations'.[73]

This plan was agreed. The priority was to work out how to get the infantry and artillery into positions in Flanders by 28 September 1918, the date fixed for the attack. In conditions of great secrecy the various Batteries needed to head north toward Ypres and this process began on 18 September 1918 when the men arrived at Longueau for the train journey to Arnèke and then by road for the short trip to billets at Rubrouck, some 116 miles from their starting point on the outskirts of Amiens. As shown in Illustration 21, the long trek north and east for the Brigade – and Vaughan Williams – had begun. This journey would ultimately cover over 250 miles before the men, horses, wagons, supplies and guns reached Beveren, on the perimeter of Antwerp.

Longueau to Rubrouck	*dep. 18.9.18*	*arr. 19.9.18*	*116 miles*
Rubrouck to Herzeele	*dep. 22.9.18*	*arr. 22.9.18*	*10 miles*
Herzeele to Ypres areas	*dep. 24.9.18*	*arr. 24/25.9.18*	*17 miles*
Ypres areas to Lendelede	*dep.18.10.18*	*arr. 18.10.18*	*20 miles*
Lendelede to Beveren	*dep.23.10.18*	*arr. 24.10.18*	*50 miles*
Beveren to Knokke	*dep.3.11.18*	*arr. 4.11.18*	*44 miles*

Illustration 21: Chart showing details of the 86th Brigade's long trek north and east into Belgium, 1918.

A whole Battery on the march might stretch well over a quarter of a mile, the rear being brought up with general wagons, field kitchens, water-cart, mess-cart and so on. The roads were crowded with traffic: signal companies, pigeon units, ambulances, staff cars and myriad other kinds of vehicles and men.

On 22 September, the 141 Heavy Battery was in Herzeele, on the road to Dunkirk a few miles from the Belgium border and the rest of the Brigade arrived in holding positions to the east of Ypres on 23/24 September 1918. These holding positions included Alexander Farm, English Farm and the well-known Ramparts. Ypres itself, as shown in Photo 48, was an awful ruin. Preparations were now under way for the *Fifth Battle of Ypres* which started on 28 September. No preliminary bombardment was to be fired; batteries were to remain silent on 26-27 September with gunnery positions and measurements being finalised.

Photo 48: Ypres in 1918.

The train journeys and marches north were not without risk. Considerable care was needed when travelling in areas recently vacated by the retreating Germans. There were many narrow escapes from delayed-action time-bombs, exploding mines and ammunition dumps. Some of these mines would explode eight days after the enemy retreat. Ernst Jünger, a Lieutenant in the German infantry, described what steps the Germans took in such a retreat:

'Among the surprises we'd prepared for our successors were some truly malicious inventions. Very fine wires, almost invisible, were stretched across the entrances of buildings and shelters, which set off explosive charges at the faintest touch. In some places, narrow ditches were dug across roads, and shells hidden in them; they were covered over by an oak plank, only just above the shell-fuse. The space was measured so that marching troops could pass over the spot safely, but the moment the first lorry or field gun rumbled up, the board would give, and the nail would touch off the shell...'[74]

This movement of troops and artillery was part of: 'A gigantic drive across the country by a great line of Armies'[75] of which the *Official History of the Great War* commented:

'The stumbling in the mud, the cries and curses of the excited troops and the roar of the barrage must be imagined. Noise and darkness, either natural or artificial, were the features of the fighting'.[76]

For the *Fifth Battle of Ypres* the British Second Army had five field artilleries and eight RGA brigades, including, from 27 September, the 86th Brigade, RGA, and, of course, the 141 Heavy Battery – with Ralph Vaughan Williams.[77] The 60-pounders selected forward firing positions to the east of Ypres, in a location called English Farm.

Zero Hour was set at 5.30 am on 28 September with another 'creeping barrage' being registered to extend to 4,000 yards. Intense counter-battery firing would be carried out on all known hostile positions, A proportion of enemy targets would be neutralised by gas shells. Vaughan Williams's Unit began a bombardment of Westrozebeke, to the north-east of Ypres, with 4,750 rounds being fired on 28 September alone. On 29 September the Batteries moved to a new position east of Ypres and were attached to the British 36th Division.

The initial battle on 28 September was successful, with considerable ground secured by the Belgian Army and the British Second Army, including the greater part of Ypres Ridge and Houthulst Forest. On 29 September very nearly as much was achieved toward the fresh objective of capturing Gheluvelt. Heavy rain on the night of 29/30 September, however, slowed progress such that the transport of guns and ammunition was almost impossible. As the *War Diary* of the 86th Brigade, RGA put it on 30 September: 'Roads were blocked and unpassable for heavy artillery'. Despite these handicaps, the troops advanced to the slope down to Gheluvelt where intense German fire halted the momentum. The weather improved a little on 1 October and heavy artillery was brought forward to fire on Menin. A significant part of Gheluvelt was secured on 2 October and at 7.45 pm that day the British forces were ordered to consolidate the ground already secured and make no further attacks until further orders.

The battle was over with the Allies holding the high ground above Ypres although at significant cost – 4,675 British casualties were counted by 1 October. The gains are shown in Illustration 22.

Vaughan Williams had now been engaged in both the *Battle of Amiens* and the *Fifth Battle of Ypres*. The trek northward toward the retreating Germans continued, as shown in Illustration 21, although bad weather hampered the movement of the gun batteries. The 86th Brigade reached Lendelede, east of Ypres, in West Flanders on 18 October 1918 setting up HQ at Villa Rodemont near the town. The Brigade now took part in the closing stages of the *Battle of Courtrai*, directing heavy bombardments on 20 October in the direction of the retreating Germans.

The *Battle of Courtrai* marked a renewal of the offensive in Flanders that had been delayed from 3 October owing to the weather and the state of the roads. The British Second Army now totalled 10 divisions alongside significant Belgian and French forces amounting to 28 divisions overall.[78] The Second

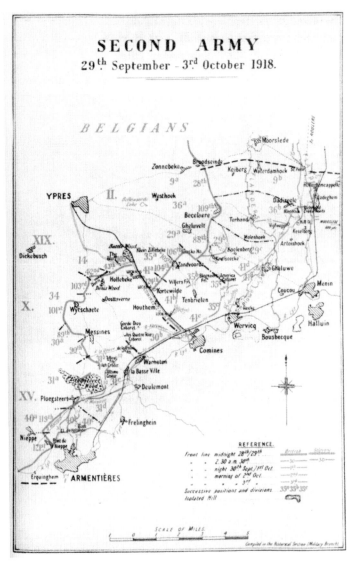

Illustration 22: Allied gains in the Fifth Battle of Ypres, 1918.

Army formed the flank guard for the proposed operation by seeking to hold the line of the River Lys down to Harlebeke north of Courtrai. Zero Hour was fixed for 5.35 am on 14 October 1918. Following heavy fighting, partial bridgeheads were established over the Lys and around 6,000 German prisoners were captured by the Allies.[79] Courtrai was regained late on 19 October and by the next day the troops of the Second Army were able to cross the Lys, the river sometimes referred to as the Leie, its Flemish name. The 60-pounders of the 141 Heavy Battery crossed the Lys on 22 October, with the Siege Batteries of the Brigade following the next day.

Although there was little opportunity for rest conditions were now very different for the soldiers. As Harry Siepmann, an Artillery Officer, put it:

> 'The guns and the horses and the men were moving together through open country, where the fields and trees were green, the houses intact and the inhabitants in their homes. But the greatest change of all was that, after several years of being either beaten or held, we were now undoubtedly winning'.[80]

Vaughan Williams and the 141 Heavy Battery continued to march northward. The plains between the Lys and the Scheldt (Schelde in Flemish) rivers were hard going for the guns and horses owing to heavy rains creating very marshy conditions. Beveren, on the outskirts of Antwerp, in East Flanders, was reached on 24 October. Here the 60-pounders continued to assault the retreating German army. Despite the imminence of the Armistice, Vaughan Williams remained in considerable danger; during the night of 26 October alone, the Brigade faced considerable hostile shelling and 500 rounds were fired to neutralise this assault.

The 86th Brigade, RGA was now redeployed to the British 34th Division. It was vital that the heavy batteries were successful against German artillery and machine gun targets located on the east bank of the Scheldt if this strategically vital river was to be taken. Zero Hour was 5.25 am on 31 October 1918 and the artillery barrage, supplemented by machine guns, moved at the rate of 100 yards every three minutes. Fortunately, retaliation to the barrage was not severe and the offensive succeeded as the Germans had evacuated their ground and retreated across the Scheldt. The Heavy Battery supported attempts by the Allies to cross the river. A plan to cross by night with the support of all available artillery was set for Monday 11 November 1918, unless the enemy had fallen back.

On 1 November Vaughan Williams's Division was withdrawn into reserve on relief by a French battery. There was a marked decrease in enemy gunfire by 8 November and all artillery action was suspended the next day. The Brigade now relocated back to Knokke in West Flanders, on the coast near the border with Holland. The batteries were withdrawn from the front line on 10 November.

Remarkably, despite the dangers, opportunities had still been found for music during Vaughan Williams's service in the 141 Heavy Battery. W. A. Marshall remembered:

'He spent a lot of such spare time as he had in getting-up concerts, vocal, by and for the troops, mostly drivers. I can't think he enjoyed them much, in view of the talent available. I saw him once or twice, drooping despondently over the keyboard of a ghastly wreck of a piano, whilst drivers sang sentimental songs – execrably as a rule – to his accompaniment. My heart bled for him'.[81]

The long-range guns such as the 60-pounders of the 141 Heavy Battery had played a vital role in the final months of the war. Counter-batteries had dealt with German artillery; road junctions, ammunition dumps and suspected headquarter buildings had all been targeted to good effect. This had, in turn, encouraged the infantry to go farther and faster.

The Armistice was declared at 11 am on 11 November 1918 and this ended all fighting on land, sea and air between Germany and the Allies. The *Official History of The Great War* said of this moment:

'When 11 am came the troops took the occasion in their usual matter of fact way: there was no outburst of cheering, no wild sense of rejoicing. Those who could lay down to sleep. The others went quietly about their duty with the strange feeling that all danger was absent. But after dark all gave way to rejoicing, searchlights wobbled in the sky, coloured lights of every description and SOS signals illuminated the front lines, rockets went whizzing into the air, and field batteries fired their star shells'.[82]

For some there was disbelief that the war had ended; was this not another rumour? For Stephen Graham, a private in The Guards, his first thoughts were:

'No more bombs, no more shells, no more bullets; we are safe then, after all, we shall get back to our homes, to our wives, to mother and father, and all we love in Blighty'.[83]

The silence in the absence of artillery fire was unnerving; the distant rumble of an exploded German mine or ammunition dump had the soldiers wondering if the war had restarted. That night, motorcars drove by with headlights blazing and lamps were turned on in open windows, with shutters discarded for the first time in four years. The liberation of civilians led to much rejoicing among the people who could now return to their homes, if these were still intact. Without horses or mules, the returning civilians had to carry their belongings on improvised barrows. Food was still scarce but the Germans were gone and curfews were being lifted along with many other German prohibitions. On the march forward, civilians turned out to greet the Allied soldiers with many flowers and bunting displayed. Excited children seemed to be everywhere.

Vaughan Williams would have heard cries of "Vive les Anglais" and the offer of flowers and, if you were lucky, a bottle of wine, or more.

Vaughan Williams, however, did not enjoy the victory. He felt flat, seized by a fit of depression – a typical response, perhaps, after the adrenaline-filled days of fighting were over. He wrote to Gustav Holst on 16 November 1918 saying that the news of the Armistice had produced:

'A complete slump in my mind and I've never felt so fed up with my job'.[84]

The end of the war brought for many a great sense of anti-climax. Vaughan Williams was also likely to have been too tired to be elated.

It was in the week beginning 11 November 1918 that plans for a march through Belgium and into Germany were developed at British Army HQ in Cambrai. The terms of the Armistice included the evacuation of all German territory on the left (western) bank of the Rhine. This river became a temporary frontier from Switzerland to Holland. The occupation by the Allies of three bridgeheads, each of around 20 miles into Germany, along the Rhine between Mayence, Coblence (now Koblenz) and Cologne, was authorised[85] and sections of the British Second and Fourth Armies, including the 1st and 2nd Canadian Divisions comprising 107,000 troops and 25,000 horses, were ordered to take part in the advance.[86]

Ralph Vaughan Williams was now part of this Army of Occupation. After the Armistice his Unit was known as the 86th (Mobile) Brigade, RGA, and consisted of the following batteries:

141 Heavy Battery (6-60 pounders)
1/1 Wessex Heavy Battery (6-60 pounders)
203 Siege Battery (6-six inch guns)
324 Siege Battery (6-six inch guns) [87]

The 86th (Mobile) Brigade joined the 9th and 29th Divisions, within the Second Army, and these forces were ordered to prepare for the forward move. They were to hold the northern sector of the newly created neutral zone – American and French divisions concentrated further south, with the French focused on Mayence. For the British troops, Cologne marked the centre of their area of responsibility, with Bonn at the southern extremity – see Illustration 23.

Vaughan Williams was unlucky to be deployed in one of only 16 Divisions, out of a total of 61, that had been selected to advance to Germany on 17 November 1918.[88] The remaining troops were to stand fast. Although the *Story of the 29th Division* says that 'To our great joy and pride we found that we were chosen as

Illustration 23: The march through Namur and Charleroi to Germany, late 1918.

one of the two British infantry divisions (in the Second Army) selected to lead the advance into Germany,'[89] Vaughan Williams did not agree with this sentiment. He said that this was not a job he relished, 'either the journey or its object'.[90] The soldiers faced immense difficulties on the ground, including dealing with shell-ravaged roads and dangers from mines and delay-action charges in the territory newly evacuated by German troops. Many wells and springs had also been poisoned or polluted. Dead horses and broken-down lorries were everywhere. Streams of escaped prisoners, including British, French and Belgium soldiers, often in extreme distress through starvation, added to the burden on those making their way to the German frontier. The weather, too, was deteriorating and winter clothing was in short supply. The march northeast was a stern test of endurance especially as the men were utterly worn out.

Why did Vaughan Williams object to the journey and its objectives? He was, as the letter to Holst on 16 November 1918 shows, thoroughly fed up. He would have wanted to get home and probably felt that an occupying force was unnecessary against what seemed a beaten and demoralised enemy. He knew, too, about the difficult circumstances on the ground which presented continuing dangers even though the war had ended. However, Vaughan Williams and his colleagues would probably, in the chaos following the Armistice, underestimate two strategic factors. Firstly, that this military operation into Germany was necessary as a deterrent to any further German aggression and, secondly, it was vital to safeguard French and Belgium borders which were, at the time, still felt to be vulnerable. The presence of Royal Garrison Artillery units in Germany, with 12 60-pounder guns in the Second Army alone, and with an allocated 300 rounds of ammunition, was a statement of enormous military and symbolic significance. Furthermore, such an occupying Army would strengthen the Allied negotiator's hand in the peace conference to come. Perhaps Vaughan Williams was simply too tired to care about these political considerations.

The march began at 8 am on 17 November and the British direction of travel toward the Rhine is shown in Illustration 23, with Charleroi first and Namur reached soon after, the troops then heading south of Liège. The British and Canadian contingents were heading for an area to the north east of Cologne, a distance of over 130 miles. Conditions were very poor, with destroyed roads, railways and bridges slowing the troops. As the Armistice was set to expire on 17 December 1918, the Army of Occupation needed to cross the Rhine by 13 December. This deadline meant for a punishing marching schedule, made all the more daunting when rations for the men frequently did not appear. Supply trains were often over 24 hours late so that at times no rations at all were available until just before the march was scheduled to begin.

Despite these difficulties, an advance section of the 29th Division entered Germany on 4 December 1918 near Malmédy. The main battalion, and the 9th Division, followed across the border over the next few days, reaching the outskirts of Cologne on 9 December. The 29th Division was to cross the Rhine by the Hohenzollen Bridge heading for a final position on the bridgehead perimeter, some 20 miles northeast of Cologne.[91]

The march to Cologne and Bonn was largely completed by 12 December 1918, with instructions issued to all units to cross the Rhine by that day, even though some would struggle to achieve this deadline. On arrival, Cologne and Bonn were out of bounds to the soldiers in the early days of the occupation although this ban was relaxed on 20 December 1918.

The inhabitants of the Rhineland seemed largely indifferent to the arriving troops although some were curious and a few relieved to see the British and Canadian forces. For this minority of Germans, the Allied Army seemed to offer an opportunity for stability and order in a country reeling from economic and social instability as well as the political chaos which had resulted from more than four years of war.

Confirmation that Vaughan Williams was in one of the struggling units is evident in his letter to Gustav Holst dated 12 December 1918 which says that he was still 'slowly trekking toward Germany'. Vaughan Williams added that in Belgium 'every village we pass is hung with flags and triumphal arches' and he continued:

> 'We usually march about 10 kilos or more a day and rest every 4th day – it's a tiresome job watering and feeding the horses in the dark before we start (though I must confess that there being 8 subalterns in this Bty my turn of turning out early for this only comes once a week). Then usually two or three wagons stick fast in the mud at the 1st start off and worry and delay ensues, and finally when one gets to one's destination one has to set up one's horse lines and find water and fill up nose bags etc. and if *this* has to be done in the dark it beggars description'.[92]

Even in these difficult circumstances, Vaughan Williams told Holst that he had: 'Started a singing class and we are practising Xmas carols and *Sweet and Low*'.[93] This was a reference to a part song, with words by Tennyson, that would have appealed to the marching soldiers:

> *Sleep and rest, sleep and rest,*
> *Father will come to thee soon;*
> *Rest, rest on thy mother's breast,*
> *Father will come to thee soon.*

Vaughan Williams added that he had seen Namur (see Photo 49) and Charleroi and was not impressed with either.[94] This was, perhaps, not surprising as both towns had been heavily shelled in the war, with Namur in particular being affected by the Allied defeat, against Austrian-made howitzers, as early as 18 to 22 August 1914. The roads and trench systems near Namur were in poor condition, covered by broken down and dismantled German guns and rifles. Much of these military remnants had been set on fire by the retreating Germans.

Photo 49: British and Canadian troops march through Namur, 1918.

Once in the wooded countryside to the northeast of Cologne, the troops were engaged in stopping smuggling into and out of the neutral zone. To avoid boredom, games were organised and the soldiers thought about their future while awaiting demobilisation.

While Vaughan Williams was marching towards Germany, the soldiers remaining on the Western Front wanted to get home as soon as possible and this led to much discontent in the ranks. Sir Douglas Haig had foreseen this 'general relaxation of the bonds of discipline' as early as October 1917[95] and was alarmed by what might happen next. One solution to avoid discontent, or worse, was to focus on education for the troops while awaiting their papers to return home – it was not until 29 December that long-serving men, miners and policemen begun to be demobilised. Army commanders drew up plans for various courses, concentrating on subjects that might be useful to the soldiers on their return to civilian life. Classes included French, bookkeeping and shorthand typing.

Education of a different kind, however, was now to be the focus for Ralph Vaughan Williams. Sometime late in December 1918, certainly after his letter to Holst on 12 December referred to earlier – when he clearly had no indication of an imminent move – Vaughan Williams left his horses and guns and withdrew from the Army of Occupation. Instead, he was appointed Director of Music for the First Army in France based in Valenciennes. His marching days were over.

The circumstances that led to this appointment remain unclear. It's possible that his wife, Adeline, alerted her brother Herbert Fisher, who was still serving in the Cabinet in London, to the fact that her husband remained in danger, even though it was four weeks since the Armistice had been signed. Someone with authority clearly intervened to remove Vaughan Williams from the line as the transfer of an officer between the Second Army (in Germany) and the First Army (in France) would not have been a local decision. There are no references in Vaughan Williams's Army file to cast any light on this redeployment. Most likely a senior Staff officer in the War Office in London understood, or was strongly reminded, that Vaughan Williams was a musician of stature and this, happily, resulted in the composer's return to France as Director of Music for the First Army.

As to Valenciennes, Field Marshal Haig had described it as the last important town held by the enemy in France. The town was liberated by the Allies in the first days of November 1918 and the Commanding Officer of the First Division, General Sir Henry Horne, chose 'quite a nice house' as the First Army HQ, moving in on 13 November 1918.[96] Fortunately, the area had suffered relatively little during the war although the Germans had pillaged anything of value. The important railway station had been badly damaged as the retreating Germans had dynamited the platforms and surrounding area.

Lt. E. R. Winship provided more information on Vaughan Williams's role as Director of Music in Valenciennes at this time:

> 'After the Armistice in November 1918, in order to furnish some means of recreation and employment for the troops awaiting demobilisation, officers were appointed to create interest in education, music, sport and other activities. Vaughan Williams was asked to take over the music section and, on accepting, was made Director of Music.

> The First Army HQ was at Valenciennes and on obtaining a billet there he became a member of the HQ Mess which consisted of officers with similar responsibilities in other branches.

His work entailed visiting the divisions over a wide area, finding officers and other ranks from the various units who were interested in music and getting them to act as conductors for a choral society, orchestra or to take a class in music.

At the time of his demobilisation in February 1919 there were already nine choral societies, three classes, an orchestra and a band. Included in these was the HQ Choral Society of which he was the conductor.

He engaged recruits for this society himself and once, after a church service in the town, came forward (rather an incongruous figure in uniform!) and spoke of its activities.

A friend of his at that time was Lt. Col. G. A. Sullivan, a member of the HQ Choral Society (a talented pianist) and they sometimes played duets together. Once he played a piano piece by Grieg in the Mess and seemed very amused afterwards at having been able to do so!

A rather unusual occupation for him at this time (evidently made at the request of someone) was in attempting to put together an organ which was lying in pieces on the floor of an outbuilding in the town. He spent some of his spare time here amidst the ruins of the instrument trying to sort things out!

This was evidently a restful and happy period for him, back as he was at music and awaiting demobilisation. Later on in life he sometimes referred to those happy days spent at Valenciennes'.[97]

Vaughan Williams was first demobilised (or 'Disembodied' in the language of the 'Dispersal Unit') on 15 February 1919. He was entitled to wear his uniform for one week and upon other occasions as deemed necessary. From this date, he was not entitled to draw pay. Vaughan Williams, however, retained an honorary position within the British Army as Director of Music while remaining a Second Lieutenant within the Special Reserve of Officers. His commission was relinquished on 1 April 1920 and notification to this effect was placed in the *London Gazette*. His final demobilisation from the Special Reserve was effective from 15 July 1919 – see Illustration 24.

By the end of February 1919, Vaughan Williams was back in England and living at 10 Madingley Road, Cambridge. At least, as a composer and conductor, Vaughan Williams had a good idea of what he would do after the war. This was unlike most soldiers who had no idea of what direction their life might take once they discarded their Army uniforms.

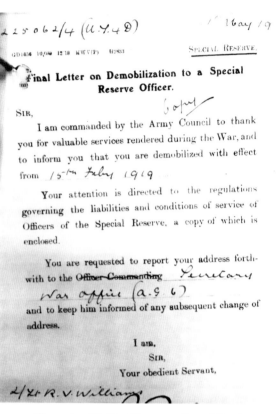

Illustration 24: Final Letter on Demobilisation.

A fascinating coda to Vaughan Williams's wartime experience then unfolded, a development not touched upon in many of the composer's biographies. On 15 October 1920 he applied for promotion to the rank of Lieutenant; he had been eligible to make such an application at any time after 24 June 1919. He completed form W.I. 4035 (M.S. 4 D.) and sent it to the War Office in London. Why did he bother to do this? Normally he was uninterested in status or formal recognition – he turned down at least one offer of a knighthood and almost certainly refused the post of Master of the King/Queen's Music. Promotion almost two years after the end of the war from 2/Lt to a full Lieutenant hardly seems worth the effort for a composer who was by now a Professor at the Royal College of Music, conductor of the Bach Choir and so on. Perhaps he was persuaded to make this formal request by his wife, Adeline, or his brother-in-law, H. A. L. Fisher, who were both more inclined to appreciate formal recognition. Alternatively, the promotion might have enhanced Vaughan Williams's pension although given his reasonable financial circumstances this seems an improbable motivation.

Most likely, Vaughan Williams felt that his appointment as Director of Music for the First Army from January 1919 merited this promotion. Lt. Winship, in the recollections quoted earlier, says that Vaughan Williams became a member of the HQ Mess at Valenciennes which consisted of officers with similar responsibilities in other branches of the Army and these officers were almost certainly full Lieutenants or higher ranks. Indeed, his friend G. A. Sullivan was a Lt. Col. This may have caused resentment and led to his formal submission in October 1920 – but even this does not sound like the modest and self-effacing Vaughan Williams of so many personal recollections.

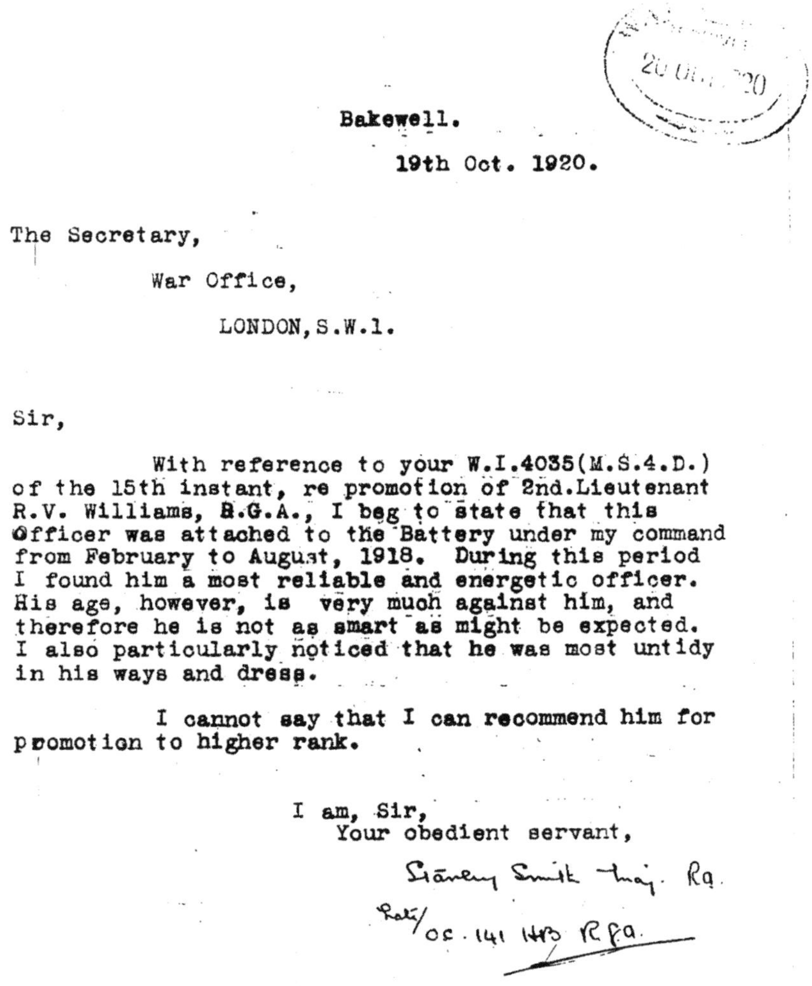

Bakewell.

19th Oct. 1920.

The Secretary,

    War Office,

       LONDON,S.W.1.

Sir,

      With reference to your W.I.4035(M.S.4.D.) of the 15th instant, re promotion of 2nd.Lieutenant R.V. Williams, R.G.A., I beg to state that this Officer was attached to the Battery under my command from February to August, 1918. During this period I found him a most reliable and energetic officer. His age, however, is very much against him, and therefore he is not as smart as might be expected. I also particularly noticed that he was most untidy in his ways and dress.

      I cannot say that I can recommend him for promotion to higher rank.

         I am, Sir,
          Your obedient servant,

Illustration 25: Reply to Vaughan Williams's application for promotion.

Whatever the motivation, the Army had the last word. Lt. General Alex Godley, Military Secretary to the War Office, duly consulted Major S. Smith, formerly Commanding Officer, 141 Heavy Battery, RGA who replied as shown in Illustration 25:

The Military Secretary duly passed this letter on to Vaughan Williams – something he could have avoided – at his new address in Sheringham, Norfolk. The covering note, dated 13 November 1920, informed Vaughan Williams that his application for promotion 'cannot be approved' for the reasons stated in the enclosed letter from Major Smith to the effect that Vaughan Williams was 'most untidy in his ways and dress'. As usual, the British Army put 'keeping the men up to the mark' as the top priority and Ralph Vaughan Williams was never remotely close to the mark.

So it came to this. After all his wartime experiences from 31 December 1914 to 15 July 1919, across different wartime fronts, in the destruction of Neuville St Vaast, the dirt and flies of Salonica, the danger of Croisilles and his participation in at least four battles (*Doiran, Amiens, Fifth Ypres* and *Courtrai*), Vaughan Williams's request was rejected on the basis that his cap was often askew. The insistence of Army commanders on irrelevant and trivial details was legendary but this was a particularly egregious example. There is no record of what Vaughan Williams thought of this reply.

Tellingly, for Vaughan Williams there would in future be no regimental dinners and no formal reunions. He welcomed seeing a few of his wartime comrades, such as Harry Steggles, but showed no nostalgia for the Army itself. The Army would not feature again in his long life.

References

1   H. A. L. Fisher *An Unfinished Autobiography*, Oxford University Press, 1940, p. 89.

2   Ursula Vaughan Williams *R.V.W. – A Biography of Ralph Vaughan Williams*, Oxford University Press, 1964, p. 125.

3   *ibid*, p. 124.

4   Anne Olivia Bell (ed.) *The Diary of Virginia Woolf, 1915-1919*, The Hogarth Press, 1977, p. 203.

5   Hugh Cobbe *Letters of Ralph Vaughan Williams 1895-1958*, Oxford University Press, 2008, p. 120.

6   Christopher Hassall *Rupert Brooke – A Biography*, Faber and Faber, 1964, p. 461.

7   *ibid*, p. 462.

8   This Military History Sheet is held in the Public Record Office at Reference WO 374/75055.

9   Ursula Vaughan Williams, *op. cit.*, p. 125.

10 Hugh Cobbe *op. cit.*, p. 218.

11 John Lewis-Stempel *Six Weeks – The Short and Gallant Life of the British Officer in the First World War*, Orion, 2010, p. 5.

12 Jean Moorcroft Wilson *Edward Thomas – From Adlestrop to Arras*, Bloomsbury, 2015, p. 413.

13 Carole Rosen *The Goossens – A Musical Century*, Deutsch, 1993, p. 50.

14 Ursula Vaughan Williams, *op. cit.*, pp. 126-127.

15 See Mollie Smith *The Military on Ashdown Forest 1793-1925*, Nutley Historical Society, 2005, p. 33.

16 As we have seen, the posting was to Salonica not Palestine.

17 'Doubling' means marching at the double, that is twice as fast as normal.

18 Vaughan Williams did go to Lydd in Kent where he was based in the Royal Garrison Artillery's Hut Town.

19 Reproduced in full in Stephen Connock *Toward the Sun Rising – Ralph Vaughan Williams Remembered*, Albion Music Ltd, 2018, p. 297.

20 Richard Bradford *Orwell – A Man of Our Time*, Bloomsbury Caravel, 2020, p. 31.

21 2/Lt Frederick Charles Hoy (1894-1978) from 'Ten Years Ago Today', written on 18 September 1928, with the instructions to be opened by his daughters Beryl and Barbara on 18 September 1938. The letter was kindly provided by his grandson John Whittaker. Additional information was provided by John Whittaker from an account of his grandfather's life.

22 For further information see Paul Cobb Battery Action! T*he Diary of a Gunner, 1916-19*, Reveille Press, 2015, pp. 32-33.

23 Letter to Ursula Vaughan Williams quoted in her book, *op. cit.*, p. 127.

24 Jean Moorcroft Wilson, *op. cit.*, p. 412.

25 This is the most likely form of words based on what other junior officers received in 1918. The original is missing.

26 Hugh Cobbe, *op. cit.*, p. 118.

27 See Joseph Mason in Stephen Connock, *op. cit.*, p. 298.

28 Max Plowman *A Subaltern on the Somme*, The Naval and Military Press, 1928, p. 4.

29 See *War Diary* 86th Brigade, WO-95-325-7.

30 I. Hogg *Allied Artillery in World War I*, The Crowood Press, 1998, pp. 65-70 and quoted in Alan Aldous *Vaughan Williams as an Officer*, *Journal of the RVW Society*, October 1999, p. 9. See also Dale Clarke *British Artillery 1914-19*, Osprey Publishing, 2005, pp. 3-19.

31 Gordon Corrigan *Mud, Blood and Poppycock*, Cassell, 2003, p. 141.

32 *ibid*, p. 144.

33 Siegfried Sassoon *The Complete Memoirs of George Sherston*, Faber and Faber, paperback edition, 1980, p. 291.

34 Huntly Gordon *The Unreturning Army – The Classic Memoir of a Field Gunner in Flanders*, Bantam Books, 2013 edition, p. 58.

35 Ursula Vaughan Williams and Imogen Holst (eds.) *Heirs and Rebels – Letters written to each other and occasional writings on music by Ralph Vaughan Williams and Gustav Holst*, Oxford University Press, 1959, p. 46.

36 Huntly Gordon, *op. cit.*, p. 98.

37 Dennis Wheatley *The Time has Come – 1914-1919 Officer and Temporary Gentlemen*, Hutchinson, 1978, p. 104.

38 James E. Edmonds and others, *Military Operations France and Belgium 1918 – The German March Offensive and its Preliminaries*, Imperial War Museum, 1935, p. 37

39 *ibid*, p. 62.

40 *ibid*, p. 70.

41 *ibid*, p. 104.

42 *ibid*, p. 120.

43 Martin Gilbert *The First World War*, The Folio Society, 2012, p. 497.

44 *War Diary, 86th* Brigade, *op. cit.*, – 21 March 1918.

45 Captain Arthur F. Behrend *Nine Days – Adventures of a Heavy Artillery Brigade of the Third Army during the German Offensive of 21-29 March 1918*, The Naval and Military Press, 1921, pp. 1-2.

46 Paul Cobb, *op. cit.*, p. 195.

47 Siegfried Sassoon, *op. cit.*, p. 424.

48   Peter Hart 1918 – *A Very British Victory*, Weidenfeld and Nicolson, 2008, p. 66.

49   Martin Gilbert, *op. cit.*, p. 503.

50   Peter Hart, *op. cit.*, p. 191.

51   *ibid*, p. 515.

52   The *War Diary* for the 86th Brigade normally only gives locations for headquarters and rarely refers to the position of individual batteries such as 141 Heavy Battery. Where the actual location of 141 Heavy Battery is provided, sometimes it may only be a part of the Unit. Broadly, the Batteries of the Brigade followed within a few miles of their respective HQ.

53   Dennis Wheatley, *op. cit.*, pp. 208-209.

54   His recollections are printed in full in Stephen Connock, *op. cit.*, p. 296.

55   Cuthbert Headlam *History of the Guards Division in the Great War, Volume 2, 1915-1918*, The Naval and Military Press, 1924, p. 77.

56   *ibid*, p. 45.

57   James E. Edmonds, *Military Operations France and Belgium, March-April 1918, Continuation of the German Offensive*, Imperial War Museum, 1937, p. 492.

58   James E. Edmonds, *Military Operations France and Belgium, May-July 1918*, Imperial War Museum, 1939, p. 4.

59   *ibid*, p. 9.

60   *War Diary* 86th Brigade, *op. cit.*, 23 April 1918.

61   Ernst Jünger *Storm of Steel*, Penguin Classics, 1961 edition, p. 30.

62   *War Diary* 86th Brigade, *op. cit.*, 8 June 1918.

63   James E, Edwards, *op. cit.*, p. 215

64   *ibid*, p. 215.

65   *ibid*, pp. 316-319.

66   Ursula Vaughan Williams, *op. cit.*, p. 130.

67   James E. Edwards, *Official History of the Great War – Military Operations France and Belgium 1918*, Volume IV, The Naval and Military Press, 1940, p. 22.

68   *ibid*, p. 34.

69   *ibid*, p. 89.

70   *ibid*, p. 154.

71   *ibid*, p. 155.

72   James E. Edwards, *op. cit.*, p. 462.

73   *ibid*, p. 462.

74   Ernst Jünger, *op. cit.*, p. 128.

75 James E. Edmonds, *Official History of the Great War – Military Operations France and Belgium 1918, Volume 5*, The Naval and Military Press, 1947, p. v.

76 *ibid*, p. vii.

77 *ibid*, p. 61. See Note 2.

78 *ibid*, p. 270.

79 *ibid*, p. 276.

80 Harry Siepmann, *Echo of the Guns – Recollections of an Artillery Officer1914-18*, Robert Hale, 1987, p. 168.

81 For the full text see Stephen Connock, *op. cit.*, p. 336.

82 James E. Edwards, *op. cit.*, p. 558.

83 Stephen Graham *A Private in The Guards*, William Heinemann, 1928, p. 258.

84 Hugh Cobbe, *op. cit.*, p. 122.

85 J. E. Edmonds, *Official History of the Great War – The Occupation of the Rhineland 1918-1929*, Naval and Military Press, 1945, p. 1.

86 See Chris Hyland *The Canadian Corps' Long March Logistics, Discipline and the Occupation of the Rhineland*, in Canadian Military History, 2015, Vol. 21, Article 2, p. 3.

87 British Expeditionary Force disposition on 11 November 1918. Information taken from www.314th.org/Nafziger-Coll.of-Battle, p. 21.

88 J. E. Edmonds, *op. cit.*, p. 12.

89 Captain Stair Gillon *The Story of the 29th Division: A Record of Gallant Deeds*, The Naval and Military Press, 1925, p. 220.

90 Quoted in Ursula Vaughan Williams, *op. cit.*, p. 131. See also letter VML 446 in the online database of *Letters of Ralph Vaughan Williams*, edited by Hugh Cobbe.

91 Stair Gillon, op.cit, p. 226.

92 *ibid*, line 3.

93 *ibid*, lines 4-6.

94 *ibid*, last line.

95 Gary Sheffield *The Chief – Douglas Haig and the British Army*, Aurum Press, 2012, p. 341.

96 Simon Robbins *British Generalship during the Great War – The Military Career of Sir Henry Horne (1861-1929)*, Ashgate Publishing Ltd., 2010, p. 221.

97 Stephen Connock, *op. cit.*, p. 336.

6   1919-1958: From 'the old man' to the 'Grand Old Man'.

Vaughan Williams may have been 'the old man' to his fellow-cadets at Maresfield Park but it was not long before he was Britain's musical 'Grand Old Man'. After demobilisation he sought to resume his musical activities and tried to adjust to civilian conditions. This was not easy and in this difficult transition he was in good company. The actor Basil Rathbone wrote in his autobiography:

> 'There was a tinge of fear about one's heart and mind as the readjustment to civilian life took shape. For so long there had been but one single purpose to one's life, a life completely disciplined and organised from "up top". This hard-earned routine was not going to be easy to escape from. So much would never be the same again. So much must be changed within myself and in relation to others…'[1]

Edmund Blunden, who had served as an officer in the Royal Sussex Regiment from 1915 until he was demobilised on almost the same day as Vaughan Williams in 1919, referred to being 'driven back by the world of peace and its puzzles to the company of the years of terror.'[2] His poem from 1922, *Behind the Line*, captured this feeling:

> *About you spreads the world anew,*
> *The old fields all for your sense rejoice,*
> *   Music has found her ancient voice,*
> *   From the hills there's heaven on earth to view.*
> *And kindly Mirth will raise his glass*
> *With you to bid dull Care go pass –*
> *And still you wander muttering on*
> *Over the shades of shadows gone.*

Vaughan Williams sought to remove the 'shades of shadows gone' by moving to Sheringham, on the north Norfolk coast, to be with his wife, Adeline, who was nursing her brother Hervey Fisher – see Photo 50. He had suffered from an injury to his spine since early childhood. When he died on 26 May 1921 it came as a great blow to both Adeline and Ralph. They rented accommodation in four different locations while in Sheringham (Northern Lights, The Sun Dial, Mainsail House and The Little House) and Vaughan Williams said in a letter to the painter William Rothenstein from Northern Lights on 22 August 1919 that: 'My plans are so vague that I don't like to make any promises to be at any particular place at a particular time'.[3]

Photo 50: Ralph and Adeline in Sheringham, 1920.

Vaughan Williams began to revise two pre-war works, *A London Symphony* and *The Lark Ascending*, and focused again on a ballad-opera that he had also worked on before the war – *Hugh the Drover*. His great friend and teacher Sir Hubert Parry had died on 7 October 1918 and been replaced by Hugh Allen as Director of the Royal College of Music. Allen had to reinvigorate the College after the war, with the number of students increasing from 200 to 600. This meant a large increase in the teaching staff and, in his first two years, Allen made 26 new appointments. One of these was Ralph Vaughan Williams who joined the teaching staff in 1919, along with Gustav Holst. Vaughan Williams was soon a member of the Board of Professors, and took over the conductorship of the Bach Choir from Hugh Allen in 1920. He also received an honorary doctorate from Oxford University in 1919 which marked an important early recognition of the composer's worth immediately after the war.

Slowly, life seemed to be returning to something like normal. As Michael Kennedy put it, Vaughan Williams 'ran himself in' – he took life more slowly with no rush to complete new music.[4] He had revised and orchestrated *The Lark Ascending* by December 1920 and it was first performed in this final version on 14 June 1921.

Individuals respond in different ways to the experience of war. Some talk of it incessantly, others never, not even to close family and friends. Vaughan Williams was in the second group, reticent to discuss his experiences at Ecoivres, Mont St Eloi, Neuville St Vaast, Salonica, Croisilles, Ypres or Namur. He reminisced with certain colleagues from the Army, but with no one else, even declining to contribute to a book on the 2/4th London Field Ambulance put together by the Unit personnel in the late 1920s and published in 1935.

Vaughan Williams began to work hard on what became the *Pastoral Symphony*, which he had started to think about at Ecoivres in Northern France while serving in the RAMC, and the importance of this work in the context of the Great War is discussed in this book, see Chapter 7.

Life went on. Despite the onset of her crippling illness, Adeline was able to join Ralph on a visit to Connecticut in North America for a performance of the *Pastoral Symphony* conducted by her husband with the Litchfield County Choral Union on 7 June 1922. Adeline wrote to her sister Cordelia:

> 'Ralph started the concert with his *Pastoral*. It went very beautifully…1,500 people and more camped outside on the grass…We have been in this nice country for a week, very green, I don't know what the audience made of the *Pastoral* but the feeling was as if they liked it…'[5]

Many folk song arrangements followed, which must have given great pleasure to the composer, including *Ca' the Yowes*, arranged for tenor solo and chorus. Vaughan Williams returned to Bunyan with his one act opera *The Shepherds of the Delectable Mountains*, first performed at the Royal College of Music on 11 July 1922. We also return to this short but important 'Pastoral Episode' in Chapter 7.

On 22 October 1922 Vaughan Williams reached 50 and Gustav Holst planned a surprise for him. Jane Joseph, a pupil of Gustav Holst, composed a birthday song which was serenaded at dusk to the composer in the front garden of his house in Cheyne Walk – all very reminiscent of *Siegfried Idyll*. The singers from Morley College included Holst and the song went as follows:

> *My comrades! Rejoice and sing*
> *Upon this day of thanksgiving.*
> *Give honour*
> *And greet the mighty one*
> *Who added grace to song.*

Vaughan Williams opened the windows of the house to listen and wave at the performers who were then invited in for drinks.[6]

In 1923 Vaughan Williams returned to hymn-book editing and this led to the publication of *Songs of Praise* in 1925. The music was jointly edited with Martin Shaw and the words edited by Percy Dearmer, the work being undertaken over

20 years after their first collaboration on *The English Hymnal*. Five original tunes were provided by Vaughan Williams, none as memorable as *Sine Nomine* or *Down Ampney*, composed for the earlier hymnal. Martin Shaw recalled of Vaughan Williams that:

> 'His wisdom, musicianship, integrity and scholarship were seen again in the hymn-book intended as an 'All Churches' hymn-book: *Songs of Praise*. His criteria included a considered opinion that warm words should be married to an austere tune, and vice versa, in order to maintain the dignity necessary to public utterance, as opposed to private, and to combine that with humanity. Secondly, the finest version of every tune, and not necessarily the earliest, should be the one printed. Thirdly, that fine melody, rather than the exploitation of a trained choir, should govern selection'.[7]

It was two years of very hard work; the *Oxford Book of Carols* (1928) caused fewer problems.

Vaughan Williams focused on folk songs in 1923 with the *English Folk Songs Suite* for military band. The slow movement, an *Intermezzo* based on *My Bonny Boy*, is quite lovely. A little later he contemplated writing the music for a ballad-opera called *John Kemp's Wager* ('The Hobby Horse') by his friend Robert Graves.[8] This came to nothing but another ballad-opera, *Hugh the Drover*, which, as we have seen, he had begun in 1910, was completed and first performed in public on 14 July 1924. This romantic and expressive work is very much in the style of the composer's lyrical pre-war years. When the original libretto by Harold Child, a *Times* leader writer, did not fit easily with the composer's vision, Vaughan Williams took a firmer hand in reshaping the text using incidents from real life that he had heard from folk song singers in his pre-war tours of English counties. How Vaughan Williams must have enjoyed revisiting folk-inspired music of such beauty after his war experiences! For example, he chose the lovely folk-song 'Tuesday Morning' to introduce Mary in Act I of *Hugh the Drover*:

Illustration 26: 'Tuesday Morning' from *Hugh the Drover*.

The open-air lyricism of the music for Hugh and his lover, Mary, recalls the *Songs of Travel* as well as *A London Symphony*. Harold Child's libretto did at least provide the composer with the opportunity to unleash his romantic impulses, as in this text for Mary, the Constable's daughter, also from Act I:

> *In the night time I have seen you riding, riding,*
> *In the night time I have heard you calling, calling,*
> *In the day time duty frights me chiding, chiding,*
> *I have feared for truth and honour falling, falling.*
>
> *In the day time I have lost you fearing, fearing.*
> *In the sunset I have sought you pining, pining,*
> *In the twilight I have found you nearing, nearing,*
> *I have dreamed your arms about me twining, twining…*

Hugh the Drover remains an underrated opera, a fine example of how the discovery of English folk song unleashed a fresh melodic inventiveness in the music of Ralph Vaughan Williams.

Flos campi (1925) is also romantic but the style is quite different, more ethereal and ecstatic. Vaughan Williams indicated in his programme note for a performance of the work in 1927 that the Latin title, translated as 'Flower of the Field', did not connote 'buttercups and daisies' but was the Vulgate equivalent of 'Rose of Sharon' – 'I am the Rose of Sharon, and the Lily of the Valleys'. However, Vaughan Williams disavows all speculation of religious inspiration by stating firmly that the music for *Flos campi* has no ecclesiastical basis – for him it is a celebration of love between a man and a woman.

The work is in six linked movements, each headed by a Latin quotation, with an English translation, added later, from the *Song of Solomon*. The restrained, lyrical opening bars set the tone, the work flowing with a remarkable sense of rhapsodic longing. The *cantabile* viola solo in the second section is quite beautiful, the wordless choir instructed to sing with 'half closed lips'. The instrumental fourth section, a march with oriental overtones, provides necessary contrast. Above all, *Flos campi* is, as Hubert Foss once put it, 'An exquisite study in pure sound'.[9]

Vaughan Williams's love for folk song was beautifully expressed in the *Six Studies in English Folk Song* (1926), distilling the essence of this traditional music into a 10-minute piece. *On Christmas Night* followed this same year – 1926 – as the composer continued to pursue his goal of reviving the English *Masque*, with dancing, singing and miming. Some of Vaughan Williams's favourite carols were included such as *The First Nowell* and *On Christmas Night*.

The major works of 1927-29 were two operas: *Sir John in Love* and a 'romantic extravaganza' called *The Poisoned Kiss*. Both are intensely lyrical and warm-hearted. *Sir John in Love*, an opera in four acts, has a libretto by the composer based on Shakespeare's *The Merry Wives of Windsor*. The work incorporates a number of delightful folk songs, including *Greensleeves*, and Vaughan Williams interpolates poems such as Ben Jonson's 'Have you seen but a bright lily grow' from *The Triumph*. This is, perhaps, one of the most beautiful of all Vaughan Williams's settings. The composer included it at the heart of a cantata for mixed chorus and orchestra that he arranged from the opera in 1931 under the title *In Windsor Forest*.

The Poisoned Kiss had to wait until 1935 for its first performances. Set to a somewhat dated libretto, much of it spoken, by Evelyn Sharp, sister of Cecil, the work is deeply expressive with moments of high drama. Neither composer nor librettist could quite make up their minds if the work was a comedy or a drama and in the end it falls uneasily between both genres. Vaughan Williams was dissatisfied with the libretto and on Evelyn Sharp's death in 1955 he purchased the rights and set about revising the work with his second wife, Ursula. Despite the difficulties, it contains music of wonderful lyricism and the opera does not deserve its almost complete neglect.

As the composer approached his sixtieth birthday in 1932, he wrote one of his outright masterpieces, *Job – A Masque for Dancing*. As Sir George Dyson put it:

> 'The point at which he reached, in my opinion, his characteristic height was when he produced that unique 'Masque for Dancing' *Job*. There is in this work the whole essence of his musical thought. And as the story of *Job* is an epitome of man's pilgrimage from joy to sorrow, and from sorrow to humility, so does the composer's music illustrate the whole range of his creative and imaginative expression, his pleasure, his pathos and his faith. He had not only found his language, but he had learnt to command and expand it to the measure of his own deep and abiding ideals'.[10]

Vaughan Williams knew both the fine Hebrew poetry of the *Book of Job*, with its theme of suffering as an important element in God's dealings with man, and the visions of William Blake contained in his *Illustrations for the Book of Job*. These *Illustrations* consist of 21 superbly engraved plates, published in 1826, shortly before the artist's death. When Vaughan Williams was asked in 1927 to write the music for a ballet based on the Blake engravings, he jumped at the chance. He had not seen the scenario for the ballet, which was being devised by the Blake scholar, Dr Geoffrey Keynes, when he accepted the commission and, in his enthusiasm for the project, he pushed on with musical ideas anyway. He used for inspiration the original Blake engravings contained in Joseph Wicksteed's book *Blake's Vision of the Book of Job* (1910).

The idea for a ballet based on William Blake's interpretation of the *Book of Job* had come from Keynes who involved his sister-in-law, Gwen Raverat, in the stage designs. A 'working scenario' was completed during 1927. The choice of Vaughan Williams, a cousin to Gwen Raverat, was inspired, as Vaughan Williams had already sought, with his friend Gustav Holst, to establish an expressly *English* style of ballet. Vaughan Williams strongly disliked the classical style of dancing *en pointe*. Instead he sought to fashion a style based on folk-traditions.

Vaughan Williams called the new work a *Masque for Dancing*, thereby explicitly linking *Job* to the Masque tradition in England, which can be traced back to Tudor times. With an emphasis on tableau-like scenes, dances and mime, Vaughan Williams further strengthened the cultural and historical links to a tradition of English ballet by including a number of court dances of the 17th century in his *Job*, including the Sarabande, Pavane and Galliard. *Job* was first performed in a concert version on 23 October 1930 and then later as a staged version on 5 July 1931 at the Cambridge Theatre in London, produced by the Carmargo Society. It was this staged version which so inspired the 20-year old Ursula Lock, later to become Mrs Ursula Vaughan Williams, that she remembered it when writing to the composer in 1938.

Given the fierce nature of the music for the Devil in *Job* and the rhythmic force of the first and third movements of the *Piano Concerto in C major* (1931), the ferocity of the *Symphony No. 4 in F minor* (1934) should not have come as a complete surprise to the audience in the Queen's Hall on 10 April 1935 when Sir Adrian Boult gave the first performance with the BBC Symphony Orchestra. Simona Pakenham remembers being 'completely knocked back by this music – I'd never heard anything like it before'.[11] Walton thought it 'the greatest symphony since Beethoven'[12] and Patrick Hadley declared that the work had 'knocked Europe sideways'.[13]

Vaughan Williams's programme note for the first performance, as always, gave no hint at what he meant by such an angry, uncompromising work. He always rejected 'interpretations' of his music, especially any implying that he was trying to capture the state of Europe, dominated by Hitler's rise to power in the 1930s, stating simply: "All I know is that it is what I wanted to do at the time". The death of his close friend Gustav Holst on 25 May 1934 may have come too late to be reflected in the music, although Holst had been ill for some time. Similarly, there may have been anger at Adeline's deteriorating health, a build-up of frustration dating from 1909. It remains an enigma.

Vaughan Williams was now very much 'Uncle Ralph' or 'The Uncle' to his friends and family. Formal recognition of his contribution to music came on 17 May 1935 when he received a letter from Buckingham Palace offering him the Order of Merit. After some thought, he accepted the award which is made to only 24 holders at any one time. In the Order, he joined H. A. L. Fisher, his brother-in-law and referee for his application for a Commission back in 1917. At a party to celebrate his award, Vaughan Williams was embarrassed and upset when a wreath was put around his neck. He always disliked such public displays of affection, however well meant.

Photo 51: Vaughan Williams in the garden of The White Gates, Dorking, 1930.

Vaughan Williams's mastery was confirmed with a number of works in the late 1930s, including the Skelton cycle *Five Tudor Portraits* (1935), the Whitman-inspired *Dona Nobis Pacem* (1936) and his moving one-act opera based almost verbatim on J. M. Synge's *Riders to the Sea*, first performed in 1937 and also discussed in more detail in Chapter 7.

Dona Nobis Pacem was largely based on the poetry of Walt Whitman who exerted a lifelong fascination for Vaughan Williams based on the freshness of the poet's language, the 'sing-able' quality of the verse and the sense of spiritual exultation which Whitman articulated. The cantata used sections from *Drum Taps* including a 'Dirge for Two Veterans' which Vaughan Williams had originally composed in 1911. The composer was aware that Whitman had served in field hospitals in the American Civil War during 1863 when he wrote some of the finest poems in *Drum Taps*. Whitman would often take it upon himself to notify parents that their soldier-son had died in his presence. That Vaughan Williams empathised with Whitman's suffering on behalf of the men he treated can be heard in his tender setting of the following text:

> *O strong dead march you please me!*
> *O moon immense with your silvery face you soothe me!*
> *O my soldiers twain! O my veterans passing to burial!*
> *What I have I also give you.*
>
> *The moon gives you light,*
> *And the bugles and the drums give you music,*
> *And my heart, O my soldiers, my veterans,*
> *My heart gives you love.*

The music is remarkably poignant and life-affirming with a quiet intensity that remains all the more moving for its understatement.

In March 1938, Vaughan Williams embarked on an affair with Ursula Wood, a married woman younger by almost 40 years. How this happened can be described briefly as follows.

Photo 52: Ursula Wood in 1936.

Ursula Wood was 26 when she first contacted Ralph Vaughan Williams in January 1938. She had been in touch with the composer via the Royal College of Music to discuss a detailed scenario which Ursula thought might form the basis for a ballet. Ursula remembered the background to this first liaison, which she referred to simply as 'lunch with Vaughan Williams' in her diary entry for 31 March 1938:

> 'In 1938 I wrote to Ralph offering him a libretto I had done called *The Ballad of Margaret and Clerk Saunders*. Ralph did not think it was a

good libretto and, through Douglas Kennedy, I agreed to write something else which was based on Spenser's *Epithalamion*. There was then a lot of correspondence going backwards and forwards so, after a while, I said to Kennedy: "For goodness sake, do ask the man to ask me out to lunch", and he did. When we met at the end of March 1938 I thought him quite beautiful, with his green pork-pie hat'.[14]

This may have turned into another professional collaboration between the composer and a writer much like, say, his work with Evelyn Sharp a few years before on *The Poisoned Kiss*. However, the relationship between Ralph and Ursula was intimate almost immediately:

'On the first day we were in a taxi waiting for the light and he put his arms around me and gave me a very passionate kiss. So I said: "Well, it's very nice but I haven't had that sort of kiss from someone like you" and he replied "well, that's alright"… We had a wonderful dinner…By the time I went to see him off at Victoria, I found I'd absolutely got it badly, very badly. I had fallen in love and that was very difficult… Later, I was lying awake all night thinking about him, how lovely he was. So I rang him up and said: "Please can you come and see me?" So he came, half his face shaved and the other half not! That was lovely'.[15]

Although both Ralph and Ursula were married, it is easy to see why they both threw caution to the wind and started a passionate affair. For Ursula, a very attractive and aspiring poet, Vaughan Williams was the perfect partner. He valued her knowledge of poetry, especially of Shakespeare, he was fun and worldly, distinguished and rugged, had money and fame, and introduced her to a social milieu of writers and musicians, including Evelyn Sharp and Gerald Finzi, with whom she would never otherwise have mixed. Her husband, Michael, was – according to the accounts of people who knew him well – a nice, quiet, decent, undemonstrative Army man who loved nothing more than coming home to his watercolours. For Vaughan Williams at 65, how could he resist such a young and romantic woman? By 1938, his wife had been crippled with arthritis for almost 30 years. They were close but there was, understandably, little in the way of a physical relationship. Ursula brought gaiety, flair, humour, style, poetry – and sex.

Ursula's influence was very significant from the start. She appealed to Vaughan Williams's frivolous side which had been stifled by his first wife and by her family – Adeline still always dressed in black in mourning for her dead brothers or some other sad event. The impact of Ursula Wood on the music of Vaughan Williams was immediately apparent. Henry Wood had asked the composer for a piece to commemorate his jubilee marking 50 years as a conductor in 1938. Ralph called Ursula and said:

> "Henry Wood wants to have 16 singers and I am thinking of Lorenzo and Jessica". I said: "What, 16 Lorenzos and sixteen Jessicas?" and he replied: "Oh no, you'll see, just wait and see". He had the poetry in his mind. I think he was rather in love with me at that time; I think it was written for me".[16]

It is a beautiful work which shows in its rapt setting of Shakespeare a man happy with himself in his new relationship with Ursula Wood. The work is certainly one of the most ravishing of all Vaughan Williams's compositions. It was Vaughan Williams who came up with the inspired idea to set the words for the 16 voices as *soloists*, the individual vocal qualities of each singer shaping the phrasing and colour of each part. The initials of each singer at the first performance were placed in the score to mark his or her individual entries. While Henry Wood and Vaughan Williams were able to agree on the names of the 16 singers, some leading soloists had to be omitted; perhaps the most disappointed was the bass-baritone Keith Falkner, a close friend of both conductor and composer.

In 1941 Ursula was pregnant. She appeared uncertain about the identity of the father – Ralph or her husband Michael Wood – though the former is more probable as she was less likely to have been intimate with Michael at that time. This was partly because he was rarely at home and also because he was not physically well. Ursula had a termination, thus resolving her awful dilemma.

Michael, died shortly afterwards on 8 June 1942 from a heart attack. Vaughan Williams took Ursula down to Dorking to recover. Adeline made a fuss of her as she always did when friends faced bereavement; after all, she had considerable experience of such sadness. Vaughan Williams had now achieved what he wanted

Photo 53: Ursula's first husband Michael Wood.

Photo 54: RVW with Seumas O'Sullivan, Dublin, 1939.

– Ursula was with him in Dorking; he even made space for her to work in his study. They could visit her flat at 7½ Thayer Street in Marylebone whenever they needed more privacy.

The Nazis rise to power in Germany during the 1930s had been watched by Vaughan Williams with increasing alarm. He took a full share in the work of the Dorking Committee for Refugees from Nazi oppression in 1938. He became close friends with Robert Müller-Hartmann, a Jewish German refugee. As one writer put it:

> 'Vaughan Williams shared a hatred of Nazi oppression and worked tirelessly to help refugees find work and assimilate into English culture'.[17]

With Great Britain once again at war with Germany, how could a 68-year-old composer contribute to the war effort? He offered the use of a large part of his garden at The White Gates in Dorking to the local council for use as an allotment and organised an air-raid shelter between his house and a neighbour. He also helped with the collection of salvage materials for wartime production. More fundamentally, Vaughan Williams tried to answer this question when he wrote in May, 1940:

> 'What is the composer to do in wartime? No bombs or blockades can rob us of our vocal chords; there will always remain for us the oldest and greatest of musical instruments, the human voice… Art is a compromise between what we want to achieve and what circumstances allow us to achieve. It is out of these very compromises that the supreme art often springs; the highest comes when you least expect it.[18]

Supreme art was indeed possible and Vaughan Williams's *Fifth Symphony* was as good an example as any. It was first performed on 24 June 1943 at the Proms and made an immediate impression. Sir Adrian Boult wrote to the composer about the symphony:

> 'Its serene loveliness is completely satisfying in these times and shows, as only music can, what we must work for when this madness is over'.[19]

The *Fifth Symphony* is modal in character, visionary, owing much in spirit and in content to the unfinished opera *The Pilgrim's Progress*, especially in the glorious third movement *Romanza*. Ursula Vaughan Williams always said that this symphony in general, and particularly the slow movement, owed much to the stimulus of their love affair.[20] There is a hope and optimism in this symphony which transcends questions about the work's origin; it is a universal statement as inspiring now as it was in 1943.

At the beginning of the Second World War, Vaughan Williams had stepped down as a professor at the Royal College of Music. With more time on his hands in Dorking, he started to take part in the war effort, including fire-watching. Ursula Wood said:

> 'He would crawl about all night for two to three nights a week, getting terribly dirty…We all wore tin hats. It could be dangerous as there was such a black-out in the early days. Ralph loved gardening and he decided to offer his garden to Dorking District Council. He'd put all his vegetables into bags for people to collect… He gave many lectures at The Ship Hotel in Dorking. He was trying to be normal, to show that everyday life could go on. It gave a sense of normality in difficult times'.[21]

During fire-watching he would spend his time preparing an English language version of Bach's *Mass in B minor*. Music was his salvation. He began to organise lunchtime concerts, called an 'Informal Hour of Music', at the White Horse in Dorking. Vaughan Williams also supported Myra Hess in her wartime concerts at the National Gallery in London. When he presented the Royal Philharmonic Society Gold Medal to her on 17 January 1942 he declared his belief in the beauty of music 'which time cannot dim and enemies cannot tarnish'.[22]

Vaughan Williams also felt that he could contribute to the war effort through film music. Starting with *49th Parallel* (1941), he went on to compose music for *Coastal Command* (1942), *The People's Land* (1943), *Flemish Farm* (1943) and *Stricken Peninsula* (1945).

As early as 1943, the BBC Music Department was considering the need for a victory anthem and Vaughan Williams accepted the commission. The work became *A Song of Thanksgiving* and it was recorded in London on 5 November 1944. Set for speaker, soprano, chorus and orchestra, it was eventually broadcast on 13 May 1945, just five days after VE Day. It is a noble piece, with 'Land of our Birth', a children's song to words by Rudyard Kipling, making a memorable impression.

Approaching his mid-seventies, Vaughan Williams was at the height of his musical powers and had successfully managed both his marriage to Adeline and his affair with Ursula. Adeline was on hand to provide stability, continuity and insight and Ursula was there with her energy, good looks, flair, fun and poetic influences. A fine and rare balance, difficult to pull off, yet he had done so.

Following the Second World War, Vaughan Williams could focus fully on composition. In 1946, he decided to revise his *Piano Concerto* of 1930-1931. The work was originally written for, and dedicated to, Harriet Cohen who gave the first performance on 1 February 1933 with the BBC Symphony Orchestra conducted by Adrian Boult. The work presented formidable technical challenges to the soloist and Harriet Cohen was simply not up to the task. The idea of a two-piano version of the work had arisen after the first performance but Vaughan Williams held back until 1946 when he agreed to a request by the husband-and-wife piano duo of Cyril Smith and Phyllis Sellick to authorise such an arrangement. The stimulus for this task was to find a suitable two-piano work for the St Cecilia's Day Royal concert on 22 November 1946 for which two orchestras and two pianists had been hired.

It was Cyril Smith and Phyllis Sellick who suggested that the pianist Joseph Cooper, later of BBC television *Face the Music* fame, should be given the job of making the new arrangement. He was still serving in Germany and looking for an excuse to come back to England. Joseph Cooper said in 1996: 'Vaughan Williams was very supportive of the re-arrangement. He felt that the original version was 'a washout', that it couldn't be played. When I had got the job half done, I took it to Cyril and Phyllis who still complained that it was too difficult and that I should take out some notes – Vaughan Williams won't spot it, they said!' Joseph Cooper confirmed that he added 27 new bars of music and that it was entirely Vaughan Williams's idea to change the ending. He wrote a new gentle *Cadenza* for the two pianos *after* the first performance on 22 November 1946 which took Joseph Cooper by surprise![23]

Increasing fame did not sit easily with Vaughan Williams. He said in the spring of 1948:

> 'It's awful. People come up to me in the lavatory and say how much they like my symphonies'.[24]

A *Sixth Symphony* was first performed on 21 April 1948, conducted by Sir Adrian Boult. The music made a profound impression. Many commentators heard, in the power, vehemence and ultimate desolation of the music, Vaughan Williams's response to the Second World War, to concentration camps, the purges of Stalin, nuclear bombs and the terrors of the advancing Cold War. Vaughan Williams strongly rejected the idea that this work was a 'War Symphony', sending a rebuke to Frank Howes for such a suggestion.[25] Vaughan Williams did, however, tell Michael Kennedy about the meaning of the unusual and disturbing last movement by quoting Prospero's speech from Act IV of Shakespeare's *The Tempest*:

> *Our revels now are ended. These our actors,*
> *As I foretold you, were all spirits and*
> *Are melted into air, into thin air;*
> *And, like the basic fabric of this vision,*
> *The cloud-capp'd towers, the gorgeous palaces,*
> *The solemn temples, the great globe itself,*
> *Yea, all which it inherit, shall dissolve*
> *And, like this insubstantial pageant faded,*
> *Leave not a rack behind. We are such stuff*
> *As dreams are made on, and our little life*
> *Is rounded with a sleep.*

'Rounded with a sleep' and 'melted into air, into thin air' do seem to be evoked in the ghostly *Epilogue* to the symphony but there is a coldness at the heart of this movement which is missing in the text, and Prospero is hardly a featureless character. In this sense, the conclusion of this symphony can more appropriately be related to the desolation of parts of *Along the Field or Motion and Stillness* from the years after the First World War. Vaughan Williams seems to be peering into the abyss and finding only emptiness.

The composer returned to film music with *Scott of the Antarctic*. It was inevitable that such a tragic story of high adventure would attract a film company and, in 1946, the director Charles Frend and the Ealing Studios associate producer Sidney Cole received the enthusiastic blessing of the Ealing boss, Sir Michael Balcon, to start work on *Scott of the Antarctic*. John Mills was well cast as Captain Scott. Ernest Irving, the music director of Ealing Studios, was briefed by Balcon and said:

> 'It did not take me fifty seconds to decide whom I should suggest as composer of the music – Ralph Vaughan William'.[26]

Vaughan Williams had by now written music for five films, including *49th Parallel* in 1940. He reacted favourably to the idea of providing music for *Scott of the Antarctic*. Despite reservations about Scott's organisation, he was inspired by the courage, leadership and fortitude that Scott showed when faced with appalling conditions. The film was first shown at a Royal Command Performance at the Empire Theatre, London on 29 November 1948.

The Scott tragedy had a deep impact on Vaughan Williams such that he started work, in the summer of 1949, on a new symphony based on the film music. This became *Sinfonia Antartica*, his Seventh Symphony. It was finished by the end of 1951 and dedicated to Ernest Irving. John Barbirolli conducted the first performance, in Manchester, on 14 January 1953, with Margaret Ritchie, a Vaughan Williams favourite, as the soprano soloist.

Photo 55: Vaughan Williams in 1950 at the wedding of Bernard and Barbara Brown.

In 1949, Vaughan Williams worked on a commission from Fanny Farrer, an old friend who was leading the National Federation of Women's Institutes, on a work for a women's chorus. Vaughan Williams thought that folk song would work for this group and went back to many of the folk songs he had collected and known for almost 50 years. The work became *Folk Songs of the Four Seasons* and was first performed in the Royal Albert Hall on 15 June 1950.

Another work of 1949, *An Oxford Elegy*, took Vaughan Williams back to the use of a speaker and chorus, a format he had adopted for the wartime *A Song of Thanksgiving*. Based on Matthew Arnold's *The Scholar Gipsy* and *Thyrsis*, it is a pastoral work, rather nostalgic yet beautiful, which Vaughan Williams compared unfavourably to Delius! The final section is most moving:

Despair I will not, while I yet descry
  That lonely tree against the western sky.
Fields where soft sheep from cages pull the hay,
  Woods with anemones in flower till May
Know him a wanderer still.

Vaughan Williams often searched for 'the light' and at these moments produced music at once rapt, noble and contemplative, infused with an inner glow of emotional intensity. So it is with his music to *The Pilgrim's Progress*.

During 1949 and into 1950, there had been plans and counter-plans regarding staging of the now largely finished *The Pilgrim's Progress* and delays occurred for many reasons. In the end, the opera was first performed at the Royal Opera House, Covent Garden on 26 April 1951, as part of the *Festival of Britain*, and was conducted by Leonard Hancock. Vaughan Williams had been thinking about music for *Pilgrim's Progress* since at least 1906. Understandably, he was very disappointed by the lukewarm reception of the work at Covent Garden which was partly down to a poor production.

Was Vaughan Williams, in his own quest to find the Celestial City, sympathetic to Christian beliefs? This is a complicated issue. Vaughan Williams's family were conventionally Christian and his First World War enlistment form records him as being 'C of E' – see Appendix 1 – notwithstanding that one of his uncles was Charles Darwin whose own faith was affected by the consequences of his research into the origin of species. At Cambridge in the 1890s, Vaughan Williams professed to be an atheist – but who wouldn't in the company of Bertrand Russell and others in the social milieu of that time? As we have seen, Vaughan Williams took on the job of editing the *English Hymnal* in 1904, yet his motivation was not religious, rather a desire to improve the quality of hymn tunes, removing much of the sentiment to be found in Victorian hymnody.

Ursula Vaughan Williams always maintained that her husband was 'never a professing Christian' even if he was to write a Mass, a Communion Service, numerous anthems, motets and original hymn tunes many of which, such as *For all the Saints (Sine Nomine)*, have become the mainstay of Sunday services throughout the Christian world. In 1922, Vaughan Williams was prompted to say after composing his *Mass in G minor* 'There is no reason why an atheist should not write a good Mass'. He was, however, deeply knowledgeable about the Authorised Version of the Bible and the Psalms and his inclusion of telling passages from these sources in his opera *The Pilgrim's Progress* shows the depth of his understanding of sacramental and ecclesiastical texts. Vaughan Williams was continually fascinated by Christian mysticism, and the sense of a spiritual journey as Pilgrim makes his way to the Celestial City via the Delectable Mountains is what gives the opera its compelling emotional and musical narrative.

Vaughan Williams certainly included more of the spiritual and pastoral elements of Bunyan's book in his opera rather than the humorous or dramatic. The composer wrote his own libretto which he described as 'a free adaptation of Bunyan's allegory'. Alongside the additions from the Bible and the Psalms, the words of Lord Lechery's song in Act III were written by Ursula Vaughan Williams.

The composer was adamant that *The Pilgrim's Progress* was 'first and foremost a stage piece'. He did not want it 'relegated to the cathedral'. Vaughan Williams recognised that the opera was not 'dramatic' and did not contain 'a love story or any big duets' that the audience might expect from a conventional opera. A later performance at Cambridge in 1954, with John Noble as Pilgrim, reassured him that the work could succeed in the theatre.

Future generations will see this work as Vaughan Williams's masterpiece.

Photo 56: RVW receives an Honorary Doctorate from Sir Winston Churchill at the University of Bristol, 1951.

In 1950 Vaughan Williams collaborated with Ursula Wood – soon to be Ursula Vaughan Williams – by including her texts in a cantata for mixed chorus and orchestra called *The Sons of Light*. He valued having a poet so close to him and turned again to her verse in both *Silence and Music* (1953) and, most poignantly, in the *Four Last Songs* of 1954 to 1958. One of these songs, 'Tired', captured the relationship between Ralph and Ursula in intimate terms:

Sleep, and I'll be still as another sleeper
holding you in my arms, glad that you lie
so near at last.

This sheltering midnight is our meeting place,
no passion or despair or hope divide
me from your side.

I shall remember firelight on your sleeping face,
I shall remember shadows growing deeper
as the fire fell to ashes and the minutes passed.

By the 1950s, Vaughan Williams was the 'Grand Old Man' of English music. He disliked this epithet saying: "I am not Grand and I am not Old".[27] Sir Winston Churchill presented him with an Honorary Doctorate at the University of Bristol in 1951 – see Photo 56. Generally strong, Vaughan Williams nevertheless suffered from a number of physical ailments in the mid-1950s including phlebitis, lumbago and, more seriously, prostate problems. He kept in touch with many of his old wartime comrades. Harry Steggles from the 2/4th London Field Ambulance recalled that while both were sitting in the 'bivvy' at Katerini in 1917, Vaughan Williams suddenly said: "Harry, when this war ends we will a) dine at Simpsons on saddle of mutton and b) see *Carmen*". Steggles went on:

'It was many years after the war when a postcard arrived saying we will a) dine at Simpsons. b) see *Carmen*. I had forgotten all about it but R.V.W. never! What a night it was, my first introduction to opera. I had gone to a lot of trouble to get myself up in the very best clothes I had fearing almost lest my shoes got dirty before I met Bob in civvy street. I duly waited outside Simpsons in the Strand for the arrival of the great man, feeling very fluttery. He suddenly loomed up with the old familiar gait I knew so well. I trembled lest he was wearing a dinner suit for I hadn't such a thing in those days. But no, he wore a huge, very old and comfortable looking Norfolk suit, complete with a large straw hat such as one would wear in the garden which was brown with age.

My fears were that he would not be dressed well enough for admission to this select restaurant. But with an outstretched hand, a "my dear Harry" and a pat on the shoulder, in we went. To my amazement the waiters bowed to him and even dusted the seat where he sat, ignoring me completely. I then had my first lesson in how to handle waiters, with saddle of mutton, redcurrant jelly, Port and Stilton, for Bob was in complete command. It also left a lasting impression in my mind that a man with the terrific personality of RVW could wear anything he chose and command respect'.[28]

Photo 57: Ralph and Ursula's wedding day, 7 February 1953.

Lt. John Tindall Robertson always remembered Vaughan Williams's birthday and on one occasion – in October 1952 – he replied:

> 'It was very nice to get a letter to remind me of the old days at Maresfield – you were a boy then and I was middle aged – now you are middle aged and I am old and toothless – but it doesn't seem to make much difference'.[29]

Following Adeline's death in 1951, Vaughan Williams was at last free to marry Ursula, which he duly did on 7 February 1953 at 12 noon – they had decided on a wedding after attending a performance of *Tristan and Isolde* on 12 January at Covent Garden. The couple took a lease on a lovely house overlooking Regent's Park at 10 Hanover Terrace. They travelled to Italy on 23 April 1953, cramming in Verona, Venice and a day in Milan before returning home on 8 May. Ralph and Ursula went to the Three Choirs Festival in Gloucester in September 1953, when Vaughan Williams conducted both *Dona Nobis Pacem* and *Job* – see Photo 58. Another trip to Italy followed in May, 1954 – Florence, Sienna and Rome, including the Vatican on 24 May – before returning home again on 29 May 1954.

Photo 58: RVW in Gloucester, 1953

Vaughan Williams's desire to catch up on lost time meant that they were soon planning to visit America to see the Grand Canyon. Keith Falkner, his old friend and at that time Professor of Music at Cornell University, suggested an American lecture tour and this took place in the autumn of 1954. Photo 59 shows an elegant Ralph and Ursula on board *RMS Queen Mary* during the eight day voyage.

At Cornell, Vaughan Williams lectured on 'Why do we make music?', 'What is music?', 'How do we make music?' and 'When do we make music?'. At Yale University, he gave a lecture entitled 'Making your own music'. The substance of these lectures was published by Cornell University in 1955 under the title

Photo 59: Ralph and Ursula on board *RMS Queen Mary*, 1954.

Illustration 27: Signed programme for a concert at Cornell University, 21 November 1954.

The Making of Music. There were concerts too (see Photo 60) and the programme for one of these, partly conducted by Vaughan Williams, is shown in Illustration 27.

Just before the lecture and concerts at Cornell and Yale, Vaughan Williams and Ursula had arrived at Niagara Falls on 9 October 1954. They travelled to California and saw the Grand Canyon on 29 October.

Travelling continued after 1954 with a visit to Athens, Crete, Messina, Venice and Vienna in September, arriving home on 2 October.

Musically, the significant work for 1954 was a cantata, *Hodie*, which beautifully captures the spirit of Christmas. Vaughan Williams conducted the première at the Three

Photo 60: Vaughan Williams conducting at Cornell University, November 1954.

Photo 62: Ralph and Ursula in Athens in 1955.

Photo 61: Ralph and Ursula in Santa Barbara, California, in 1954.

Choirs Festival in Worcester Cathedral on 8 September 1954. This work seemed to refer back to the easy lyricism of his pre-war days, especially in the wonderful setting of Thomas Hardy's *The Oxen*, which Ursula Vaughan Williams had brought to his attention:

> *Christmas Eve, and twelve of the clock.*
> *"Now they are all on their knees,"*
> *An elder said as we sat in a flock*
> *By the embers in hearth side ease,*
>
> *We pictured the meek mild creatures where*
> *They dwelt in the strawy pen,*
> *Nor did it occur to one of us there*
> *To doubt they were kneeling then.*
>
> *So fair a fancy few would weave*
> *In these years! Yet, I feel*
> *If someone said on Christmas Eve,*
> *"Come, see the oxen kneel,*
>
> *In the lonely barton by yonder coomb*
> *Our childhood used to know,"*
> *I should go with him in the gloom,*
> *Hoping it might be so.*

Vaughan Williams carried on working with immense energy. Both the *Eighth* and the *Tess*-inspired *Ninth Symphony* show Vaughan Williams exploring new

Photo 63: Ralph with Sir John Barbirolli rehearsing the *Eighth Symphony*, 1956.

orchestral sonorities, using various exotic instruments, including, as he put it: 'all the 'phones and 'spiels known to me'. He was always on the lookout for something new.

The *Eighth Symphony* was finished in 1955 and first performed on 2 May 1956 by Sir John Barbirolli, the work's dedicatee, with the Hallé Orchestra – see Photo 63. Although it is relatively short, it has a concentrated energy alongside a lightness of mood. The symphony can be linked with the *Romance for Harmonica* (1952) and the *Tuba Concerto* (1954) in its use of unusual instrumentation.

Vaughan Williams's *Ninth Symphony* was composed between early 1956 and November 1957, when the composer was well into his eighty-fifth year. It was first performed on 2 April 1958 conducted by Sir Malcolm Sargent and dedicated to the Royal Philharmonic Society – he had received the Gold Medal from the Society way back in 1929. The composer continued with his exploration of unusual instrumental sonorities, this time including three saxophones and one flugelhorn as well as a deep gong, bells and glockenspiel. The flugelhorn in particular gives the slow movement of the symphony a mellow tone and Vaughan Williams chose this instrument following a holiday in Bavaria in 1957. During a boat trip on the beautiful Königssee, the pilot suddenly stopped, turned off the engine, and produced a flugelhorn which he proceeded to play, with the melody echoing off the mountains. Vaughan Williams said at the time: 'I shall put that in my symphony'.

Both Michael Kennedy and, in much more detail, Alain Frogley[30] have shown that the *Ninth Symphony* was initially influenced by the Wessex countryside and, in particular, by Thomas Hardy's novel *Tess of the d'Urbervilles*. This book was a favourite among soldiers in the First World War; Siegfried Sassoon kept a copy in his pocket in 1916. The sketch of the first movement was originally called 'Wessex Prelude' and the final movement was called 'Landscape'. The spirit of *Tess* herself was heard in the second movement. Although no titles appear in the final published score, and the composer asserts that the programme 'got lost on the journey', the influence of Tess is real enough.

The *Ninth Symphony* has the same key, E minor, as the Sixth and also shares an enigmatic quality with the earlier symphony. As noted above, the last movement of the *Sixth Symphony* was inspired by Shakespeare's *The Tempest* and something of Prospero's wisdom and insight can also be found in Vaughan Williams's last symphony.

Vaughan Williams had planned to visit King's Lynn in July 1958 where Lionel Tertis was scheduled to play *Flos Campi*. Unfortunately, a return of his phlebitis prevented the journey but the viola player went through the score with the composer in 10 Hanover Terrace where Photo 64 was taken. It is one of the last photographs of Ralph Vaughan Williams.

Photo 64: Vaughan Williams with Lionel Tertis, July 1958.

Despite the phlebitis and that Vaughan Williams had been in hospital for major prostate surgery in 1957, his friends were not conscious of his health failing. He was working hard on his opera *Thomas the Rhymer* and a new collection of carols called *The First Nowell*. It was in early July 1958 that Austen Williams, then the vicar of St Martin-in-the-Fields, approached Vaughan Williams's friend, Simona Pakenham, with a request for her to persuade the composer to collaborate on the writing of a nativity play. She hesitated to put this to Vaughan Williams as she was aware of how busy he was. There was a production in rehearsal of *Sir John in Love* at Sadler's Wells which was the focus of much of his attention. However, she hoped she could charm Ralph into agreeing and they duly met on 6 July 1958 to consider the project. The play was to be given at the Theatre Royal, Drury Lane on 19 December 1958 in support of the Ockenden Venture, a charity that was building a village for refugee children. It would ultimately became Ockenden International which helps refugees and displaced people across the world. Simona worried that there was very little time for this composition given the deadline but, although Vaughan Williams showed little interest in the charity, she said that 'the mere mention of Christmas inspired him'. He loved Christmas carols and so agreed to contribute an arrangement of carols to a script based on medieval plays which Simona would compile. She duly delivered the script to Ralph by mid-July 1958.

Progress was difficult. Deafness prevented Ralph from speaking on the telephone but messages were relayed stating that the composer wanted a larger orchestra than could be accommodated in the Drury Lane pit. In the end, in a letter to Simona of 25 August 1958, Vaughan Williams compromised – 'very much against my will'.

The composer died in the early hours of the following morning – 26 August 1958. How poignant that one of the final pieces of music that Vaughan Williams was working on was the choral setting of the beautiful carol *The First Nowell* to the words 'and by the light of that same star', which his makeshift choir of soldiers had sung on the slopes of Mount Olympus over 40 years earlier.

Even as Ursula telephoned at dawn to tell Simona and her husband, Noel Iliff, who was producing the play, that Ralph had died, she added: 'Please do not assume that *The First Nowell* will have to be cancelled'. Roy Douglas had agreed to do what was necessary to complete the score. Rehearsals took place in the crypt of St Martin's and the performance went ahead as planned at 2.30 pm on 19 December 1958. This is what Vaughan Williams would have wanted. (See Photo 65)

Ursula had called other close friends early on the morning of 26 August 1958 to avoid them hearing about her husband's death on the 9 am radio news. John Barbirolli was in France and immediately returned to see the body; Evelyn Barbirolli recalls how moved he was by this. They had only recently been with Vaughan Williams at Cleeve Hill, the highest point in the Cotswolds, for the Cheltenham Festival, and remembered him standing outside the hotel looking at the country he knew so well. She said:

> 'He looked wonderful, like a great sculpture. He was standing quite still, transfixed'.[31]

Photo 65: Procession of the Three Kings from *The First Nowell*, Theatre Royal, Drury Lane, 19 December 1958.

A long and remarkable life had ended. This chapter has shown the extent and depth of remarkable music that Vaughan Williams composed after surviving the horrors of the First World War. We now need to reflect on and consider in more detail the deep impact of wartime service on Vaughan Williams's music in the 1920s – 'With rue my heart is laden'.

References

1   Basil Rathbone *In and Out of Character*, Limelight Editions, 1956, p. 16.

2   Edmund Blunden *Overtones of War*, Duckworth, 1996, p. 73. The poem *Behind the Line* is also from page 73 of this book and is reproduced here with the kind permission of Duckworth Books.

3   Hugh Cobbe, *Letters of Ralph Vaughan Williams 1895-1958*, Oxford University Press, 2008, p. 124.

4   Michael Kennedy *The Works of Ralph Vaughan Williams*, Oxford University Press, 1964, p. 151.

5   British Library *Collection of Ralph Vaughan Williams*, Ref. 1714/1/6 – 54.

6   See Stephen Connock *Toward the Sun Rising – Ralph Vaughan Williams Remembered*, Albion Music Ltd., 2018, p. 34.

7   *ibid*, p. 309.

8   Richard Perceval Graves *Robert Graves – The Assault Heroic 1895-1926*, Weidenfeld and Nicolson, 1986, p. 317.

9   Hubert Foss *Ralph Vaughan Williams*, Harrap and Co., 1950, p. 158.

10 Stephen Connock, *op. cit.*, p. 269.

11 *ibid*, p. 197.

12 Ursula Vaughan Williams *R.V.W. – A Biography of Ralph Vaughan Williams*, Oxford University Press, 1964, p. 205.

13 *ibid*, p. 206.

14 Stephen Connock, *op. cit.*, p. 219.

15 *ibid*, p. 219.

16 *ibid*, p. 223.

17 Steven K. White (ed.) *Dear Müller-Hartmann: Letters from Ralph Vaughan Williams to Robert Müller-Hartmann*, 2009, p. 4.

18 Ralph Vaughan Williams 'The Composer in Wartime' in *The Listener*, 16 May 1940.

19 Ursula Vaughan Williams, *op. cit.*, p. 254.

20 Comments made to the author by Ursula Vaughan Williams during interviews on 19 October 1998 and 14 December 1998.

21 Interview with Ursula Vaughan Williams in *Journal of the RVW Society*, October 2001, p. 14.

22 Marian C. McKenna *Myra Hess – A Portrait*, Hamish Hamilton, 1976, p. 170.

23 See the interview with Joseph Cooper in Stephen Connock, *op. cit.*, pp. 103-106.

24 Recounted by Eric Wetherell in the *Journal of the Ralph Vaughan Williams Society*, No. 1, September 1994, p. 4.

25 Frank Howes *The Music of Ralph Vaughan Williams*, Oxford University Press, 1954, p. 53.

26 David James *Scott of the Antarctic – The Film and its Production*, Convoy Publications, 1948, p. 144.

27 Stephen Connock, *op. cit.*, p. 171.

28 *ibid*, p. 315.

29 Hugh Cobbe *Letters of Ralph Vaughan Williams*, online database number VWL 2604.

30 See Alain Frogley *Vaughan Williams's Ninth Symphony*, Oxford University Press, 2001.

31 Stephen Connock, *op. cit.*, p. 91.

7 'With rue my heart is laden' – War and the Music of Ralph Vaughan Williams

Vaughan Williams's peacetime life appeared to resume where it had left off in 1914. His willingness to take on new teaching and conducting roles must have given him fresh energy and a sense that he was leaving the war behind. However, the emotional impact of wartime experiences as intense as the Great War would take many years to heal – indeed for some a lifetime. Philip Larkin mused on the impact of the First World War[1] in his poem *MCMXIV* (1914), which concludes:

> *Never such innocence,*
> *Never before or since*
> *As changed itself to past*
> *Without a word – the men*
> *Leaving the gardens tidy,*
> *The thousands of marriages,*
> *Lasting a little while longer:*
> *Never such innocence again.*

Siegfried Sassoon in his *Memoirs of an Infantry Officer* wrote: 'We were the survivors; few among us could ever tell the truth to our friends and relations in England. We were carrying something in our heads which belonged to us alone, and to those we had left behind in the battle'.[2]

The painter and poet David Jones, who served in the Royal Welch Fusiliers as a private from December 1915 to March 1918, wrote in the Preface to his war book *In Parenthesis*:

> 'I think the day by day in the Waste Land, the sudden violences and the long stillnesses, the sharp contours and unformed voids of that mysterious existence, profoundly affected the imaginations of those who suffered it.'[3]

It is, perhaps, significant that Vaughan Williams set part of *Psalm 90* in his motet *Lord, Thou Hast Been Our Refuge* so soon after the war, including a telling use of the hymn tune *O God our help in ages past* (St Anne) as a descant:

> *O God our help in ages past,*
> *Our hope for years to come,*
> *Our shelter from the stormy blast,*
> *And our eternal home.*

The wartime associations of this hymn are obvious; it was sung at services of remembrance during the First World War and thereafter, including at the annual Remembrance Day Service in London.

It was also significant that Vaughan Williams should compose a Latin Mass, his *Mass in G minor*, in 1920/1 – which was within a year of his demobilisation. The influence of both Gustav Holst, the work's dedicatee, and Sir Richard Terry can be heard in the polyphonic style and the recapturing of a Tudor liturgical spirit and atmosphere. However, it is the visionary and mystical expressiveness of the work which relates it to Vaughan Williams's war experiences. As Hubert Foss put it:

'The whole work glows, quietly but brightly, with an inner fire that is at once religious and musical'.[4]

The return of the gentle theme from the opening 'Kyrie eleison' at the close, as the choir sing the 'Agnus Dei', is deeply moving and provides a satisfying sense of unity to the work:

O Lamb of God, that takest away the sins of the world, have mercy upon us.
O Lamb of God, that takest away the sins of the world, grant us peace.

Such a spiritual setting of the Mass reminds us all of the sacrifice of Christ, who was 'standing at the edge of death' along with the true meaning of mercy and peace. This came within just two years of Vaughan Williams's most hazardous period of combat, during the *Spring Offensive* of March and April 1918, when he stood at the edge of death and there were over 75,000 British casualties between 21 and 26 March 1918 alone. Writing a Mass at this time was no coincidence, but part of Vaughan Williams's innermost responses to the First World War, with music that is subtle, sincere, comforting and compassionate.

In 1922 Vaughan Williams also composed *O Vos Omnes* ('Is it Nothing to You?'), a work very much in the style of the *Mass in G minor*. As a setting for eight-part chorus of three verses from Chapter 1 of *The Lamentations of Jeremiah* (vv. 12-14) it anticipates the *Mass* in its understanding of Christ's suffering. It is hard not to feel Vaughan Williams's response to the pity of war in this sombre and dignified setting, which opens with:

Is it nothing to you, all ye that pass by?
Behold, and see if there be any sorrow like unto my sorrow,
which is done unto me, wherewith the Lord
hath afflicted me in the day of his fierce anger.

Equally importantly, the impact of the war found expression in Vaughan Williams's continuing fascination with Bunyan's *The Pilgrim's Progress*. He carried the book with him into France and Salonica, and the metaphors in Bunyan's allegory – the Slough of Despond, Christian's heavy burden on his back, the Valley of the Shadow of Death where: 'lay blood, bones, ashes, and mangled bodies of men, even of Pilgrims that had gone this way formerly', the City of Destruction and so on resonated with the composer with even greater intensity after 1918.

It is no surprise, therefore, that one of the first works that Vaughan Williams wrote after the war was a 'Pastoral Episode' founded upon *The Pilgrim's Progress* called *The Shepherds of the Delectable Mountains*. First performed on 11 July 1922, Pilgrim asks three Shepherds the way to the Celestial City:

> Pilgrim: *Is the way safe, or dangerous?*
> Shepherd: *Safe, for those for whom it is to be safe, but many shall fall therein.*

It is noteworthy that Vaughan Williams called the work *A Pastoral Episode*. As Paul Fussell says in his superb book *The Great War and Modern Memory*:

> 'If the opposite of war is peace, the opposite of experiencing moments of war is proposing moments of pastoral. Since war takes place outdoors and always within nature, its symbolic status is that of the ultimate anti-pastoral…Recourse to the pastoral is an English mode of both fully gauging the calamities of the Great War and imaginatively protecting oneself against them. Pastoral reference, whether to literature or to actual rural localities and objects, is a way of invoking a code to hint by antithesis at the indescribable; at the same time it is a comfort in itself, like rum, a deep dugout or a woolly vest'.[5]

Pastoral requires shepherds and their sheep and these are provided in abundance in *Shepherds of the Delectable Mountains*, as indicated by the following passage:

> Pilgrim: *Whose delectable mountains are these? And whose be the sheep that feed upon them?*
> Shepherd: *These mountains are Emmanuel's land, and the sheep also are his, and he laid down his life for them.*

The music at this stage is deeply restrained and lyrical, with solo viola prominent. It expresses Vaughan Williams's English Eden and the contrast with the violence of the sustained artillery barrages in the *Fifth Battle of Ypres* in 1918 could not be starker. However, the work's Great War associations are not only in antithesis – references to death and destruction occur throughout the text.

Pilgrim sings 'Fain would I be where I shall die no more, in the Paradise of God' and the inclusion of *Psalm 23* – 'Yea, though I walk through the valley of the shadow of death, I will fear no evil' – reminds us of the relevance of this Psalm to the soldiers in the Great War and to Ralph Vaughan Williams.

The first performance of *The Shepherds of the Delectable Mountains* took place on 11 July 1922 at the Royal College of Music. It was conducted by Arthur Bliss, of 13th Royal Fusiliers and Grenadier Guards, who had lost his beloved brother, Kennard, on 28 September 1916. The cast featured Keith Falkner, of the Royal Naval Air Service, singing the role of Third Shepherd and the conductor of the off-stage orchestra was Gordon Jacob, of the Royal Fusiliers, who had also lost his brother, Anstey, in the *Battle of the Somme*. How moving it must have been for these veterans to perform this dignified and lyrical opera.[6]

With pastoral imagery invoked as a deliberate antithesis to the indescribable features of war it can again be no coincidence that Vaughan Williams focused on a third symphony, which he tellingly called *Pastoral Symphony*, after returning from active service in 1919. Vaughan Williams began to think about this work while he was based at Ecoivres in 1916 and it was largely completed by 1921. The symphony was first performed on 26 January 1922, conducted by Sir Adrian Boult. Ursula Vaughan Williams recalled what her husband had said about this symphony in a letter to her soon after they had met in 1938:

> 'It's really war-time music – a great deal of it incubated when I used to go up night after night with the ambulance wagon at Ecoivres and we went up a steep hill and there was a wonderful Corot-like landscape in the sunset – it's not really lambkins frisking at all as most people take for granted'.[7] (See Photo 66)

Photo 66: The 'Corot-like landscape' looking west from Mont St Eloi.

The French and English landscapes seem to merge in this moving symphony. Herbert Howells described the work as 'the Malvern Hills when viewed from afar' and the work's understated quality owes something to the quiet of the Cotswolds near where Vaughan Williams was born. The work also shows the influence of Maurice Ravel, Vaughan Williams's teacher for a short period in early 1908, especially in the impressionistic first movement. Here, too, folk song is deeply sublimated – as in so much of Vaughan Williams's works – lending a notable elegiac tone to the symphony.

The opening *molto moderato* is quiet and contemplative. A solo violin introduces a gentle arabesque. Much solo work follows, for flute, oboe, harp and horn, built around a descending four-note phrase. Despite the slow tempi, there is a powerful underlying momentum. The ruminative mood is continued in the second movement, marked *lento moderato*, which includes a natural E flat trumpet, one without valves, playing a haunting solo against muted strings. This magical episode originated when Vaughan Williams heard a bugler practising in the woods when he was based at Bordon, Hampshire, during the war. There is a forlorn *Last Post* quality about this episode, making it all the more surprising that early audiences and commentators did not grasp the significance of the wartime influence on this symphony. Vaughan Williams described the third movement, *moderato pesante*, as 'in the nature of a dance'. The first real climax of the work is reached before a short fugal coda dissolves into silence.

It is in the finale that Vaughan Williams allows the pent-up emotions of war, and the pity of war, to fully emerge. Now the loss of so many friends and comrades is felt. The movement begins with a wordless soprano vocalise, both visionary and ethereal, unharmonised except for a drum-roll, which seems to conjure up the 'desolate area of no-man's land some called the Edge of Beyond'. From this poignant moment the most expressive and heartfelt theme of the symphony is heard on lower strings. The music becomes even more impassioned, led by flutes and strings, leading to a fulsome restatement of the soprano's melody for full orchestra. The disembodied voice returns, this time accompanied by a high note held by muted strings, before dying away, leaving so much unsaid. As Wilfred Owen put it in *Spring Offensive*: 'Why speak they not of comrades that went under?'

The *Pastoral Symphony* is intense, absorbing music as Vaughan Williams gives expression to his innermost feelings of loss and regret, and allows himself, and us, to mourn for those that suffered. This grieving is universal, a benediction recollected in tranquillity and expressed with total sincerity.

The nearest parallel to this moving work is, perhaps, Arthur Bliss's 'symphony on war' *Morning Heroes*. Bliss began to compose the work in 1929 and explained:

> 'Although the war had been over for more than ten years, I was still troubled by frequent nightmares; they all took the same form. I was still there in the trenches with a few men; we knew the armistice had been signed, but we had been forgotten; so had a section of the Germans opposite. It was as though we were both doomed to fight on till extinction. I used to wake with horror.
>
> I was now at last decisively to exorcise this fear. If sublimation, the externalising of an obsession, can be thought of as a cure, then in my case I have proved its efficacy'.[8]

Vaughan Williams continued with a number of folk-inspired works some of which, including the romantic and tuneful opera *Hugh the Drover*, had been, as noted earlier, largely composed before the war. Others, such as *Old King Cole*, date from 1923. However a new musical language was developing around this time which was simpler, even austere, with a quality of detachment which could not be ascribed to any of Vaughan Williams's pre-war works. As well as the *Mass in G minor*, this new style can be heard in the *Two Poems by Seumas O'Sullivan* (1925), the *Four Poems by Fredegond Shove*, *Sancta Civitas* (both completed in 1925) and the one-act opera *Riders to the Sea* (1925-32).

To understand this new style it is worth examining the four songs set to poems by Adeline Vaughan Williams's niece Fredegond Shove. This choice of text marks a fresh development for the composer, for example in his selection of 'Motion and Stillness':

> *The sea shells lie as cold as death*
> *Under the sea.*
> *The clouds move in a wasted wreath*
> *Eternally.*

Or this from 'The New Ghost', the third of the four songs:

> *And he cast it down, down, on the green grass,*
> *Over the young crocuses, where the dew was.*
> *He cast the garment of his flesh that was full of death,*
> *And like a sword his spirit showed out of the cold sheath.*

This preoccupation with death in his choice of poems was different to, say, the metaphysical themes of the *Four Hymns* of 1914 and was quite understandable given Vaughan Williams was himself living 'on the edge' from 1916 to the end of 1918. The music for 'Motion and Stillness' is remote and spare, the open fifths of the piano accompaniment clearly showing a new direction, as does the setting of 'The New Ghost' with, remarkably, no accompaniment at all in the first two lines. It is very sparse after that too, with the piano remaining in the upper register. Putting aside folk songs, can you imagine Vaughan Williams in his pre-war song cycles choosing to have no accompaniment for the first lines? The impact of the war on Vaughan Williams, the man and his music, cannot be underestimated.

On a much larger scale, *Sancta Civitas* (Holy City), an oratorio for baritone and tenor soloists, chorus and orchestra, continues with novel harmonies and a complex, rarefied musical style, both archaic and yet modern. In what he said was his favourite choral work, Vaughan Williams takes the text from the apocalyptic imagery of the *Book of Revelation*, with some minor additions from Taverner's Bible and other sources. He prefaced the work with a short quotation from the *Phaedo* of Plato stated in Greek without translation. English versions vary widely but can be reasonably given as follows:

> 'Now to assert that these things are exactly as I described them would not be reasonable. But that these things are something like them, are truly concerning the souls of men and their habitations after death, especially since the soul is shown to be immortal, this seems to me fitting and worth risking to believe. For the risk is honourable, and a man should sing such things in a manner of an incantation to himself'.

Here we find again that preoccupation with death as the dying Socrates reflects on the soul's immortality – the likelihood of life after death.

The slow orchestral prelude in C opens with a rising progression in the lower strings, soon to be accompanied by flutes and a distant oboe. The narrator recounts St. John's vision of heaven. A trumpet motif and quiet *alleluias* continue the mystical atmosphere of the music before an *allegro* section ushers in a vision of heaven. The destruction of 'Babylon the great' follows, with Babylon in this context symbolic of anti-Paradise. Soon a magical section, led by solo violin, begins with 'And I saw a new heaven and a new earth'. Vaughan Williams chooses lines from the *Book of Revelation* (22:2) that in the 1920s would have had enormous symbolic meaning for him:

> And I saw a pure river of the water of life, and on either side of the river was there the tree of life: and the leaves of the tree were for the healing of nations.

Another vision of Eden, or Paradise, is envisaged. The water of life and the tree of life are metaphors to represent a new world of beauty, happiness and blessedness. There will be a 'new order of things' which will sustain meaningful life. The idea of the 'healing of nations', inspires Vaughan Williams to write music which is both rapt and expressive, especially toward the end of the oratorio when a tenor solo is introduced for the first time:

> *Behold I come quickly.*
> *I am the bright and the morning star.*
> *Surely I come quickly.*

These words, also from the *Book of Revelation* (22: 7, 16, 20), provide hope for the dawning of a new day, a time of peace and prosperity. John Foulds set these same words in Part 2 of his *A World Requiem* (1918-21) with similar optimistic intent.

Sancta Civitas is one of Vaughan Williams's most personal compositions, in which he allows the mystical element in his character to give us a vision of a new world order just a few years after he had directly experienced the horrors of the old one. He chose from the *Book of Revelation* symbols which were able to capture his hopes for the future, and composed music of an expressive quality that matched this optimistic vision. In this, *Sancta Civitas* is a direct product of the First World War, exactly as Fould's *A World Requiem* was. As Percy Young put it: 'The *Sancta Civitas* (Holy City), in Vaughan Williams's philosophy, was the only hope of humanity in the period of post war bewilderment'.[9]

A further work which can be attributed to the effects of the war on the composer is the song cycle *Along the Field* for voice and violin. Vaughan Williams returned to the poet A. E. Housman (1859-1936) in eight songs taken either from *A Shropshire Lad* or *Last Poems*. Vaughan Williams had first discovered Housman's lyrics at Cambridge and his memorable settings of the poet, in *On Wenlock Edge* (1909), from *A Shropshire Lad* (1896), had been written shortly after the composer's period of study with Ravel. Housman's poetry, with its restrained lyricism, always moved the composer and he carried *A Shropshire Lad* with him throughout the First World War. The six evocative poems for *On Wenlock Edge* were right for Vaughan Williams at that stage of his development. As is well known, Housman loathed the music and was particularly upset at Vaughan Williams for dropping some of his words. Vaughan Williams would say at the time: "Oh well, poor chap, he'll have to get used to it".

Along the Field was published in 1954, with selected poems from *A Shropshire Lad* and *Last Poems* in the following order:

1 We'll to the woods no more (*Last Poems*)
2 Along the field (*A Shropshire Lad*)
3 The half-moon westers low (*Last Poems*)
4 In the morning (*Last Poems*)
5 The sigh that heaves the grasses (*Last Poems*)
6 Goodbye (*A Shropshire Lad*)
7 Fancy's knell (*Last Poems*)
8 With rue my heart is laden (*A Shropshire Lad*)

He completed the work in 1927 when there were just seven songs and the work was called *Seven Housman Songs*. The cycle then expanded to nine songs and, as late as the 1954 edition of *Grove*, was called *Nine Housman Songs*, including 'The Soldier' as number four. This song was removed when the composer revised the work for publication in 1954.[10] It is not clear why it was deleted although Ursula Vaughan Williams always claimed she was behind this decision as she felt both the poem and music were weak. Ursula said:

> 'I told him to take one of the songs out. It was a bad song. The words were unsuitable. I was cross about it being included and he was rather pleased that I was cross. He agreed to take the song out'.[11]

The reference in the removed poem to 'Filth in trench from fall to spring' suggests an autobiographical and wartime significance which may have felt much less appropriate to the composer and his wife in the 1950s. When Vaughan Williams gave a copy of the newly published score of *Along the Field* to Ursula in 1954, he wrote at the top of the title page: 'They looked away'[12] – see Illustration 28.

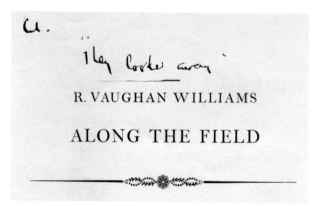

Illustration 28: Title page of *Along the Field*.

This is a quote from the second stanza of 'In the morning', the fourth song of the cycle, which has a rhapsodic violin part. What did he mean by this? It may have had a very personal significance to Ursula and himself or, perhaps, he was unhappy that the cycle had been infrequently performed as it had taken over 25 years to be published. Alternatively, he may have felt that the underlying sadness and haunting quality of the music had been misunderstood, with commentators 'looking away' rather than seeing the trenchant war-inspired meaning.

Vaughan Williams chose to write this cycle for voice and violin, following Gustav Holst's example in his *Four Songs for Voice and Violin* of 1916-17. Indeed, the more inward and austere style of Holst's music following *The Planets* most likely had a significant influence on Vaughan Williams, even if he admitted to not understanding the *Ode to Death* (1919).

The opening song, 'We'll to the woods no more' sets the valedictory tone. However the most haunting, even harrowing, episode in the cycle is 'The sigh that heaves the grasses', with atmospheric double-stopping effects from the violin:

> *The sigh that heaves the grasses*
> *Whence thou wilt never rise*
> *Is of the air that passes*
> *And knows not if it sighs.*
>
> *The diamond tears adorning*
> *Thy low mound on the lea,*
> *Those are the tears of morning,*
> *That weeps but not for thee.*

It is not easy to listen to this cycle, so profound are the references to death and separation. Both 'Goodbye' and 'Fancy's knell' show the influence of folksong and are more declamatory. However, the final song returns to the sad and fading imagery:

> *With rue my heart is laden*
> *For golden friends I had,*
> *For many a rose-lipt maiden*
> *And many a light foot lad.*
>
> *By brooks too broad for leaping*
> *The light foot boys are laid;*
> *The rose-lipt girls are sleeping*
> *In fields where roses fade.*

The essence of Housman is here: the pastoral imagery, the innocent lads and maidens, the fading of dreams, the elegy for doomed youth. Vaughan Williams composes music of a quiet simplicity, with the voice and violin in straightforward counterpoint, He recalls the 'golden friends', such as George Butterworth and Ernest Farrar, that he had lost in the First World War. As Butterworth's lovely unfinished *Fantasia for Orchestra* (1914) shows, in the completion by Martin Yates, his compositional technique was deepening – what a loss to Vaughan Williams and to music his death was! Ernest Farrar, too, was killed before he could realise his full potential. He died on 18 September 1918 at the *Battle of Epéhy*, after just two days at the Front following his commissioning as an officer in the Devonshire Regiment. Farrar's *English Pastoral Impressions* (1915) was dedicated to Vaughan Williams.

Photo 67: George Butterworth.

Photo 68: Ernest Farrar, 1918 –
his last photograph.

There is one further work of the 1920s that has a possible metaphorical wartime association – the one-act opera *Riders to the Sea*. Vaughan Williams began to compose this opera in 1925 and there are certain stylistic similarities with *Sancta Civitas* of that same year. He completed the opera in 1932 but the work was not performed until 1937.

The opera is an almost-verbatim setting of a short play by the Irish playwright J. M. Synge (1871-1909). Synge had visited the Aran Islands, off the west coast of Ireland, in 1898 and was deeply moved by the islanders' response to the forces of nature, the violence of the sea and the constant threat of death. The fortitude of the people of Aran provided Synge with rich source material for his play, including the one-act *Riders to the Sea*, which was completed in 1901 and first performed in 1904 in Dublin.

The play, and Vaughan Williams's opera, features Maurya who has lost her father, husband and four sons at sea. One of her two remaining sons, Michael, has been missing for nine days. A bundle of clothes from a body found in the sea has been given to Maurya's two daughters who, fearing these might belong to Michael, hide them away from their mother. Maurya's youngest son, Bartley, despite all that has happened to his grandfather, father and brothers, is determined, with all the courage – or recklessness – of youth, to take some horses across the sea to Galway Fair. Maurya sees an apparition of Michael on the grey mare which Bartley is riding and realises that her two remaining sons will never return. Soon Michael's death is confirmed and Maurya begins her poignant final lament: "They are all gone now, and there isn't anything more the sea can do to me".

The haunted, sorrowful but ultimately peaceful response of Maurya to the death of the menfolk of her family stimulated music from Vaughan Williams of remarkable concentration, subtlety and, in the final pages, an overwhelming tenderness and nobility, as she sings: "No man at all can be living forever, and we must be satisfied".

Vaughan Williams was clearly responding to the courage and fortitude of Maurya against the hostile forces of nature, a theme he would return to in the film music for *Scott of the Antarctic* in 1948. Some might argue with conviction that this is the key to the work and interpretations should be taken no further. However, the themes of death, grief and personal bereavement might, in addition, show that Vaughan Williams saw the loss of Maurya's father, husband and six sons as a metaphor for the losses sustained by so many other families between 1914 and 1918. Wilfred Owen used another metaphor in his poem *The Parable of the Old Man and the Young*[13] based on an important incident in *Genesis* v. 22. Abram bound his son with belts and straps for suggesting a lamb be sacrificed for a burnt-offering. When an Angel calls from heaven saying lay not thy hand upon the lad for behold there is a ram caught in a thicket, offer the ram instead, the poem continues:

But the old man would not do so, but slew his son,
And half the seed of Europe, one by one.

Vaughan Williams's choice of this particular play by Synge, involving the death of all the menfolk in Maurya's family, may be coincidental but he would have been only too aware of the devastating impact of the war on family life back home. Max Plowman, a subaltern on the Somme with the 10th Battalion, Yorkshire Regiment, told of a pitiable letter he received in October 1916 setting forth the case of a mother nearly demented because two of her three sons were killed in the trenches after 1 July 1916. She was in mortal fear of what might happen to her remaining son, a boy in Plowman's company named Stream. The officers promised to see what could be done to release the boy to less dangerous duties. A few days later a large shell dropped in the trench, killing one soldier. The body was blown to pieces so no one knew who it was. Quickly, the dead soldier's pay-book and identity disc are found – the name is Stream. Plowman says:

> 'Stream! Good God! This boy blown to pieces so that there is literally nothing left to bury!
>
> What will it mean to the lad's mother?'[14]

Vaughan Williams was only too aware of many other such tragic incidents suggesting that 'coincidence' in relation to the choice of text for *Riders* seems unlikely.

Another deeply poignant element in *Riders to the Sea* was the daughter's reluctance to tell their mother of the death of Michael. In the Great War, thousands of parents, husbands and wives, faced the loss of a child or partner. As Winston Churchill put it: 'There are few homes in Britain where you will not find the empty chair and the aching heart'.[15] Sir Arthur Conan Doyle lost his eldest son, Kingsley, on 1 November 1918. He described him thus:

> 'My only son by my first marriage was one of the grandest boys in body and soul that ever a father was blessed with. He had started the war as a private, worked up to acting captaincy in the 1st Hampshires, and been very badly wounded on the Somme. It was pneumonia which slewed him in London…'[16]

Clare Delius lost her only son, Hugh, in Morlancourt on 8 August 1918, just three days before the Armistice. It was almost certainly his first day in the trenches. She wrote in the biography of her brother *Frederick Delius* (1935):

> 'I, in common with millions of mothers, was trying to present to the world the approved picture of the Spartan mother who had dedicated her only son to a great cause…I was tortured like every woman with a serving son at the time, looking upon all telegraph boys and postmen as the forerunners of doom, and hardly daring to glance at those long, long casualty lists that filled the papers in those days…'[17]

The Prime Minister, Herbert H. Asquith, was told of the death of his son Raymond on 17 September 1916; he had also been shot during the *Battle of the Somme*. The Prime Minister later wrote to a friend:

> 'I can honestly say that in my own life he was the thing of which I was truly proud, and in him and his future I had invested all my stock of hope. This is all gone, and for the moment I feel bankrupt'.[18]

Families received Army Form B 104-82 as a letter or telegram with the dreadful, yet formal message: 'It is my painful duty to inform you…' Wilfred Owen's parents, Tom and Susan Owen, received one on 11 November 1918, the day the war ended. Rudyard Kipling received another following the death of his son, John Kipling, on 27 September 1915. He was a 2/Lt. in the Irish Guards and had died in the *Battle of Loos* aged just 18. Rudyard Kipling was devastated, not least because he had facilitated his son's enlistment given that the boy had poor eyesight. His 1916 poem *My Boy Jack*, written for Jack Cornwall, a 16-year-old who died on board ship during the *Battle of Jutland*, captured the anguish Kipling must have felt on his own son's death, along with all parents who lost a son or daughter in the First World War:

> *"Have you news of my boy Jack?"*
> *Not this tide.*
> *"When do you think that he'll come back?"*
> *Not with this wind blowing, and this tide.*

The third stanza of the poem asks:

> *"Oh, dear, what comfort can I find?"*
> *None this tide,*
> *Nor any tide,*
> *Except he did not shame his kind –*
> *Not even with that wind blowing, and that tide.*

The composer and conductor Cecil Coles, a close friend of Gustav Holst, died on 26 April 1918 at Crouy, near Soissons on the Western Front. He was just 29 and left a wife, son and baby daughter. His widow had received a letter stating that he had died from shock and would not have suffered any pain.[19] Imogen Holst recalled that her father dedicated his *Ode to Death* 'For C.C. and the others' in 1919.[20]

Sometimes terrible news was sent in error. Robert Graves's mother received a letter on 22 July 1916, two days before his 21st birthday, saying:

> 'I very much regret to have to write to tell you that your son has died of wounds. He was very gallant, and was doing so well and is a great loss'.[21]

Fortunately, this proved to be false and Graves's mother was able to establish by 30 July that her son was alive, albeit wounded in one lung, finger and thigh. By 5 August 1916 he was recovering in London.

Bereavement caused by the war had not spared Vaughan Williams's family or friends. As we have noted in Chapter 2, his brother-in-law Charles Fisher had died, like Jack Cornwall, in the *Battle of Jutland*, on 1 June 1916. This, together with the death of another brother-in-law, Edmund Fisher, in 1918, left Adeline Vaughan Williams grieving for the rest of her long life. George Butterworth's father had received a personal message concerning his only son from the Adjutant of the 13th Durham Light Infantry, dated 6 August 1916, saying:

> 'The Commanding Officer, Capt. G. White, has asked me to write to inform you of the very serious loss we have suffered in the death of your son.
>
> His talents as a Company Commander were undoubtedly great, and on the night of 4/5th inst, when he was ordered to bomb up a trench and hold an important post, he personally supervised this work, so that now, as I write, the post, 20 yards from the enemy, remains in our hands.
>
> Unfortunately it was this thoroughness in supervision which indirectly led to his death. The trench had been so knocked about by bombs and shells that some places were very exposed, and a German saw him soon after dawn on the 5th...'[22]

Vaughan Williams especially mourned the unfulfilled potential of his composer friend. Butterworth had left most of his manuscripts to Vaughan Williams. Alexander Kaye Butterworth, the composer's father, pulled together a *Memorial Volume* to his only son, a copy of which he presented to Vaughan Williams in May 1918 inscribing it: *Ralph Vaughan Williams from A. Kaye B*. George Butterworth had signed up for the Durham Light Infantry early in the war and, as we have seen, Vaughan Williams wrote to Gustav Holst in 1916 saying: 'Out of those 7 who joined up together in August 1914 only 3 are left'.[23]

Against this background of both profound personal loss and the grieving of parents across the country in the First World War, Maurya's lament in *Riders to the Sea* would have assumed a universal significance for Vaughan Williams:

They are all together this time, and the end is come.
May the Almighty God have mercy on Bartley's soul,
And on Michael's soul,
And on the souls of Sheamus and Patch,
And Stephen and Shawn,
And may he have mercy on my soul,
And on the soul of every one is left living in the world.

The work can be viewed as Vaughan Williams's personal lament for a lost generation, for the one in ten British men between the ages of 20 and 45 who had died in the war. In total, 744,000 soldiers did not return home in 1919, or ever again.[24]

By 1928, Vaughan Williams had largely exorcised the ghosts of the First World War as shown by the beautiful *Six Studies in English Folk Song* (1926) and his lyrical folk-inspired opera *Sir John in Love* (1928). Of course, anguished music was still to come, including the angry and uncompromising *Symphony No. 4 in F minor*, composed between 1931 and 1934. However, the harsh dissonances of this symphony and other works were a more generalised response to Vaughan Williams's underlying feelings in the 1930s rather than the direct expression of wartime grief as in the *Pastoral Symphony*.

The three great works of the early and mid-1920s represent the pity of war (*Pastoral Symphony*), grief and family loss (*Riders to the Sea*) and hope for the 'healing of nations' (*Sancta Civitas*). Taken together, they are Vaughan Williams's Great War Trilogy.

After this, Vaughan Williams was at last able to move on.

References

1   The poem *MCMXIV*, was published in *The Whitsun Weddings*, Faber and Faber, 1964, p. 28. It is reproduced here under a License Agreement from Faber and Faber Ltd., dated 25 January 2021.

2   Siegfried Sassoon *The Complete Memoirs of George Sherston*, Faber and Faber, paperback edition, 1980, p. 449.

3   David Jones *In Parenthesis*, Faber and Faber paperback edition, 2018, p. xii.

4   Hubert Foss in a programme note for a Henry Wood Promenade Concert on 9 January 1951, p. 12.

5   Paul Fussell *The Great War and Modern Memory*, Oxford University Press, 1975, p. 235. See also the evocative analysis of pastoral influences on English music in Eric Saylor *English Pastoral Music – From Arcadia to Utopia 1900-1955*, University of Illinois, 2017.

6   For a more detailed analysis of the links between the opera and the Great War see Andrew Green 'The Shepherds of the Delectable Mountains: A Pastoral Episode – Vaughan Williams's Secret Salute to the Fallen of the Great War?' in *Journal of the Ralph Vaughan Williams Society*, No. 75, June 2019, pp. 3-11.

7   Ursula Vaughan Williams *R.V.W. – A Biography of Ralph Vaughan Williams*, Oxford University Press, 1968, p. 121.

8   Arthur Bliss *As I Remember*, Faber and Faber, 1970, p. 96.

9   Percy M. Young *Vaughan Williams*, Dennis Dobson Ltd., 1953, p. 60.

10 I am grateful to John Francis for pointing out that the cycle originally comprised seven songs. The words of 'The Soldier', from Housman's *Last Poems*, Riverside Press, 1922, p. 23, are:

> *Soldier from the wars returning,*
>   *Spoiler of the taken town,*
> *Here is ease that asks not earning;*
>   *Turn you in and sit you down.*
>
> *Peace is come and wars are over,*
>   *Welcome you and welcome all,*
> *While the charger crops the clover*
>   *And his bridle hangs in stall.*
>
> *Fear no more of winters biting,*
>   *Filth in trench from fall to spring,*
> *Summers full of sweat and fighting*
>   *For the Kaiser or the King.*
>
> *Rest you, charger, rust you, bridle;*
>   *Kings and Kaisers, keep your pay;*

Soldier, sit you down and idle
At the inn of night for aye.

11 From an interview with the author in 1998.

12 An inscribed score: a gift to Stephen Connock from Ursula Vaughan Williams in 1996.

13 C. Day Lewis (ed.) *The Complete Poems of Wilfrid Owen*, Chatto and Windus, 1963, p. 42.

14 Max Plowman *A Subaltern on the Somme* in 1916, E. P. Dutton, 1928, pp. 130-142.

15 Winston Churchill, quoted in Andrew Roberts *Churchill – Walking with Destiny*, Allen Lane, 2018, p. 266.

16 From Arthur Conan Doyle *Memories and Adventures*, Wordsworth Literary Lives, 1923, and quoted in *The Arthur Conan Doyle Encyclopaedia* at www.arthur-conan-doyle.com/kingsley.conan.doyle.

17 Clare Delius *Frederick Delius*, Ivor Nicholson and Watson Ltd., 1935, pp. 194-195.

18 Quoted in Jeremy Paxman, *Great Britain's Great War*, Viking Press, 2013, p. 191.

19 See sleeve notes by John Purser in a Hyperion disc of music by Cecil Coles on Hyperion CDA 67293, 2003, pp. 7-8.

20 Imogen Holst *A Thematic Catalogue of Gustav Holst's Music*, Faber Music, 1974, p. 141.

21 Robert Graves *Goodbye to All That*, Cassell and Co. Ltd., 1957 edition, p. 194.

22 *Memorial Volume* dedicated to George Butterworth, YouCaxton Publications, 2015, p. 84.

23 Ursula Vaughan Williams *R.V.W. – A Biography of Ralph Vaughan Williams*, Oxford University Press, 1964, p. 122.

24 Andrew Roberts, *op. cit.*, p. 263.

8 Conclusions

For a man of 42 with an increasingly frail wife, Vaughan Williams's decision to enlist on New Year's Eve 1914 showed considerable courage and strength of character. Given his importance to English musical life by 1914, as Sir Hubert Parry well understood, he need not have taken such a risk by joining the Army; it was not until 1918 that conscription embraced his age group when the Military Service (No. 2) Act increased the upper age limit to 50. Signing up for a four-year term in late 1914 reflects a number of considerations: his sense of duty and national pride, his character and that he respected the actions of his close friends and family.

Vaughan Williams's sense of civic duty first led him to join the Special Constabulary in the summer of 1914. He felt a strong sense of nationalism as he wrote in 1914:

> 'A nation is made up of individuals bound together by ties of race, of domestic relationships, of common laws, customs, institutions and sympathies…'[1]

In all Vaughan Williams's musings on national character, he would focus on broad-minded sympathies, on realising the merits of the 'humblest singer of folk-song', on the importance of community, of customs, language, art, tradition, of acting without artifice or subterfuge, of being true to oneself. He wrote:

> 'Local patriotism… (has) a deep rooted instinct which we cannot eliminate if we would: and which we ought not to want to eliminate. I believe that the love of one's country, one's language, one's customs, one's religion, are essential to our spiritual health. We may laugh at these things but we love them nonetheless'.[2]

This 'love of one's country' led many men to volunteer to serve for 'King and Country' in 1914 and Vaughan Williams had genuine integrity such that it would have seemed insincere not to have enlisted. In this, his character fitted his ideals. He had remarkable inner strength and what Michael Kennedy referred to as an 'iron personality'.[3] He was a man of firm convictions, a dogged perseverance, a singleness of purpose, a big heart, an astonishing capacity for hard work and an ability to laugh at himself and others. He needed all these qualities between 1914 and 1918. As to the actions of his friends, seeing George Butterworth, R. O. Morris, Bevis Ellis and so many others sign up in August 1914 would have meant much to him. It would have been unthinkable for

Vaughan Williams to stand aside when many of his close friends and family members were enlisting.

Vaughan Williams's choice of joining the Royal Army Medical Corps was, as we have seen, dictated more by his age than by a strong desire to enter the Ambulance Service, although the influence of Walt Whitman may be relevant. His flat feet would also have ruled out an infantry role. Nevertheless his long walks around Leith Hill Place, in the Cotswolds and elsewhere, meant that he was reasonably fit. He rarely reported sick, with one day in hospital for bronchial catarrh on 22 January 1915 and four nights in hospital between 10 and 14 November 1916 for 'PUO' – a fever of unknown origin. Vaughan Williams was, however, generally untidy in his physical appearance, for which he cared little. In civilian life, he seemed always to wear the same tweed jacket, pork-pie hat or knitted jumper with the stitches loosened by numerous cats. This was a nightmare for the Army and for him. On 30 November 1916 he was admonished and fined two pence for 'losing by neglect his cap and badge' the day before[4] and, as noted above, being 'untidy in his ways and dress' cost him promotion in 1920. He was fortunate to find, in Harry Steggles, John Tindall Robertson, A. J. Moore and others, Army colleagues who would help him with his puttees and getting his cap on straight for parade. At least one of the benefits of becoming an officer was that he had the help of a batman for his period of service up to December 1918.

Taking part in war can lead to unusual friendships. George Butterworth was enthusiastic about joining the Durham Light Infantry because he was able to lead a group of Durham miners. Vaughan Williams would never have met Harry Steggles, a salesman for the General Electric Company, in the normal course of life. Yet they became close friends during and after the war. As Harry Steggles put it:

> 'R.V.W. of Charterhouse and Cambridge, myself of London County Council Old Kent Road School. What a contrast; old enough in years to be my father, yet young enough in heart to be my comrade. The gap in our social standards was terrific, but I was always at ease in his company, in fact the great guiding influence he had upon me is with me to this day'.[5]

Vaughan Williams was modest and self-effacing. His good humour, often self-deprecating, and emotional stability made him a fine companion. Very few in the RAMC or later in the Royal Garrison Artillery were aware that he was one of this country's leading and most accomplished composers, with two symphonies and many works of distinction, such as the *Fantasia on a Theme by Thomas Tallis*, to his name. He took his turn with the most basic of Army tasks, from the lowest form of fatigue duties, to digging latrines, filling sandbags and so on. Like most soldiers, he was more at peace with himself in the fighting areas when he felt that he was contributing to the war effort. His untidy dress mattered less in the ambulance wagon toiling between Ecoivres and Neuville St Vaast night after night in 1916, or hauling the 60-pounder guns in the *Battle of Amiens* in 1918 – and there were fewer parades to worry about.

Vaughan Williams was not perfect. He could be quick to show anger and when he did it was like an Old Testament wrath. This would, however, dissipate quite quickly and he rarely held grudges against people. He was a stickler for keeping to time; for example, delays in starting a rehearsal would infuriate him. He would also become frustrated if he felt people were not giving their best to any effort, something he expected of himself and others. As we have seen, he hated displays of public admiration and increasingly avoided public gatherings even though he was quite a lively speaker, with a quick sense of humour and a self-deprecating wit.

He was courageous too. As Harry Steggles put it:

'The trenches held no terrors for him; on the contrary, he was thrilled one day when he was allowed to peep at the German front line trenches. He had no knowledge of fear; at times I was anxious because of this'.[6]

On at least two occasions, firstly when in the 2/4th London Field Ambulance in 1915 and secondly at Bordon in Hampshire, he agitated for a posting overseas showing that he was always prepared to place himself more at risk, perhaps also to prove himself. As Joseph Mason, one of his colleagues at Maresfield Park in 1917 put it:

'He devoted himself wholeheartedly to the military service of his country – England – in whatever way possible. That took precedence over everything else in his life… Music was left behind; the war was in front of him and therein lay his duty which he would pursue at all costs'.[7]

At all costs. Although Vaughan Williams survived the war without apparent physical injury – there were no 'wound stripes' for him – the one issue that was to cause lasting damage was his loss of hearing.

Close proximity to thousands of high explosive and shrapnel shells being discharged by the 60-pounders for eight months in 1918 contributed to this problem although it may have been partly hereditary. His grandfather, Sir Edward Vaughan Williams, had to retire as a judge because of his deafness. For a composer to lose his hearing was most unfortunate, as Beethoven would have agreed, and Vaughan Williams bore this burden with considerable stoicism. By the mid-1940s he was, as he put it, 'oboe-deaf' and he also struggled to hear high violins and flutes. He was able to converse one-on-one without too much difficulty but found large gatherings increasingly difficult. Vaughan Williams had conventional hearing aids, of the sort shown in Photo 69, which he found 'squeaky'. He also had an old-style inverted ear trumpet, or coffee-pot, hearing aid that he would ask people to speak into. In later years, rehearsals and concerts became more problematic which meant he relied on Roy Douglas and others to help out with matters of interpretation. Phone calls were an issue, too, and by the early 1950s Ursula Vaughan Williams would often take such calls and pass on messages to her husband. We noted this earlier in relation to the composition of *The First Nowell* in 1958.

Photo 69: Vaughan Williams with hearing aid in the early 1950s.

Many others suffered similar hearing loss in the First World War. For example, Robert Ford of 157 Battery, Royal Field Artillery, was supporting the gunners in April 1918. He said:

'The noise! I thought someone had cut my throat! I got partly accustomed to it, but after about two hours my right ear was completely deaf...My left ear came back after two days, but my right ear never recovered'.[8]

Vaughan Williams's decision to apply for a commission in the Royal Garrison Artillery, following the recommendation of the Brigadier-General of the 60th Division, placed him in greater danger because of Germany's final major offensive in the spring of 1918. Vaughan Williams would not, of course, have been aware of this last desperate German push to the Channel ports in March 1918 but by the time he joined the 141 Heavy Battery, 86th Brigade, in the sector of the Western Front south of Arras, near Croisilles, the British retreat was well under way. Transporting guns and ammunition by horses with the Germans engaged in counter-battery offensives was a duty of considerable risk. Fortunately for Vaughan Williams, by August 1918, it was the enemy in retreat and he began that long trek through Northern France and into Belgium taking part, as we have seen, in three battles on the way, the *Battle of Amiens*, the *Fifth Battle of Ypres* and the *Battle of Courtrai*.

Serving twice on the Western Front, as well as almost eight months on the Salonica Front, gave Vaughan Williams contrasting war experiences. There was the proximity to sick, wounded and dying soldiers night after night in the ambulance wagons from Ecoivres to Neuville St Vaast and back, always with the danger of shellfire or mines exploding. Then there were the mosquitoes, dirt, dust, rain, snow and winds in Salonica with long periods of fatigue duties, including washing those wretched red stones which caused him so much anguish. Next, in 1917, he had another challenge in mastering the technology of howitzers and 60-pounders on gunnery courses in Maresfield Park, Lydd and Rouen before heading back to the Western Front with the Royal Garrison Artillery in the early spring of 1918. Here the dangers of counter-battery fire, enemy aircraft and infantry attacks were continuous during the German *Spring Offensive* which began on 21 March 1918. He was a considerate officer; he wrote in May 1918 that:

'I consider it the duty of every officer to do all he can for the welfare of those under his command...'[9]

Finally, after handling those 200 horses through northern France and into Belgium, up to the Scheldt, until the Armistice on 11 November 1918, and then into Germany as part of the Army of Occupation, he took on the role of Director of Music for the First Army at their HQ in Valenciennes sometime in late December 1918.

With the important exception of his involvement in the Army of Occupation, Vaughan Williams did, perhaps, have a fortunate war. In almost four years of military service, he spent half of his time training in England. His decision to join the Royal Army Medical Corps as a wagon orderly took him to Ecoivres to the north of Arras and, in mid to late 1916, this was a relatively quiet sector. Next he avoided the Somme battlefields by being relocated with his Division to Salonica in November 1916. Here malaria was a greater danger than enemy action. Finally, his experiences as a junior officer with the Royal Garrison Artillery in northern France were generally between five and eight miles behind the front line. Serious dangers remained, as we have seen, especially when the German *Spring Offensive* was under way. However, it was preferable to being a subaltern in the infantry or the field artillery where life expectancy was very low.

It was also fortunate, too, that Vaughan Williams was able to find time, even in the most hazardous circumstances, for music. He formed a band and a choir while at Saffron Walden and the music went with him to France and Greece and back to France in 1918. There were concerts in England, in France and on the slopes of Mount Olympus where, most memorably for all concerned, there was a seasonal concert on Christmas Day 1916 when the *Sussex Carol* was sung – 'On Christmas night all Christians sing…' There were more carols in December 1918 when Vaughan Williams was marching toward the Rhine. He was also able to finish his military service as Director of Music for the First Army.

Vaughan Williams was, at least, consistent in his musical objectives before and after the First World War. His focus on 'National Music', with Gustav Holst, continued in the 1920s, particularly with the folk-based ballets *Old King Cole* (1923) and *On Christmas Night* (1926). He also continued to improve the musical health of the nation with hymn books and carol collections such as *Songs of Praise* (1925) and *The Oxford Book of Carols* (1928). His commitment to supporting amateur music-making was undiminished and he would continue to provide alternative scoring for his works to allow for as many types of musical performance as possible. In all these important respects the war did not alter or deflect his mission even though it almost certainly added a more extreme range of emotions to his music for the rest of his life.

Being generally 'fortunate' between 1915 and 1919 did not mean that Vaughan Williams avoided the horror and pity of war – far from it. As a wagon orderly, he witnessed and had to deal with incredible suffering in others and death was a constant feature of his Army life. He would also have seen first-hand in 1918 the fear and destruction caused by an enemy offensive. These harrowing experiences led Vaughan Williams to a marked change of musical style and emotional content in many of his works in the 1920s.

Sir Thomas Armstrong, who was also an officer with the Royal Garrison Artillery in 1917-18, recalled that Vaughan Williams was:

> 'Very thankful and indeed fortunate to have been one of the tragically small handful of young men who survived the terrible ordeal, but had to carry for the rest of their lives the dreadful memories of their experiences'. [10]

Now, over 100 years since the end of the First World War, it is this war-inspired music that brings us closer to what Vaughan Williams and countless others experienced between 1914 and 1918. In his great wartime trilogy we hear the composer's profound responses to the reality of war: the pity of war in the *Pastoral Symphony*, parental loss and grief in *Riders to the Sea* and a vision of a new heaven and a new earth in *Sancta Civitas*. The desolate nature of warfare is also heard in the song cycle *Along the Field* and his pleas for mercy and peace in the *Mass in G minor* remain unforgettable.

We are confronted here with the full range of Vaughan Williams's war-inspired memories and emotions. We can share his deep sense of grief and profound hope for the future. In doing so, we can also empathise with all that he and his colleagues suffered on our behalf and for generations to come. Protective Providence decided to save Ralph Vaughan Williams. As Max Plowman would have put it: 'He gave Death the chance. Death did not take it'. [11]

Toward the end of the Second World War, in 1944, Vaughan Williams set words from *Henry V* in his *Song of Thanksgiving* which could equally apply to his own safe return from the Great War:

> *O God, thy arm was here, and not to us,*
> *But to thy arm alone ascribe we all.*
> *Take it, God, for it is none but thine.*

References

1   David Manning (ed.) *Vaughan Williams on Music*, Oxford University Press, 2008, p. 43.

2   R. Vaughan Williams *National Music and Other Essays*, Oxford University Press, paperback edition, 1996, p. 154.

3   See the interview with Michael Kennedy in Stephen Connock *Toward the Sun Rising – Ralph Vaughan Williams Remembered*, Albion Music Ltd., 2018, p. 171.

4   Vaughan Williams's personal file is in the National Archives at WO 374/75055.

5   Quoted in Stephen Connock, *op. cit.*, p. 312.

6   *ibid*, p. 313.

7   *ibid*, pp. 298-299.

8   Quoted in Lyn MacDonald *To the Last Man, Spring 1918*, Viking Press, 1998, p. 345.

9   See the online database of *Letters of Ralph Vaughan Williams*, edited by Hugh Cobbe, letter number VWL 443.

10 Quoted in Rosemary Rapaport (ed) *Thomas Armstrong – A Celebration by his Friends*, Thames Publishing, 1998, p. 122.

11 Max Plowman *A Subaltern on the Somme*, The Naval and Military Press, 1928, p. 54.

Appendix 1:
Vaughan Williams's Form of Attestation, 31 December 1914.

Appendix 2:
Vaughan Williams's Medical Inspection Report, 31 December 1914.

Appendix 3:
A British Army Infantry Division in 1915.

Divisional Headquarters
(Major General commanding and staff)

1 signal company

Artillery
HQ Divisional Artillery
12 batteries of 18 pdr guns (total 48 guns)
3 batteries of 4.5 inch howitzers (total 16)
1 heavy battery (4 x 60pdr)
1 Divisional ammunition column

Engineers
HQ Divisional Engineers
3 field companies Royal Engineers

Infantry
3 brigades, total 12 battalions, each battalion 4 x Vickers medium machine guns

Mounted Troops
1 squadron cavalry, one cyclist company

Pioneers
1 pioneer battalion

Service and Support
3 field ambulances
1 motor ambulance workshop
1 sanitary section
1 mobile veterinary section
 Divisional train

Total All Ranks: 19, 614

Appendix 4:
List of Units of the 60th Division.

Divisional Headquarters	based at Villers-Châtel
HQ Royal Artillery	"

Royal Field Artillery
> 300th Brigade – four Batteries
> 301st Brigade – four Batteries
> 302nd Brigade – four Batteries
> 303rd Brigade – three Batteries (Howitzers)

Divisional Ammunition Column	based at St Michel-sur-Ternoise
HQ Royal Engineers	based at Villers-Châtel

> 3/3th London Field Company Royal Engineers
> 2/4th London Field Company Royal Engineers
> 1/6th London Field Company Royal Engineers

179th Infantry Brigade
> HQ   based at Ecoivres
> 2/13th Battalion (London Regt.)
> 2/14th   "
> 2/15th   "
> 2/16th   "
> H.G. Company

180th Infantry Brigade
> HQ   based at Penin
> 2/17th Battalion (London Regt.)
> 2/18th   "
> 2/19th   "
> 2/20th   "
> H.G. Company

181st Infantry Brigade
> HQ   based at Chelers
> 2/21st Battalion (London Regt.)
> 2/22nd   "
> 2/23rd   "
> 2/24th   "
> H.G. Company

Pioneer Battalion 1/12th North Lancs

HQ and 517 Company, Divisional Train		based at Tincques
518	"	based at Acq
519	"	based at Doffine
520	"	based at Chelers

2/4th London Field Ambulance		(with 179th Brigade)
2/5th	"	(with 180th Brigade)
2/6th	"	(with 181th Brigade)

Divisional Sanitary Company　　　　　　based at Villers-Châtel

Mobile Veterinary Section　　　　　　based at Villers-Châtel

Divisional Transport:
Bicycles
Wagons for postal services
Water carts
Wagons for baggage and cooks
Motor cars
Wagons for supplies, ammunition, signals company, field artillery, field ambulances, mobile veterinary section, gunnery company, infantry battalions and others.

414 vehicles in total

Appendix 5:
Extracts from Notes on the Evacuation of the Wounded in the Neuville St Vaast area by the 2/4th London Field Ambulance, June-October 1916.

1   The Field Ambulance evacuated the casualties on the line held by the 179th and 180th Brigades. The 179th Brigade held the centre sector with Regimental Aid Posts (RAPs) in the centre, right and left sectors of the line.

2   From these RAPs, Field Ambulance bearers brought the patients to two Collecting Posts (CPs). That for the Centre Sector was in the Territorial Trench. The road from the first CP forms a wide trench covered with duck boards without many zig-zags and this carry was not a difficult one although it was about 1,200 yards. From the second CP the carry was along the Territorial Trench about 800 yards. It was however a most difficult one in a narrow trench where for part of the distance the stretcher had to be carried on the shoulders instead of the hands and, where it was wide enough to carry the stretcher in the ordinary way, there were numerous traverses. From this CP to the Advanced Dressing Station (ADS) the carry was by Territorial Trench and included going underneath the Arras – Bethune road.

That for the right sector was in Neuville St Vaast, situated in a cellar in a ruined house. A trolley line runs from the RAP to the Aux Rietz – Neuville St Vaast road and thence down to the ADS. It was a carry of 800 yards after which it was sometimes possible to bring them by trolley line direct to the ADS. When this was not available it was a long carry – 1,500 yards as the crow flies which probably means 2,000 yards by the trench.

3   The ADS was situated in the dug-outs on the south-east side of the Maroeuil – Neuville St Vaast road, south west of the Aux Rietz crossroads and consisted of five trenches opening on to the road with dug-outs and trenches. Evacuation from the ADS to the Main Dressing Station (MDS) was by motor ambulance at night time. Authority was given to send a motor ambulance to the ADS by day in the event of urgent cases only.

4   The route which the cars used to take to the ADS was through Maroeuil and thence by Farm Brunhaut to the ADS where they had to turn round in order to come back. This last is a most difficult procedure as the car has to back several times in order to get round and in doing so must get the back wheels across the light railway, leading to the possibility of the whole road being blocked supposing a car broke down while the turning was in process. An attempt was made to obviate this by sending the cars up one way and bringing them back by the Aux

Rietz – La Targette crossroads. This, however, had to be given up owing to the difficulty at the crossroads. At this point two trolley lines converge onto the engineer dump and the road goes steeply downhill through the wood and is quite dark except for the light from hurricane lamps in the hands of people moving about, which only tend to make it more difficult rather than easier. Further, the crossroads at Aux Rietz and La Targette are both dangerous corners.

5   The question of evacuation in the event of an advance was considered. The road Neuville St Vaast to Thelus would be useful; however, parts of the road were very bad with shell holes which became more numerous as time went on and scattered with debris from surrounding houses. It was crossed by three trenches: Denis – Laroque – Brecon Line and a small one between these. The first was already bridged, for the second two timber was prepared so that a bridge could be put across each with little labour. This piece of roadway could then have been made passable to wheeled stretchers by means of a large working party working during one night.

Major Layton, Officer Commanding, 2/4th London Field Ambulance
30 November 1916

Appendix 6:
Application for a Temporary Commission with the Royal Garrison Artillery.

Application for Admission to an Officer Cadet Unit with a view to appointment to a Temporary Commission in the Regular Army for the period of the War, to a Commission in the Special Reserve of Officers or to a Commission in the Territorial Force.

The candidate will complete the following particulars and obtain certificates below as to character and educational qualification.

1. Name in full { Surname.		*Vaughan Williams*
Christian names.		*Ralph*
2. State whether desirous of appointment to—		*Temporary commission in the Regular army*
(i) A temporary commission in the Regular Army.		
(ii) A commission in the Special Reserve of Officers.		
(iii) A commission in the Territorial Force.		
3. State *in order of preference* the branch of the Service in which desirous of serving, *e.g.*, Cavalry, Artillery, Engineers, Infantry, Army Service Corps, etc.		*Royal Garrison Artillery*
NOTE.—Unless otherwise stated it will be assumed that a candidate is prepared to accept a commission in any branch of the Service.		
4. Unit (if any) to which desirous of being appointed.		
(If for the Army Service Corps state whether for Motor Transport, Horse Transport, or Supply.)		
NOTE.—No guarantee can be given for appointment to a particular unit.		
5. Date and place of birth.		*Oct 12th 1872. Down Ampney Vicarage Glos England*
6. Whether married.		*No*
7. Whether of pure European descent.		*yes*
8. Whether a British subject by birth or naturalization. (State which, and if by naturalization attach a certificate from the Home Office.)		*British subject by birth*
9. Nationality by birth of father (if naturalized, state date.)		*English*
10. Occupation of father.		*Holy Orders church of England*
11. Permanent address of candidate.		*13 cheyne walk chelsea london s.w*
12. Present address for correspondence.		*2/4 london field ambulance RAF*
13. Schools or Colleges at which educated.		*charterhouse school; Trinity College Cambridge*
14. Occupation or employment in civil life.		*Doctor of Music*
15. Whether able to ride.		*yes*
16. Whether now serving, or previously served, in any branch of His Majesty's Naval or Military Forces, or in the Officers Training Corps. If so, state :—		
(a) Regiment, Corps, or Contingent		*2/4 London field ambulance RAMC*
(b) Date of appointment		*Dec 31st 1914*
(c) If serving in the ranks state whether on an ordinary peace engagement or for the period of the war only		*period of war*
(d) Rank		*Private*
(e) Date of retirement, resignation or discharge		
(f) Circumstances of retirement, resignation or discharge		
(g) Whether in possession of Certificate A.		
(h) Whether in possession of Certificate B.		

Appendix 7:
Vaughan Williams's Military History Sheet, 20 December 1917.

The Entries on this page only require to be made from time to time as they occur.

No. 2033   Name Vaughan-Williams R.

MILITARY HISTORY SHEET.

1. Service.

Place.	From	To	Years	Days
Home	31.12.14	21.6.16	1	173
B.E.F	22.6.16	18.11.16		150
BSF	19.11.16	16.6.17		210
Home	17.6.17	20.12.17		190
			2	358

		Initials of Officer making the entry
2. Passed classes of Instruction † †This includes any authorised class of instruction		
3. Campaigns (including actions) medals and decorations	Home 31.12.14 t 31.6.16 B.E.F 22.6.16 t 18.11.16 BSF 19.11.16 —	

Appendix 8:
Extracts from *War Diary* of 86th Brigade, Royal Garrison Artillery. 8 August to 16 August 1918 inclusive.

8 August 1918
Brigade opened fire at 4.20 am on neutralising and harassing targets and concentrations. Ceased firing at 10.30 am – targets out of range. Advanced sections of batteries moved forward. 141 HB Brigade under 3rd Canadian Division from 12.30 pm.
6.30 pm remaining sections of batteries ordered to join forward sections.

9 August
Brigade attached to 32nd Division for further advance. Brigade HQ moved forward to MAISON BLANCHE on AMIENS – ROYE road.
141 HB came into action.

10 August
Brigade advanced to BEAUFORT.
141 AND 1/1 HBs in action by 2 pm GRUNY, FRESNOY and CRÉMERY bombarded by Heavies 4/5.30 pm.
Harassing fire through night in LA CHAVATTE and road and trench junctions south of FRANSART and HATTENCOURT.

11 August
Bombardment 9.30 am FRESNOY, LA CHAVATTE.
2.40 pm roads south-east of FRESNOY.
5.30/6 pm FRESNOY – GRUNY Road and Cemetery north-east of GOYENCOURT.
9 pm SOS answered by Batteries.
32nd Division relieved by 3rd Canadian Division during night of 11/12th.

12 August
Brigade supported attack on PARVILLERS by 7th, 8th and 9th Infantry Brigades. Opened fire at 5.30 pm to 7 pm Night harassing fire by 141 HB on LIANCOURT, CRÉMERY AND GRUNY.
Many 'NFs' answered during the day.

13 August
Quiet. Reverted to CCHA at 12 noon.

14 August

434 Siege Battery attached to Brigade. 6 GFs and 7 NFs taken by Brigade. 16 rounds of gun harassing fire on LIANCOURT WOOD. 160 rounds 60-pdr on FRESNOY, CRÉMERY and LIANCOURT and Roads.

15 August

6 inch gun fired 6 rds. Neutralising and harassing fire on roads east of HATTENCOURT from 5 pm in view of enemy relief. 13 NFs taken up. Harassing fire through the night on HALLU WOOD and roads in LIANCOURT – FONCHETTE area.

16 August

Bursts on hostile batteries at 4.15, 4.25 and 4. 40 am 12 NFs taken up during the day. Neutralising fire on 10 HBs from 12.15 pm. Back areas harassed by 6 inch gun. Night harassing fire on HALLU WOOD and trenches north and east of HALLENCOURT.

Glossary

HBs – Heavy Batteries such as the 141 Heavy Battery.

GFs is a signal used for communication between artillery units or with the Royal Air Force and indicates the movement of enemy troops.

NFs is another signal which refers to a specific position from which enemy guns are firing. Map coordinates are normally provided after an NF signal.

SOS indicates that a barrage fire is required immediately (certainly within three minutes).

CCHA is the Canadian Corps Heavy Artillery.

Select Bibliography

General books on the First World War

Arthur, Max, *Last Post – The Final Word from our First World War Soldiers*, Phoenix Paperback, 2005.

Blunden, Edmund, *Undertones of War*, Penguin Classics, 1928, reprinted 2000.

Churchill, Sir Winston, *The World Crisis 1911-1918*, Penguin Books, paperback edition 2007.

Clark, Christopher, *The Sleepwalkers – How Europe Went to War in 1914*, Allen Lane, 2012.

Clarke, Dale, *British Artillery 1914-19 – Heavy Artillery*, Osprey Publishing, 2005.

Corrigan, Gordon, *Mud, Blood and Poppycock – Britain and The Great War*, Cassell, 2004.

Edmonds, Charles, *A Subaltern's War*, Peter Davies Ltd., 1929. Reprinted by Icon Books, 1964.

Ellison, Norman F., *Remembrances of Hell – The Great War Diary of Writer, Broadcaster and Naturalist – Norman Ellison*, edited by David Lewis, Airlife Publishing, 1997.

Falls, Captain Cyril, War Books – *A Critical Guide*, Peter Davies Ltd, 1930.

Ferguson, Niall, *The Pity of War 1914-1918*, Penguin Books, 1998.

Fussell, Paul, *The Great War and Modern Memory*, Oxford University Press, 1975.

Gilbert, Martin, *The First World War*, The Folio Society edition, 2011.

Graham, Stephen, *A Private in the Guards*, Macmillan, 1919. Reprinted by William Heinemann, 1928.

Graves, Robert, *Goodbye to All That*, Cassell and Co. Ltd., 1957.

Jacques, Alain, and others (eds.) *Somewhere on the Western Front – Arras 1914-1918*, Leclerc Publications, 2003.

Hart, Peter, *1918: A Very British Victory*, Weidenfeld and Nicolson, 2008.

Hastings, Max, *Catastrophe: Europe Goes to War 1914*, William Collins, 2014.

Heffer, Simon, *Staring at God: Britain in The Great War*, Penguin Random House, 2019.

Holmes, Richard, *Tommy: The British Soldier on the Western Front, 1914-1918*, HarperCollins, 2004.

Huntly, Gordon, *The Unreturning Army – The Classic Memoir of a Field Gunner in Flanders*, Bantam Books, 1967.

Jünger, Ernst, *The Storm of Steel*, Penguin Classics, 1929, reprinted 1961.

Keegan, John, *The First World War*, Hutchinson, 1998.

Lewis-Stempel, John, *Six Weeks – The Short and Gallant Life of the British Officer in the First World War*, Orion Paperback, 2010.

MacDonald, Lt. J. A. (ed), *Gun-Fire – An Historical Narrative of the 4th Brigade, Canadian Field Artillery in the Great War (1914-18)*, The Naval and Military Press, 1929.

MacDonald, Lyn, *1915: The Death of Innocence*, Headline Books, 1993.

MacDonald, Lyn, *To the Last Man – Spring 1918*, Viking, 1998.

MacMillan, Margaret, *The War That Ended Peace – How Europe Abandoned Peace for the First World War*, Profile Books, 2013.

Miles, Captain Wilfrid, *Official History of the Great War: Military Operations France and Belgium 1916*, Imperial War Museum, 1938.

Plowman, Max, *A Subaltern on the Somme*, The Naval and Military Press, 1928.

Richter, Donald C., *Lionel Sotheby's Great War: Diaries and Letters from the Western Front*, Ohio University Press, 2009.

Robbins, Simon, *British Generalship during the Great War, the Military Career of Sir Henry Horne (1861-1929)*, Ashgate Publishing Ltd., 2010.

Robbins, Simon, *The First World War Letters of General Lord Horne*, Army Records Society, 2009.

Russell, Bertrand, *Justice in War-Time*, Spokesman, paperback edition, 2005.

Priestley, J. B., *Margin Released: A Writer's Reminiscences and Reflections*, Harper and Row, 1962.

Sassoon, Siegfried, *The Complete Memoirs of George Sherston*, Faber and Faber, 1980.

Sheffield, Gary, *The Chief: Douglas Haig and the British Army*, Aurum Press, 2012.

Siepmann, Harry, *Echo of the Guns – Recollections of an Artillery Officer, 1914-18*, Robert Hale, 1987.

Talbot Kelly, R. B., *A Subaltern's Odyssey – A Memoir of the Great War 1915-1917*, William Kimber, 1980.

Vaughan, Edwin Campion, *Some Desparate Glory – The Diary of a Young Officer, 1917*, Frederick Warne, 1981.

Wallace, Edgar, *Kitchener's Army and the Territorial Forces – The Full Story of a Great Adventure*, George Newnes Ltd, 1916. (Paperback edition published in 2017.)

West, Arthur Graeme, *Dairy of a Dead Officer*, Printed by Amazon, undated.

Wheatley, Dennis, T*he Time Has Come 1914-1919 – Officer and Temporary Gentleman*, Hutchinson, 1978.

Books on the Medical Services in the First World War

Bayly, Hugh, *A Medical Officer in Khaki – The Story of a Doctor in the First World War*, 1935, and republished as a Kindle Edition, 2017.

Brown, Kevin, *Fighting Fit – Health, Medicine and War in the Twentieth Century*, The History Press, 2008.

Cohen, Susan, *Medical Services in the First World War*, Shire Publications, 2014.

Dearmer, Mabel, *Letters from a Field Hospital*, Macmillan, 1916, now published by Elibron Classics.

Horton, Charles H., *Stretcher Bearer! – Fighting for Life in the Trenches*, Lion Books, 2013.

MacDonald, Lyn, *The Roses of No Man's Land*, Macmillan, 1980.

Mayhew, Emily, *Wounded – From Battlefield to Blighty 1914-1918*, The Bodley Head, 2013.

McCracken, Timothy, *The Royal Army Medical Corps in the Great War – Rare Photographs from Wartime Archives*, Pen and Sword, 2017.

Meyer, Jessica, *An Equal Burden – The Men of the Royal Army Medical Corps in the First World War*, Oxford University Press, 2019.

Rorie, Col. David, *A Medico's Luck in the War*, Naval and Military Press, 1929.

Tales of a Field Ambulance 1914-1918, Told by the Personnel, Borough Printing, 1935.

Trevelyan, G. M. *Scenes from Italy's War*, Jack and Co. Ltd., 1919.

Books on the First World War that are directly relevant to Ralph Vaughan Williams

Behrend, Captain Arthur F., *Nine Days – Adventures of a Heavy Artillery Brigade of the Third Army during the German Offensive of March 21-29 1918*, The Naval and Military Press, 1921.

Cave, Nigel, *Vimy Ridge – Arras*, Battleground Europe Series, Pen and Sword Ltd, 1996.

Clarke, Dale, *World War I Battlefield Artillery Tactics*, Osprey Publishing, 2014.

Cobb, Paul, *Battery Action! The diary of a Gunner 1916-19*, Reveille Press, 2015.

Dalbiac, Col. P. H., *History of the 60th Division (2/2nd London Division)*, Naval and Military Press, 1927.

Edmonds, J. E., *Official History of the War – Military Operations France and Belgium, 1918 – The German March Offensive and its Preliminaries*, Imperial War Museum, 1935.

Edmonds, J. E., *Official History of the War – Military Operations France and Belgium, March to April 1918*, Continuation of the German Offensive, Imperial War Museum, 1937.

Edmonds, J. E., *Official History of the Great War – Military Operations France and Belgium, May-July 1918*, Imperial War Museum, 1939.

Edmonds, J. E., *Official History of the Great War – Military Operations France and Belgium 1918, Volume IV*, Naval and Military Press, 1940.

Edmonds, J. E., *Official History of the Great War – Military Operations France and Belgium, 1918, Volume 5*, Naval and Military Press, 1947.

Edmonds, J. E., *Official History of the Great War – The Occupation of the Rhineland 1918-1929*, Naval and Military Press, 1945.

Falls, Captain Cyril, *Official History of the Great War; Macedonia – Volume 1, from the outbreak of war to the Spring of 1917*, The Naval and Military Press, 1932.

Falls, Captain Cyril, *Official History of The Great War, Macedonia – Volume 2, from the Spring of 1917 to the end of the war*, The Naval and Military Press, 1934.

Gillon, Captain Stair, *The Story of the 29th Division: A Record of Gallant Deeds*, Naval and Military Press, 1925.

Headlam, Cuthbert, *History of the Guards Division in the Great War, Volume 2, 1915-1918*, The Naval and Military Press, 1924.

Keech, Graham, *Bullecourt – Arras, Battleground Europe Series*, Pen and Sword Books, 1999.

Mann, A. J., *The Salonika Front*, A. & C. Black Ltd., 1920.

Kingham, W. R., *London Gunners – The Story of the H.A.C. Siege Battery in Action*, Methuen, 1919, reprinted in paperback edition (no date provided) by The Naval and Military Press.

60th Division, RAMC, 2/4th London Field Ambulance, *War Diary 1 September 1915-31 December 1915*, Naval and Military Press, 2015.

Smith, Wayne (ed.), *George Butterworth Memorial Volume*, YouCaxton Publications, 1915.

Strong, Paul and Marble, Sanders, *Artillery in the Great War*, Pen and Sword Military, 2013.

Wakefield, Alan and Moody, Simon, *Under the Devil's Eye – The British Military Experience in Macedonia 1915-1918*, Pen and Sword Military, 2017.

To these books should be added a facsimile of the *War Diary* of the 2/4th London Field Ambulance, 1 September 1915 to 31 December 1915, published by The Naval and Military Press, in association with The National Archives. See www.naval-military-press.com.

General books on Ralph Vaughan Williams

Adams, Byron and Robin Wells (eds.), *Vaughan Williams Essays*, Ashgate, 2003.

Alldritt, Keith, *Vaughan Williams – Composer, Radical, Patriot – A Biography*, Robert Hale, 2015.

Cobbe, Hugh (ed.), *Letters of Ralph Vaughan Williams 1895 – 1958*, Oxford University Press, 2010.

Connock, Stephen (ed.), *The Complete Poems of Ursula Vaughan Williams*, Albion Music Ltd., 2003.

Connock, Stephen, Ursula Vaughan Williams and Robin Wells (eds.), *There was a Time – A Pictorial History of Ralph Vaughan Williams*, Albion Music Ltd., 2002.

Connock, Stephen, *Toward the Sun Rising – Ralph Vaughan Williams Remembered*, Albion Music Ltd., 2018.

Day, James, *Vaughan Williams*, The Master Musicians Series, Oxford University Press, 1998.

Dineen, Frank, *Ralph's People – The Ingrave Secret*, Albion Music Ltd., 1997.

Douglas, Roy, *Working with Vaughan Williams – The Correspondence of Ralph Vaughan Williams and Roy Douglas*, The British Library, 1988.

Douglas, Roy, *Working with R.V.W.*, Oxford University Press, 1972.

Foreman, Lewis (ed.), *Vaughan Williams in Perspective*, Albion Music, 1998.

Foss, Hubert, *Ralph Vaughan Williams – A Study*, Harrop and Co. Ltd., 1950.

Frogley, Alain (ed.), *Vaughan Williams Studies*, Cambridge University Press, 1996.

Frogley, Alain and Aidan J. Thomson (eds.), *The Cambridge Companion to Vaughan Williams*, Cambridge University Press, 2013.

Heffer, Simon, *Vaughan Williams*, Faber and Faber Ltd., 2008.

Howes, Frank, *The Music of Ralph Vaughan Williams*, Oxford University Press, 1954.

James, David, *Scott of the Antarctic – The Film and its Production*, Convey Publications, 1948.

Kennedy, Michael, *The Works of Ralph Vaughan Williams*, Oxford University Press, 1980.

Manning, David (ed.), *Vaughan Williams on Music*, Oxford University Press, 2008.

Mellers, Wilfrid, *Vaughan Williams and the Vision of Albion*, Albion Music Ltd., 1997.

Norris, John and Neill, Andrew (eds.), *A Special Flame – The Music of Elgar and Vaughan Williams*, Albion Music Ltd., 2004.

Pakenham, Simona, *Ralph Vaughan Williams – A Discovery of his Music*, Macmillan and Co. Ltd., 1957.

Pike, Lionel, *Vaughan Williams and the Symphony*, Toccata Press, 2003.

Rushton, Julian (ed.), *Let Beauty Awake – Elgar, Vaughan Williams and Literature*, Albion Music Ltd, 2010.

Savage, Roger, *Masques, Mayings and Music-Dramas*, Boydell Press, 2014.

Saylor, Eric, *English Pastoral Music – From Arcadia to Utopia 1900-1955*, University of Illinois, 2017.

Spalding, Frances, *Gwen Raverat – Friends, Family and Affections*, Harvill Press, 2001.

Tennant, Janet, *Mistress and Muse: Ursula - the second Mrs Vaughan Williams*,

Albion Music Ltd., 2017.

Vaughan Williams, Ursula, *R.V.W. – A Biography of Ralph Vaughan Williams*, Oxford University Press, 1964.

Vaughan Williams, Ursula, *Paradise Remembered – An Autobiography*, Albion Music Ltd, 2002.

Young, Percy, *Vaughan Williams*, Dennis Dobson Ltd., 1953.

For a complete Research and Information Guide to Vaughan Williams, see Ross, Ryan, Ralph Vaughan Williams – *A Research and Information Guide*, Routledge, 2016.

The Journal of the Ralph Vaughan Williams Society is essential for a better understanding of the life and works of Vaughan Williams. It is published three times a year for members of the RVW Society. For membership details see **www.rvwsociety.com**

Notes on Sources and Copyright Issues

A Appendices

1. Vaughan Williams's Form of Attestation, 31 December 1914 – from Vaughan William's personal Army file, Public Record Office, file WO 374/75055.

2. Vaughan Williams's Medical Inspection Report, 31 December 1914 – from Vaughan William's personal Army file, Public Record Office, file WO 374/75055.

3. A British Army Infantry Division in 1915 – reproduced with permission from Gordon Corrigan *Mud, Blood and Poppycock: Britain and The Great War*, Cassell, 2004, p.111.

4. List of Units of the 60th Division – material drawn from Colonel Dalbiac *History of the 60th Division*, Naval and Military Press, 1927 and *War Diary*, 2/4th London Field Ambulance, Public Record Office, WO 95/3029.

5. Extracts from Notes on the Evacuation of the Wounded in the Neuville St Vaast area by the 2/4th London Field Ambulance June – October 1916 – from *War Diary* 2/4th London Field Ambulance, Public Record Office, file WO 95/3029, Volume III.

6. Application for a Temporary Commission with the Royal Garrison Artillery – from Vaughan Williams's personal Army file, Public Record Office, file WO 374/75055.

7. Vaughan Williams's Military History Sheet, 20 December 1917 – from Vaughan Williams's personal Army file, Public Record Office, file WO 374/75055.

8. Extracts from *War Diary* of the 86th Brigade – 8 August to 16 August 1918 inclusive – from Public Record Office, WO 95-325-7.

B Illustrations

1. *Bushes and Briars* melody and text, 1903 – with thanks to P. J. Clulow.

2. Title page for *Linden Lea*, 1912 edition – from the score published by Boosey and Hawkes, 1912, front cover.

3. *SS Connaught* – from *Wikipedia* entry for *RMS Connaught*, 1897 – see info@coastmonkey.ie

4. Primary rail routes from Le Havre – from The Long, Long Trail website. (www.longlongtrail.co.uk)

5. The casualty evacuation chain, 1916 – from Col. David Rorie *A Medico's Luck in the War*, The Naval and Military Press, 1929, facing p. 5.

6   The area covered by the 60th Division in July 1916 – from Col. P. H. Dalbiac *History of the 60th Division*, The Naval and Military Press, 1927, facing page 42.

7   Location of the Advanced Dressing Station at Aux Rietz, south of La Targette – from John Giles *The Western Front Then and Now – From Mons to the Marne and back*, After the Battle Publications, 1991, p. 146.

8   Layout of the ADS at Aux Rietz – from Col. David Rorie *A Medico's Luck in the War*, The Naval and Military Press, 1929, facing page 78.

9   Trench system near Neuville St Vaast – reproduced with permission from Nigel Cave *Vimy Ridge – Arras*, Leo Cooper, 1997, p. 96.

10   Camp Dudular, near Salonica – from the International Committee of the Red Cross, www.avarchives.icrc.org (Ref: V-P-HIST-03062-29). Reproduced under licence from the ICRC.

11   The Salonica Front 1915-1918 – reproduced with permission from Alan Wakefield and Simon Moody *Under the Devil's Eye – The British Military Experience in Macedonia 1915-1918*, Pen and Sword Military, 2004, p. 4.

12   Mount Olympus at nightfall – painting by William T. Wood from *The Salonica Front*, 1920, p. 24.

13   Eastern end of Lake Doiran, Salonica Front – painting by William T. Wood from *The Salonica Front*, 1920, p. 144.

14   The MDS at Kalinova – from *Tales of a Field Ambulance*, Borough Publishing, 1935, p. 120

15   Notification of attendance at Maresfield Park – from Vaughan Williams's personal Army file, Public Record Office, file WO 374/75055.

16   A field clinometer from 1917 – Mark V, 1917 from Imperial War Museum, OPT 511 at www.iwm.org.uk. Reproduced under licence from the IWM.

17   British Army forces deployed on 21 March 1918 – reproduced with permission from The Imperial War Museum *Official History of the Great War, Military Operations France and Belgium, 1918*, 1935, sketch 14 facing page 161.

18   The German advance south of Arras in March 1918 – from Huntly Gordon *The Unreturning Army*, Bantam Books, 1967, facing page 193.

19   The Guards Divisions hold the line around Mercatel – reproduced with permission from The Imperial War Museum *Official History of the Great War, Military Operations France and Belgium 1918 (March – April)*, sketch 9 facing page 61.

20   Map showing the British, French and German lines on 8 August 1918 near Amiens – reproduced with permission from The Imperial War Museum *Official History of the Great War, Volume 4, (8 August-26 September 1918)*, The Naval and Military Press, 1940, sketch 2, p. 626.

21 Chart showing details of the 86th Brigade's long trek north and east into Belgium, 1918 – compiled by Stephen Connock from the *War Diaries* of the 86th Brigade, see file WO 372/21/201416.

22 Allied gains in the *Fifth Battle of Ypres*, 1918 – reproduced with permission of the Imperial War Museum *Official History of the Great War, Volume 5, (26 September – 11 November 1918)*, 1947, sketch 9, p. 685.

23 The march through Namur and Charleroi to Germany, late 1918 – see Frontispiece of the *Official History of the Great War – The Occupation of the Rhineland 1918-1929*, by J. E. Edmonds, The Naval and Military Press, 1945.

24 Final Letter on Demobilisation – from Vaughan Williams's personal Army file, Public Record Office, file WO 374/75005.

25 Reply to Vaughan Williams's application for promotion – from Vaughan Williams's personal Army file, Public Record Office, file WO 374/75005.

26 'Tuesday Morning' from *Hugh the Drover* – with thanks to P. J. Clulow.

27 Signed programme for a concert at Cornell University, 21 November 1954 – from collection of Stephen Connock.

28. Title page of *Along the Field* – from collection of Stephen Connock.

C Photographs

Front Cover – Ralph Vaughan Williams in late 1917, with his Sam Browne belt – from the collection of Ursula Vaughan Williams and reproduced with permission of the Vaughan Williams Charitable Trust (VWCT).

After title page – Vaughan Williams in 1915, with cap askew! – from the collection of Ursula Vaughan Williams and reproduced with permission of the VWCT.

All photos marked *UVW* were provided for this book from the collection of Ursula Vaughan Williams and are reproduced with the kind permission of the VWCT.

1 Arthur Vaughan Williams. (*UVW*)

2 Margaret Wedgwood (née Darwin), Ralph's mother, on 18 July 1856, aged 13. (*UVW*)

3 Ralph in 1876. (*UVW*)

4 Hervey and Maggie on 28 January 1873. (*UVW*)

5 Ralph at Rottingdean, March 1885. (*UVW*)

6 Charterhouse School – from Robert Graves *Goodbye to All That*, Cassell and Co. Ltd., 1957 edition, facing page 89.

7 Ralph at Charterhouse, 1890. (*UVW*)

8   Ralph and Adeline in 1897 at Leith Hill Place. (*UVW*)

9   Maurice Ravel in 1908. (*UVW*)

10   Vaughan Williams around 1910. (*UVW*)

11   Major T.B. Layton, CO 2/4th London Field Ambulance – from *Tales of a Field Ambulance*, Borough Publishing, 1935, frontispiece.

12   Vaughan Williams in 1915 near Dorking. (*UVW*)

13   Garth House Hospital, Dorking – from Garth House website (www.caringhomes.org/garth-house-in-Dorking).

14   The 2/4th London Field Ambulance practising with the 'wounded', 1915 – from *Tales of a Field Ambulance*, Borough Publishing, 1935, facing page 25.

15   Vaughan Williams (back row, far left) relaxing, 1915. (*UVW*)

16   The only ambulance wagon in 1915, Saffron Walden – from *Tales of a Field Ambulance*, Borough Publishing, 1935, facing p. 24.

17   RAMC motor and horse ambulances, 1915 – from a postcard issued by the Royal Army Medical Corps in 1915.

18   RVW in the RAMC, 1915. (*UVW*)

19   Vaughan Williams (far left) on firewood fatigues, 1915. (*UVW*)

20   Pte. R. Vaughan Williams, 1915. (*UVW*)

21   The Unit at Saffron Walden. Vaughan Williams is in the middle of the second row. (*UVW*)

22   The 2/4th London Field Ambulance Band in Saffron Walden, 1915. Vaughan Williams is standing at the back, with cap askew. (*UVW*)

23   The huts at Sutton Veny – from *Tales of a Field Ambulance*, Borough Publishing, 1935, facing page 43.

24   Vaughan Williams, with Harry Steggles standing on the left, on Salisbury Plain in early June 1916 a few weeks before leaving for France. (*UVW*)

25   Vaughan Williams (far right) and Harry Steggles and the Motor Ambulance, Ecoivres, 1916. (*UVW*)

26   Neuville St Vaast in 1915 – reproduced with permission from Nigel Cave *Vimy Ridge – Arras*, Leo Cooper, 1997, p. 21.

27   Arras Cathedral and belfry, 1916 – from a postcard issued by Newspaper Illustrations Ltd. in 1916.

28   The 2/4th London Field Ambulance at Ecoivres, 1916. Vaughan Williams is in the back row, fourth from the right. (*UVW*)

29   The twin towers of Mont St Eloi in World War 1 – taken from World War 1 photos centenary website 2014-2018 by Paul Reed, See www.greatwarphotos.com/tag/mont-st-eloi.

30 The front of the building that housed the MDS at Ecoivres in 1999 – from collection of Stephen Connock.

31 Captain Francis Bevis Ellis – reproduced from the website of Christ Church, Oxford University and with acknowledgements to the North East War Memorials Project. See www.newmp.org.uk/article.php.

32 The church at Ecoivres – taken from www.flickr.com/photos. Copyright permission is acknowledged to Pierre Moulin.

33 A Bulgarian infantry attack at Monastir – from *Wikipedia* entry for Monastir in World War 1.

34 Vaughan Williams's band in Katerini, near Salonica, 1917 – reproduced with permission of A. J. Fairchild.

35 Sir Francis Darwin – from a painting by Walter Stoneman 1918, in the National Portrait Gallery. See www.npg.org.uk. Reproduced under licence from the National Portrait Gallery.

36 H. A. L. Fisher in 1940 – from Fisher's *An Unfinished Autobiography*, Oxford University Press, 1940, frontispiece.

37 Adlestrop Station, sadly now closed – from www.adlestrop.org.uk/2014/06/24/adlestrop-poem-centenary.

38 Maresfield Park main building – from a postcard of 1912 photographed by Arthur Windsor-Spice. Reproduced with the kind permission of Wendy Fraser, granddaughter of the photographer.

39 Vaughan Williams in the Royal Garrison Artillery, 1917. (*UVW*)

40 Royal Garrison Artillery camp at Lydd, 1916 – from a postcard reproduced at www.lyddtownmuseum.co.uk.

41 RGA training at Lydd – from a postcard reproduced at www.lyddtownmuseum.co.uk.

42 2/Lt. Vaughan Williams and Adeline when on leave, Cheyne Walk, late 1917 or early 1918. (*UVW*)

43 A Heavy Battery of the RGA towing 60-pounder guns in Northern France – from The Long, Long Trail; see www.longlongtrail.co.uk.

44 A 60-pounder gun moving up in support – from a postcard issued by the Ministry of Information.

45 Vaughan Williams in front of a 60-pounder, 1918. (*UVW*)

46 This British large-calibre gun was destroyed during shelling, near Fontaine-les-Croisilles, 1918 from *Somewhere on the Western Front: Arras 1914-1918*, Arras Archaeological Service, 2017, p. 195.

47 German prisoners captured during the *Battle of Amiens* – from www.pinterest.co.uk.

48 Ypres in 1918 – from a postcard issued by the *Daily Mail* as an Official War Photograph.

49 British and French troops march through Namur, 1918 – from Canadian War Museum, No. CWM 19930065-475 and included in Canadian Military History, Volume 21, 2015, p. 9. It is reproduced under licence and with the kind permission of the George Metcalf Archival Collection, Canadian War Museum – Accession Number CWM 20020001-012.

50 Ralph and Adeline in Sheringham, 1920. (*UVW*)

51 Vaughan Williams in the garden of The White Gates, Dorking, 1930. (*UVW*)

52 Ursula Wood in 1936. (*UVW*)

53 Ursula's first husband Michael Wood. (*UVW*)

54 RVW and Seumas O'Sullivan, Dublin, 1939. (*UVW*)

55 Vaughan Williams in 1950 at the wedding of Bernard and Barbara Brown. (*UVW*)

56 RVW receives an Honorary Doctorate from Sir Winston Churchill at the University of Bristol, 1951. (*UVW*)

57 Ralph and Ursula's wedding day, 7 February 1953. (*UVW*)

58 RVW in Gloucester, 1953. (*UVW*)

59 Ralph and Ursula on board *RMS Queen Mary*, 1954.

60 Vaughan Williams conducting at Cornell University, November 1954 – from *Ralph Vaughan Williams – The Making of Music*, Cornell University Press, 1955, front cover.

61 Ralph and Ursula in Santa Barbara, California in 1954. (*UVW*)

62 Ralph and Ursula in Athens in 1955. (*UVW*)

63 Ralph and Sir John Barbirolli rehearsing the *Eighth Symphony*, 1956. (*UVW*)

64 Vaughan Williams with Lionel Tertis, July 1958. (*UVW*)

65 Procession of the Three Kings from *The First Nowell*, Theatre Royal, Drury Lane, 19 December 1958 – provided by Simona Pakenham for this book.

66 The 'Corot-like landscape' looking west from Mont St Eloi – from collection of Stephen Connock.

67 George Butterworth – from the *Memorial Album for George Butterworth*, privately printed in 1918, frontispiece.

68 Ernest Farrar, 1918 – his last photograph – www.pagesofthesea.org.uk/soldier/ernest-bristow-farrar.

69   Ralph Vaughan Williams with hearing aid in the early 1950s – photo by David Farrer and taken from *English Folk Songs*, English Folk and Dance Society, 1912, front cover.

70   The cemetery at Ecoivres – from collection of Stephen Connock.

71   Vaughan Williams in the RAMC, 1915. (*UVW*)

72   2/Lt. R. Vaughan Williams in 1919. (*UVW*)

Publisher's Note

Every attempt has been made to trace and secure appropriate permissions and/or licences from copyright holders for the Appendices, Illustrations and Photographs contained in this book. In the event of any errors or omissions please contact Albion Music at albionslc@aol.com.

Index of Vaughan Williams's Musical Works

The following musical works of Vaughan Williams are referred to in this book.

*Although Michael Kennedy in *A Catalogue of the Works of Ralph Vaughan Williams* (1996) refers to the third symphony as *A Pastoral Symphony*, Hugh Cobbe says that the correct title from the sources is *Pastoral Symphony*. This simpler format has been adopted throughout this book.

General Index

Corps:

6th Corps, 53

King's Royal Rifle Corps, 28, 31

Divisions:

3rd, 113

9th, 126, 129

22nd, 79

26th, 79, 82

29th, 98, 126, 129

32nd, 98, 116, 119

34th, 98, 113

36th, 98, 123

46th (North Midland), 54

47th (London), 37, 44, 54

51st (Highland), 55

56th, 67

60th, 1, 3, 33-34, 37, 39-42, 45, 55, 64-65, 71, 79, 83, 89, 191, 199-200

Guards, (1st and 3rd), 112, 113, 114, 173

Infantry Line Regiments and Brigades:

179th Brigade, (60th Division), 33, 39, 42, 65-67, 71, 75, 79, 81-82, 86

Artists Rifles, 90

Devonshire Regiment, 180

Duke of Cornwall's Light Infantry, 28

Durham Light Infantry, (13th Battalion), 28, 184

Gloucestershire Regiment, (2/5th Battalion), 28

Hampshire Regiment, 182

Leicestershire Regiment, (1/4th and 1/5th), 54

Liverpool Scottish, (2nd Battalion), 49

Norfolk Regiment, 6th (Cyclist) Battalion, 29

Northumberland Fusiliers, 65

Queen's Royal Regiment (West Surrey), 28

Royal Fusiliers, (13th (Service) Battalion), 28, 173

Royal Sussex Regiment, 141

Royal Welch Fusiliers, 29, 60, 170

Suffolk Regiment, (1st Battalion), 31

West Yorkshire Regiment, 29

Yorkshire Hussars, 63

Dudular Camp, 74, 82
Dulce et Decorum est, (Owen), 115
Dvořák, Antonin, 21
Dyson, Sir George, 18, 146

Eaucourt-sur-Somme, 67, 71-72
Ecoivres, 1, 4, 52, 55-56, 59-60, 62-67, 82, 98, 110, 142-143, 174, 190, 193
Edinburgh University, 11
Elgar, Sir Edward, 14, 17
Ellis, Francis Bevis, 4, 28, 65, 188
Ellis, Roland, 65
Ellison, Norman, 3
English Pastoral Impressions, (E.J. Farrar), 180
Épange, 71-72
Epstein, Sir Jacob, 1
Étaples, 72

Falkner, Keith, 151, 161, 173
Farrar, Ernest J., 4, 180
Farrer, Fanny, 156
Ferdinand, Archduke Franz, 27, 70
Fermont, 111
Fieffes, 118
Fischeux, 110, 113
Fisher, Adeline; see Vaughan Williams, Adeline,
Fisher, Arthur, (Jack), 98
Fisher, Charles, 4, 29, 98, 184
Fisher, Cordelia, ('Boo'), 16, 143
Fisher, Edmund, 4, 29, 184
Fisher, Emmie ('Jane'), 28
Fisher, Florence, 16, 85
Fisher, H. A. L., 20, 85-87, 132, 134, 148
Fisher, Hervey, 98, 141
Fisher, Herbert William, 16
Fisher, Mary, 16
Fisher, Sir William, 29
Foch, Field Marshal Ferdinand, 87
Folies, 119
Fontaine-les-Croisilles, 112

Ford, Robert, 191-192
Forster, E.M.,
Fortel-en-Artois, 67

Foss, Hubert, 145, 170
Foulds, John, 177
Franck, César, 13
Frend, Charles, 155
Fresnoy, 205-206
Frogley, Alain, 164
Fussell, Paul, 172

Gallipoli Peninsula, 29, 70
Garth House Hospital, Dorking, 37
German Offensives:
    Mars, 107
    Michael, 107
Gheluvelt, 123
Gilbert, Sir Martin, 107
Gladstone, Dr. F. E., 13
Glastonbury Festival, 31-32
Godalming, Surrey, 12
Goodbye to All That, (Graves), 3, 12
Goossens, Adophe, 90
Goossens, Eugene, 90
Goossens, Léon, 90
Gordon, Huntly, 3, 101-102
Gounod, Charles, 12
Graham, Stephen, 126
Granados, Enrique, 46
Graves, Robert, 3, 12, 29, 60, 144, 184
Gray, Alan, 14
Grieg, Edvard, 133
Grove Dictionary of Music, 90, 178
Gurney, Ivor, 3, 4, 28, 32, 58-59

Hadley, Patrick, 4, 90, 96, 147
Haig, General (later Field Marshall) Sir Douglas, 66-67, 87, 104-105, 114, 116-117, 131-132
Hall, Sydney, 94, 108

Stevenson, Robert Louis, 18
Struma, River, 74
Sullivan, Lt. Col. G. A., 133, 135
Summer Hill Camp, Salonica – see Dudular
Sutton Veny, 44, 64
Swinburne, Algernon Charles, 17
Synge, J. M., 180-181

Tallis, Thomas, 19
Targette, La, 52-53, 56-57, 60, 66, 202
Taylor, Bishop Jeremy, 23
Tempest, The, (Shakespeare), 155, 164
Tennyson, Alfred Lord, 11, 130
Terry, Sir Richard R., 170
Tertis, Lionel, 164-165
Tess of the d'Urbervilles, (Thomas Hardy), 163-164
Thaxted, 38
Thomas, Edward, 89, 95
Times, The, 27, 144
To Gratiana Singing and Dancing, (W. Denis Browne), 29
Tono-Bungay, (H. G. Wells), 23
Toye, Geoffrey, 28
Trees so High, The, (Hadley), 90
Tristan and Isolde, (Wagner), 160
Trevelyan, George M., 14

Urchanta, 74, 82

Valenciennes, 132-133, 192
Valetta, 73
Vardar, River, 71, 74, 79-80, 97
Vaughan Williams, Adeline, 3, 16, 20, 27-28, 30, 32, 34, 79, 97-98, 132, 134, 141, 143, 147, 150, 154, 160, 175, 184
Vaughan Williams, Arthur, 10
Vaughan Williams, Hervey, 10-11
Vaughan Williams, Jane Margaret, 10
Vaughan Williams, Margaret Susan, 3, 10-11, 27
Vaughan Williams, Meggie, 10-11

Wood, Charles, 14, 17
Wood, Francis Derwent, 33
Wood, Michael, 151
Wood, Sir Henry, 150-151
Wood, Ursula – see Ursula Vaughan Williams
Woolf, Virginia, 16, 87
World Requiem, A, (John Foulds), 177

Yale University, 161
Yates, Martin, 180
Young, Percy, 177
Ypres, 4, 28, 101-2, 104, 107, 116, 121-123, 142

Photo 70: The cemetery at Ecoivres.

Postscript

'I remember, I remember how we lived so snug and warm
In a paradise of blankets and we thought there was no harm,
But oh! for Eden's innocence – we reck'd without our host –
A Milton came upon the scene and Paradise was lost,
Like Michael with his two-edged sword, he swooped upon his prey,
But far from clothing us in leaves he took our clothes away…

From 'Happy Days' by an anonymous member of the 2/4th London Field
Ambulance, published in 1935.

Photo 71: Vaughan Williams in the RAMC, 1915.

Photo 72: 2/Lt. R. Vaughan Williams in 1919.

Reviews of
Toward the Sun Rising – Ralph Vaughan Williams Remembered
by Stephen Connock

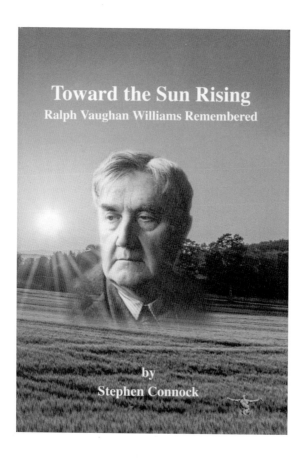

'A job well done. Indeed, as a Vaughan Williams companion, Connock's rewarding anthology (timed to mark the 60th anniversary of the composer's death) is hard to beat, and enthusiasts will surely derive much lasting pleasure from it.'

Andrew Achenback, The Gramophone, *September 2018.*

'Altogether, a charming and richly detailed introduction to the composer and his circle'.

Daniel Jaffé, BBC Music Magazine, *July 2018.*

'It is the recollections of 67 people that form the background to this tremendous book…These recollections alone would have marked down the book an indispensable and invaluable contribution to our knowledge and appreciation of the composer, but there is far, far more…The icing on the cake is what is described as a 'Biographical Note Informed by the Memories'. Some note! At 75 pages it is a book in itself, and a delightful picture of a great composer and great human being'.

Martin Bird, The Elgar Society Journal, *December 2018.*

'All Vaughan Williams enthusiasts and scholars owe Stephen Connock a debt of gratitude for his initiative…The section on Adeline Vaughan Williams is particularly original and probing. A collection of rare articles on Vaughan Williams completes this invaluable resource for future researchers'.

David Manning, Journal of the RVW Society, *June 2019.*

'In all, the 'Primary Memories' are a goldmine of information about Vaughan Williams…Toward the Sun Rising is an important (and thoroughly enjoyable) addition to the Vaughan Williams literature…It calls for a sustained round of applause both for Stephen Connock and for Albion Music'.

Allan Atlas, North American British Music Studies Association, Fall 2018.

Albion Music
Ltd